The Author

E. CLINTON GARDNER is a graduate of Vanderbilt University, Yale Divinity School, and Yale University (Ph.D.). He has held pastorates in New York and Connecticut and has taught at North Carolina State College. He is now Professor of Christian Ethics, Emory University.

The Church as a Prophetic Community

The Church as a

Prophetic Community

by

E. Clinton Gardner

THE WESTMINSTER PRESS · PHILADELPHIA

LIBRARY OF CONGRESS CATALOG CARD No. 67–10612

Published by The Westminster Press ®
Philadelphia, Pennsylvania

PRINTED IN THE UNITED STATES OF AMERICA

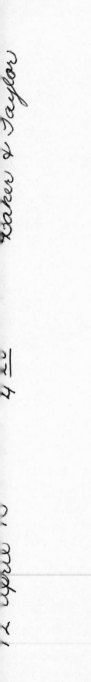

To my

Mother and Father

ACKNOWLEDGMENTS

While it is impossible to mention the names of all those individuals and groups who have contributed to the preparation of this essay, a special word of appreciation is due the administrative officials of Emory University — particularly Dean William R. Cannon, of the Candler School of Theology — for arranging a sabbatical leave in which to pursue research relative to the present project. The author is also greatly indebted to the American Association of Theological Schools for its assistance in making such a leave possible through the award of a Faculty Fellowship for the academic year 1962–1963. In addition, the Emory University Research Committee generously provided funds for travel and for the preparation of the final draft of the manuscript.

The author also wishes to acknowledge his indebtedness to his colleagues in the Candler School of Theology — especially Earl D. C. Brewer, Merrill M. Parvis, Norman Perrin (now of the Divinity School of the University of Chicago), Frederick C. Prussner, and Theodore R. Weber — for their suggestions and criticisms at various stages of the project. James Luther Adams, of the Harvard Divinity School, Charles C. West, of Princeton Theological Seminary, and J. Robert Nelson, of the Boston University School of Theology, also gave valuable assistance during the earlier phases of the research.

The volume as a whole has been greatly enriched by the author's relationships to a number of denominational and ecumenical groups with which it has been his privilege to be associated in recent years. The following groups and persons, in particular, have contributed to his understanding of the social responsibility of the church: the Commission on Christian Social Concerns of The Methodist Church (A. Dudley Ward and Roger Burgess); the Department of Racial and Cultural Relations (Oscar Lee and Will Campbell) and the Department of the Church and Economic Life (Cameron Hall) of the National Council of Churches; the Ecumenical Institute of the World Council of Churches (H. H. Wolf and N. A. Nissiotis); the Evangelical Academy at Bad Boll (Erich Wolf); and the Sheffield Industrial Mission (Brian Cordingly). In addition, the Evanston Assembly of the World Council of Churches (1954), the Sixth World Order Study Conference (St. Louis, 1965), and the continuing fellowship of the American Society of Christian Ethics have contributed significantly to the formation of the perspective represented in this study.

A word of special appreciation is due the staff of The Westminster Press for their encouragement and counsel in the preparation of the manuscript for publication. The writer is also grateful to Union Theological Seminary in Virginia for permission to make use of the substance of an article on " Religious Pluralism and the Churches," which previously appeared in *Interpretation*, Vol. XIX, No. 4 (Oct., 1965).

Finally, the author wishes to acknowledge his deep appreciation to his wife for her encouragement and assistance throughout the entire period of research, travel, and writing in which this study has been brought to completion.

E. C. G.

CONTENTS

Introduction   11

PART ONE: THE CRISIS IN THE CHURCH

I. A Fellowship of Class   19
  A. Social Classes in the United States   19
    1. Class Consciousness   19
    2. The Class Structure   21
    3. The New Meaning of Poverty in an Affluent
      Society   28
  B. Social Stratification and the Churches   31
    1. Church Membership   31
    2. Church Leadership   40
    3. Church Literature   45
  C. The Dilemma of the Churches   47

II. A Fellowship of Race   50
  A. The Rise of Racial Barriers in the Churches   51
  B. Segregation in the Churches: 1945–1960   59
    1. The Statistical Picture at the End of World
      War II   59
    2. Cracks in the Wall of Segregation: 1945–
      ca. 1960   61
  C. The Gap Between Tokenism and Brotherhood   67

D. The Churches and the Civil Rights Movement:
   Prior to 1963   70
   1. The Default of Leadership by the White
      Churches   70
   2. The Negro Church   73
E. Involvement in the Struggle for Human Rights:
   1963 ff.   75
F. The Depth of the Racial Problem in the
   Churches   77

III. Religious Pluralism and the Churches   80
A. The Disestablishment of the Churches   82
B. The Growth of Religious Pluralism   87
C. Facing the Realities of Pluralism   93
   1. A Secular Society   94
   2. The Need for Dialogue and Involvement   95
   3. Beyond Separationism   97

PART TWO: THE BIBLICAL VIEW OF THE CHURCH
AND THE WORLD

IV. The Faith of Israel   101
A. The Faith of Israel and the Faith of the Church   101
B. Israel as a Covenant Community   105
C. Radical Monotheism   117

V. The Church in the New Testament   132
A. The New Covenant Community   133
B. The Body of Christ   140
C. The Koinonia   147

VI. The Church and the World in the New Testament   156
A. The Church Vis-à-vis the World   156
B. The World in Biblical Thought   158
   1. The World as God's Creation: The Sphere
      of Human Activity   159
   2. The World as Fallen: The Sphere of Sin,
      Alienation, and Anxiety   161

3. The World as the Object of God's Reconciling Love   167

C. The World as the Sphere of the Church's Work   168

D. Bonhoeffer: The Church Exists for the World (Humanity)   173

PART THREE: TOWARD A PROPHETIC COMMUNITY

VII. The Tension Between the Church and Culture   179

A. Typical Relationships of the Church to Culture   181

    1. Withdrawal from Culture   183

    2. The Folk Church   185

    3. A Pattern of Creative Tension   188

B. The Goal of the Church: The Transformation of Individuals and Communities   191

C. Freedom and the Prophetic Community   194

    1. The Church and External Society   196

    2. Freedom Within the Koinonia   199

VIII. Renewal Through Engagement with Culture   207

A. The Contemporary Secular World   208

B. Dialogue and Involvement: Prerequisites for Relevance   211

C. God at the Center of Life: The Recovery of the Public World   215

D. Where Church and World Meet: Our Common Humanity   218

E. The Christian Life as Deputyship   226

F. The Ecumenical Movement and the Christian's Social Conscience   231

Notes   239

Index   249

INTRODUCTION

The church today is confronted with a twofold crisis in its own self-understanding. In the first place, it is in danger of losing its true identity as a community of faith which is rooted in the experience and heritage of a historical community. In the second place, it is confronted with the necessity of making a new appraisal of its relationship to society in a radically new cultural situation, variously described as pluralistic and post-Christian. These two problems are closely related, and, indeed, it is impossible to consider either of them adequately in isolation from the other.

Both these questions — the self-identity of the church and its role in relationship to secular society — are directly related to the renewal of the church. Discussion of the relevance of the church to contemporary life leads inevitably to a consideration of both themes. The first of these questions is the more basic, but it cannot be satisfactorily answered without some attention being given to the second. Moreover, the answer which any church gives to the question concerning its proper relationship to culture is largely determined by its underlying conception of its own nature.

In a fundamental sense, neither of these problems is new. In essence, Israel wrestled continually with both as she sought to understand the meaning of her existence as a covenant community. From her beginning Israel recognized that it was due entirely to God's gracious election that he had established a covenant with her. God had chosen her for his own purposes; he had called her to be his people. As her understanding of the divine will deepened, she came to see that God demanded justice and mercy among men and humility before himself (Micah 6:8, KJV). His demand for righteousness extended not only to individual and family relationships but also to the corporate, public life of the nation as a whole.

Moreover, through her wrestling with the divine will in the midst of her sufferings and her national calamities, Israel was led to a more profound conception of her own historical destiny as the people of God. Thus she came to a deepening understanding of her vocation among the nations. Instead of her election being a sign either of her own special virtue or of divine capriciousness, God had chosen her to be his servant to proclaim his salvation to all peoples even to the ends of the earth.

Similarly, from New Testament times onward, the Christian church has also been confronted with both of these questions. Each has appeared in many different forms, and each has appeared in many different cultural situations. The early church, for example, was faced with the necessity of understanding its own identity over against Judaism and the efforts of the Judaizers to confine Christianity within the limits of a Jewish cult. Again and again throughout its history, the church has been forced to rediscover its true identity as a historical community of faith in God as revealed in Jesus Christ over against many rival forms of faith, including Gnosticism, Manichaeism, humanism, Fascism, and Communism. Again and again it has been tempted to substitute faith in some ideology, faith in some social group, or even faith in religion itself for faith in God who has revealed himself in those events to which the Scriptures bear witness. Again and again it has bowed down to these idols of secular society and taught men to worship them.

Similarly, the church has also been torn with divisions that deny its unity and universality. Sometimes these divisions have

been based upon doctrines, sometimes upon wealth, sometimes upon racial and ethnic differences, and sometimes upon
personalities. But, whatever their sources, such divisions have
resulted in a contradiction between the church as a single community of faith and its concrete embodiment in factions and
schismatic groups. Like all other human organizations, the
church, too, has been tempted to seek its own institutional
growth — in numbers, in power, in wealth, in prestige — as an
end in itself. It has become conformed to the world, and in so
doing it has lost its power to speak with authority, to cast out
demons, to do the reconciling deed, and to leaven the society
in which it is set. Hence, again and again, it has been summoned to repentance; it has been forced to examine its integrity and rediscover its true identity. It has been forced to ask
to whom it belongs and what common faith binds it together
into a single community.

Each renewal in the church's understanding of its own essential nature has also led to a new wrestling with the problem of
its relationship to society. The need for such a reexamination
of its cultural responsibility has been made necessary not only
by the church's recovery of its true sense of identity but also
by the changing cultural situation itself. The eschatological expectations of the early church have receded so that a much
longer historical future is anticipated for the present world.
Even more significant is the fact that the responsibility of Christians and the church for the historical future has greatly increased due, on the one hand, to the vast increase in the membership of the churches and due, on the other hand, to the
growth of democratic institutions. Taken together, these developments have created far greater opportunities for the churches
to influence the formation of public policy, especially in the de-
mocracies of the West, than were present in the period in
which the New Testament was being written.

Throughout the New Testament period and indeed prior to
Constantine, the state was generally hostile to Christianity or,
at best, merely tolerant of it. Moreover, this has been the lot

of the church in large sections of the world down to the present. When Christians have not been permitted to occupy positions of power and where the freedom of the church has been denied, there has been little opportunity for these groups to work directly for social justice. Under such circumstances Christians have had to seek the meaning of obedience to God within the context of a society whose institutional forms they could not change.

Beginning with Constantine, however, the church began to occupy a far more favorable position in society, especially in relationship to the state. Christianity subsequently became the official religion of the Holy Roman Empire; and, following the Reformation, the newly emerging national states generally adopted some form of Protestant or Roman Catholic establishment. During this period the churches attempted to impose their rule upon society through the state. They occupied positions of power, and they attempted to make society Christian through the imposition of both Christian faith and Christian morality. This pattern of an established church was transferred, with few exceptions, to America, where it continued throughout the colonial period and, in a number of states, well into the nineteenth century. Indeed, in many respects Protestantism has continued to have the status of semiofficial establishment in this country on into the second half of the twentieth century.

The attempt to implement the Constantinian ideal of the church ruling society led to the illusion that Western society was Christian. This myth was symbolized in Europe, particularly in the Middle Ages, by the concept of Christendom and by the vision of a Christian civilization; subsequently it has been typified in this country by the widely held assumption that American civilization was Protestant Christian, both in its foundations and in its basic value orientation. But the illusion of such a Christian society has been shattered, both in Europe and in America, in the present century. The churches are now faced with the reality of a secular, pluralistic society. The Constantinian era of the church ruling society is past. Moreover, this is essentially the situation that confronts the churches all over the world — in communist lands, in Asia, and in Africa, as well as in the Christian-democratic West.

This new situation has only recently begun to be recognized in this country, and it is forcing the church to reexamine its relationship to the public, political life of the nation as a whole. It can no longer be taken for granted that the national ethos, or underlying structure of values, in our society is Christian. The churches can no longer assume that Christian morality and Christian values do in fact constitute a commonly accepted norm of public as well as private life; nor can they impose their own distinctive standards and values upon the entire nation. On the contrary, the churches must now enter into the formation of public policy as one special interest group among many; and they must do so without any built-in political advantage. As concrete embodiments of the church, the churches do in fact have political power and political interests. But when they are true to their own nature and mission in the world, their aim is not to rule the world but to minister to the needs of all men in all political parties and states. Such a ministry does not, however, require the abandonment of political power; on the contrary, it requires the use of this power, not for the churches' own glory, but as an instrument of neighbor-love, including love for secular man, for humanists, and for atheists, as well as for adherents to other religious faiths.

It is the thesis of this book that the renewal of the church and the recovery of its relevance to modern life depend upon its learning to understand itself once again as a prophetic community. This means that the church must take its stand in a particular tradition as part of a continuing community of faith whose spiritual roots reach back into the faith and history of Israel. This is its starting point in its understanding both of itself as a community and of its mission in the world. On the basis of this faith, which has been given to it as its ultimate perspective for understanding the meaning of human existence, the church is called to proclaim the divine will to men, in word and in act, in order that they may be confronted with the truth about themselves to the end that they may be made whole. It is called to proclaim the divine judgment upon men and nations, for the judgment of God reveals the final truth about man; but the church is also called to summon men to repentance in order that they may enter into the promise of reconciliation and being made new. Nothing can be more relevant to human life than such a prophetic word, but such a word cannot be spoken by the church when it loses its identity as a community of faith and confronts men only as the sanctifier of culture.

This study is intended as a contribution to the recovery of a deeper understanding of the nature of the church and its relevance to secular society. Part One deals primarily with a sociological, descriptive analysis of the contemporary churches. The first two chapters are devoted to an examination of the extent to which the churches reflect the divisions of secular society along class and racial lines in terms of their membership, leadership, and value orientation. The third chapter traces the emergence of religious pluralism in the United States and calls attention to some of the major implications of this new situation for the churches.

Part Two consists of an examination of the historical, Biblical conception of the church and its mission in the world. Whereas Part One is essentially descriptive in method, this section of the study is normative and Biblical, or theological, in character. It deals with the New Testament conception of the church, the spiritual rootage of the church in the faith of Israel, and the relationship of the church to the world.

Finally, in Part Three attention will be focused upon some of the implications of the Biblical view of the church vis-à-vis the world for the church today as it seeks to recover its relevance to the life of contemporary, secular man. It is the thesis of the present study that the church can preserve its integrity as a community of faith while at the same time giving itself for the world (humanity) only if it maintains a relationship of creative tension with society. Such a relationship of tension implies a fundamental freedom of the church over against society and also a corresponding freedom of society over against the rule of the church. It implies the engagement of the church with culture rather than the division of life into two separate spheres, one sacred and the other secular. Finally, such a relationship of tension implies the need for the church to participate in the search for answers to the most urgent and perplexing social problems that man faces; and in this task, in particular, the laity have an especially crucial contribution and witness to make. Moreover, in our increasingly pluralistic world, it is essential that the search for renewal and relevance of the church be made in the context of the ecumenical movement; and the latter, in turn, must include an effort toward a greater understanding of, and cooperation with, the non-Christian religions.

PART ONE: THE CRISIS IN THE CHURCH

I

A FELLOWSHIP OF CLASS

In the present chapter we shall examine the extent to which the churches in this country both reflect and reinforce the class alignments that are found in secular society. In order to provide a more adequate perspective for understanding the far-reaching significance of cleavages based upon class in the life of the church, it is necessary, first of all, to consider briefly the nature and significance of the class structure in American society as a whole. Then, in the remainder of this chapter, we shall analyze some of the major ways in which the class alignments of secular society are reflected in the churches, both at the local church and at the denominational levels. In particular, we shall examine the impact of class alignments upon the membership, the leadership, and the religious literature of the churches.

A. SOCIAL CLASSES IN THE UNITED STATES

1. Class Consciousness

While most Americans recognize that there are vast differences of wealth, power, and prestige in our society, they differ a great deal in regard to the significance they attach to these differences. Due to the equalitarianism represented both in our democratic tradition and in our Judeo-Christian heritage, there is widespread resistance to any attempt to draw sharp lines between the various social strata. Indeed, many forces — the frontier, public education, the rapidly changing character of our society, industrialization, urbanization, and the adoption of such legislation as antitrust laws, graduated income and inheritance taxes, social security, unemployment compensation, minimum wages, and medical care — have operated to keep class lines from becoming sharp and rigid in this country as a whole.

Patterns of social stratification vary greatly from one locality to another, and the degree of class consciousness varies widely between different status groups. In older, more stable communities, for example, the class lines are likely to be more sharply drawn and the population more rigidly divided into a number of status groups. In rapidly expanding urban areas, on the other hand, it is extremely difficult to define class lines in very precise terms due to the complex and changing character of city life. Here the symbols of wealth and power play more important roles in the establishment of class identification than is frequently the case in smaller, more stable, more tradition-oriented communities.

Insofar as class consciousness is concerned, this seems to be most pronounced among the upper and lower classes as compared with the middle class. In addition to the very top and the very bottom status groups, class consciousness is also particularly pronounced (a) among persons who have recently risen on the social scale but feel apprehensive about their acceptance at their new level and (b) among those who have held a certain status for a long time but feel their position threatened either by the processes of social change or by the rising position of persons who presently possess a lower status but are climbing up the social ladder.

Among the upper class, recognition of differential status groups is likely to be most precise among the more stable segment of this stratum — among the "power elite," for example, who have developed a systematic conception of the status structure of the entire community through long experience of working with various levels of community leadership. At the other end of the scale, members of the lower class are constantly reminded of their low status by the poor environment in which they live and the constant frustrations that they experience in the effort to attain even the minimal necessities of life. Slums, poverty, unemployment, inadequate education, broken homes, membership in a low status group itself, and, frequently, discrimination based on their racial or ethnic identification present well-nigh insuperable obstacles to any significant improvement in their standard of living. Members of this group are vividly aware of their rejection by society, and they respond both with apathy and with aggression toward society at large.[1]

On the whole, the broad middle status groups appear to draw the class lines less sharply than the groups at either end of the scale. A number of public-opinion polls indicate that the overwhelming majority of Americans think of themselves as belonging to some median status group which they may identify either as the "middle class" or the "working class." Apparently most Americans consider it undemocratic and snobbish to claim membership in the top social stratum, but they also avoid identifying themselves with the lowest status group since the term "lower class" connotes moral approbrium as well as low economic position. In general, members of the middle status groups look upon the class structure as being fluid and open, so that anyone who has either sufficient ability or a little luck is able to move upward on the social scale. They tend to explain the present unequal distribution of the various social rewards or status symbols in terms of *individual* differences rather than in terms of fixed social classes.

2. The Class Structure

Analyses of the degree of class consciousness and surveys of self-identification on the class scale are significant as indices of the depth of social cleavages in a community or nation. We have been concerned with them here because they suggest a general recognition of the existence of differential status groups in our society while at the same time they reveal that the cleavages between these groups are not nearly so sharp as they are in many other societies.

But such general subjective and largely impressionistic perceptions of class consciousness do not tell us much about the specific ways in which class status influences the value systems, beliefs, and actions of members of different status groups. In order to provide a more adequate understanding of the significance of social stratification in these areas, systematic analyses of the class structure in relationship to the major aspects of community life as a whole are needed, and an impressive number of such studies have been made in recent decades. Sociologists have examined a wide variety of communities — old and new, stable and transitional, rural and urban — in different sections of the country. Taken together these studies shed a great deal of light upon the relationship of the churches to the class structure. In the first place, they indicate the existence in most communities of a larger number of socially significant status groups than Americans generally suppose; and, more significantly, they reveal, in the second place, the extent to which such class patterns influence the totality of the life both of individuals and of communities.

There is no single reliable index of class status and, indeed, no single symbol which is always more important than any other. Rather, there are many important factors, both objective and subjective, which interact with each other to determine the prestige and influence of an individual. Among the objective factors influencing the social position and power of people are such things as occupation, source and amount of income, place of residence, education, membership in certain organizations and clubs, and responsibility or power; among the subjective factors involved are the attitudes, ideologies, and goals or aspirations that people hold. Hence, there is a tendency among sociologists to describe social classes in terms of a " style of life " rather than in terms of a series of relatively discrete indices. Taken together, a variety of factors such as those to which we have just referred largely determine the way people live – what they do, where they live, who their friends are, how they spend their leisure time, the number and kinds of gadgets they own, where they spend their vacations, where their children go to school, what their economic and political views are, and what churches they attend. In relation to each of these activities people are drawn together by a common set of values which serve to integrate their lives and give meaning to their existence.

Fortunately in our society, however, as we have seen, the class lines are not sharply drawn, and the integrating values of the different classes are not mutually exclusive. The status system resembles a continuum more than a hierarchy of sharply delineated groups, and the class structure is open in that there is, theoretically and also to a lesser extent in actual practice, the possibility of moving up the social scale. Hence, there are no class conflicts in our society such as Marx envisaged and such as are found in more rigidly structured and sharply divided societies typified by prerevolutionary Russia, Germany before World War II, pre-Communist China, and many parts of Latin America.

Nevertheless, the social stratification that has taken place in the United States has created cleavages in our community life that run counter to our democratic and religious traditions and are of sufficient magnitude to cause serious concern. Their consequences are evident in the inequalities in community life – in housing, public schools, employment opportunities, recreational facilities, medical care, and security in old age. While some kinds of social stratification are functionally useful and even necessary for the ordering and integration of any society, other forms are dysfunctional and obstruct the achievement of genuine community. A class system that rests upon inherited privilege, for example, is unjust and oppressive; it also becomes socially divisive when the special values that serve to unify a particular class come to outweigh in importance the values that the society as a whole holds in common.

In his book *The American Class Structure*, Joseph A. Kahl speaks of five major social classes in contemporary American society.[2] Inasmuch as each of these represents a generally recognizable style of life that distinguishes it in significant respects from the other four, it will be helpful if we examine each of the five groups briefly. Since there is considerable variation in the class structure from one community to another, Kahl's typology does not, of course, represent a precise description of social stratification in every American community. It does, however, provide a useful instrument for calling attention to the typical occupational characteristics, values, beliefs, and associational (residential, civic, religious) patterns of some of the major segments of American society. It indicates the manner in which all these forms of behavior interact to produce a general pattern of life centered around a particular set of values, beliefs, and moral standards that has special relevance to the status position of the particular group. Each status group tends to develop its own peculiar values and beliefs into an ideology and judge the values and beliefs of other groups in ethnocentric terms.

In the following analysis special attention will be focused upon the characteristic forms of employment in each of the five major classes. While occupation is by no means the sole criterion of social status, it is obviously a very important factor, since it represents the primary source of income needed to make possible the general way of life — the type of housing, education, recreation, and civic organizations — that is deemed appropriate for people in the same status group. After looking briefly at each of these five major classes, we shall turn to an examination of the extent to which the division of society into various social strata is reflected in the churches.

The upper class is composed of the richest, most powerful, and most exclusive families in a community. In part, members of this elite have inherited positions of wealth and prestige; in part, they are self-made folk who have risen to the very top positions in business or the professions. Characteristically, up-

per-class men are members of the boards of directors of busi-
nesses, banks, universities, and community chests. They are the
people who either make the big decisions or are at least con-
sulted when these decisions are made. They derive their income both from inherited wealth and from high salaries based
on their skills in management. Members of the upper class are
usually conservative and tend to feel superior to other groups.
They live in exclusive neighborhoods or suburbs and emphasize the values of tradition, family lineage, and graceful living.

The upper-middle class consists primarily of the families of
successful business and professional men whose incomes and
responsibilities place them just below the top levels in these
occupations. Income is mainly from current occupational
sources rather than from inherited or accumulated property.
The men in this group are specialists in business and the professions, and they have the responsibility for making the numerous day-to-day decisions affecting the business and professional life of their less prestigious colleagues and employees.
They do not hold jobs but occupy positions; they do not work
but pursue careers. Typically, they are "organization men,"
and their lives center around making a success in their careers.
They are active and other-directed. They join numerous civic
and social organizations, but in these groups they associate almost exclusively with each other. They live either in luxury
apartments in the city or in fashionable suburbs.

In view of the increasingly dominant role that the upper-
middle class plays in American society due to the growing impact of industrialization, urbanization, and the accompanying
organizational revolution of modern society, the following description of the characteristic beliefs of this group is particularly significant for a realistic understanding of both the
strengths and the weaknesses of contemporary churches:

What do they believe? Primarily, they believe in themselves and in organization. They stress individual initiative combined with smooth group functioning. They have

faith that anything can be accomplished by this combination. They say that a man must be smart, must be educated, must be energetic, but at the same time he must be cooperative, must not stand out too much from his crowd of equals, must not be eccentric or " controversial." These are the values of the upper levels of most bureaucratic structures. They are very effective in their proper situation; they may not produce great art or literature or scientific theory, but they certainly produce efficient organizations.

. . . They stress planning for the future and not too much regard for the past; they stress activity, accomplishment, practical results; they stress individualistic achievement within the framework of group cooperation and collective responsibility. They are not much interested in tradition, in art, in any sort of theory for its own sake. They always ask of an idea, " What good is it; how can you use it? " [3]

The lower-middle class is composed largely of the less successful members of business, the professions, and government, and the more successful manual workers. While this group consists predominantly of white-collar people who are at the bottom of various ladders that may potentially lead to much higher positions in business and the professions, it also includes such blue-collar workers as foremen, many skilled craftsmen, and some operatives. In many ways this is the least clearly defined of the five groups. There is frequently little difference either in income or in prestige between members of the lower-middle and the working classes.

Lower-middle class families live in the same sections of town in either small apartments, multiple-family dwellings, or small single-family houses. In the main, the adults are high school graduates, and some have had additional specialized training. In contrast to routine, nonspecialized wage workers, they pride themselves on having stable jobs. Members of this group frequently aspire to identification with the upper-middle class, but they are quite aware that they have neither the positions of responsibility nor the income that are associated with the latter. They want their children to go to college and move up the social scale even if they are unable to do so themselves. If the key goal of the upper class is graceful living and that of the upper-middle a successful career, the central aim of the lower-middle stratum is to achieve respectability; and among the signs of respectability are such things as a steady job, ownership of one's own home, a relatively strict pattern of morality, well-behaved children, and regular church attendance.

The working class is composed largely of the families of semi-skilled factory operatives. Typically, the men in this group dropped out of high school before graduation. Since they have no specialized training for particular types of work, they drift from job to job as the labor market shifts. There is little opportunity for advancement in income or responsibility such as is characteristic of a career; hence, the primary aim of the working group is to " get by " in their jobs. They derive their greatest satisfaction out of their paychecks rather than from the work they do. Thus they are tragically alienated from their work because they are not able to express their real selves in it in a vital, creative way. Moreover, they also feel largely alienated from contemporary community life since they do not participate in the policy-forming, decision-making processes either of the factory or of other major community organizations. On the whole, the values that are most important to semiskilled industrial workers differ significantly from those that are typical both of the career- and of the respectability-oriented middle classes.

The lower class is made up of people who have the most poorly paid jobs, work irregularly, and live in slums. The members of this group are at the bottom of the social scale, where they are caught in a vicious web of circumstances that makes life seem hopeless and filled with despair, bitterness, and boredom. Unemployment is concentrated in this group, especially

among members of racial and ethnic minorities. Usually their
education is limited to the grammar school, and many have not
finished it. The problem posed by dropouts from the public
schools, which has been the center of national attention in recent years, is particularly acute among the lower class. Family life is unstable. The incidence of disease, delinquency, and
crime is high. The victims of injustice, oppression, and indif-
ference on the part of society as a whole, members of the lower
class tend either to fight back — as in the racial riots in Harlem,
Rochester, and Philadelphia in 1964, in Los Angeles in 1965,
and in Cleveland and Atlanta in 1966 — or to become apa-
thetic. Because of the inequalities imposed upon them by the
circumstances in which they are caught, the members of this
group desperately need economic assistance and social justice.
In particular, they need the provision of realistic opportunities
for self-help in terms of education, specialized training, and
employment; they need better housing, medical care, police
protection, and recreational facilities. In short, they need to be
incorporated as participants into the total community so that
they can achieve genuine human dignity in relationship to society as a whole.

3. The New Meaning of Poverty in an Affluent Society

In attempting to assess the significance of the class structure
in this country for the mission of the churches, it is important
to recognize that poverty has taken on a new meaning in our
society of abundance and growing interdependence. It is one
thing for people to be in want in a society in which there is
general scarcity; it is quite another matter to be in want in a
society — even a world — in which the resources are available
to meet the basic needs of the population as a whole. Under
such circumstances there is what Adlai Stevenson once called a
"revolution of rising expectations." This escalation in human
expectations and demands stems in part out of a vision of new
possibilities and an awakening of new desires, but it stems also
in part out of an increase in human needs, objective as well as

subjective, in an increasingly complex, specialized, and inter-dependent world.

Since the dawn of the atomic age we have heard a great deal about the possibility of abundance for all. The standard of living has increased so rapidly in this country and the benefits of this increase have been distributed to such an unprecedented proportion of the population that we have frequently lost sight of those groups which have not shared in this general prosperity. In the prosperous '40s and '50s, people in the upper and middle classes, living in the suburbs and more desirable sections of the cities, were shocked to learn that there were pockets of poverty in this country — segments of our society in which large numbers of people lived at the level of barest economic necessity. More recently, as a nation we have been surprised and dismayed to discover that in the even more affluent '60s more than 34 million people — between a fifth and a sixth of the national population — are living in a state of poverty.

The Federal Government and other agencies have determined that families with incomes under $3,000 a year and un-attached individuals with incomes under $1,500 a year live in poverty.[4] On the basis of these definitions, 8.9 million families, including an estimated 29.2 million people, and an additional 5 million unattached individuals in this country were living in poverty in 1963. More tragically still, 5.1 million of these families — including about 16.7 million people — had incomes under $2,000, and 3.2 million of these unattached individuals had incomes under $1,000 a year. Thus, the incomes of approximately 20 million persons — more than a tenth of the nation — needed to be increased by at least 50 percent in order to raise them above the poverty level.

In addition to the 34 million people who were living in poverty in this country in 1963, an additional 32 million persons were living in a state of deprivation, since their incomes fell considerably below the requirements for a " modest but adequate " budget, estimated at $6,000 for families and $2,750 for unattached individuals. Included in this group were an estimated 8.6 million families, consisting of approximately 30 million people, with annual incomes between $3,000 and $5,000 and 1.9 million unattached individuals with incomes ranging between $1,500 and $2,500. Thus, a total of more than 66 million Americans, or about 35½ percent of the nation, lived either in poverty or in deprivation in 1963.[5]

The existence of this widespread poverty and deprivation in the midst of our unprecedented general prosperity has been recently dramatized through the adoption of a number of specialized programs for people living in distressed areas and for the unemployed and unemployable. National concern for the latter groups culminated in the enactment of the Economic Opportunity Amendments of 1965. It should not be forgotten, however, that such economically depressed groups have long existed in our society side by side with the affluent segments of the population, and we have just begun to discover their presence and the blighting consequences of such poverty, both in terms of the individuals who are its victims and in terms of society as a whole.

As we have seen, the churches in this country tend to be divided along class lines; for this reason their conceptions of social justice tend to reflect the special interests of the particular socioeconomic groups they represent. But there is a far greater and more dangerous gap between what Barbara Ward, the noted English economist, has called "the rich nations and the poor nations." This gap also vitally affects not only the peace of the world but also the integrity and unity of the church as a universal community. Compared with the vast majority of mankind, most of the thirty-four million persons living in poverty in this country have relatively high incomes. Indeed, most of the latter undoubtedly have far higher levels of consumption than many people who are not considered poor in India, China, and Africa. As Leon H. Keyserling points out, poverty is a relative concept, and its meaning is determined in part by the available technology, wealth, and capabilities of a society.[6] But the world is fast becoming one in terms of its economic potential and the expectations of the underdeveloped countries. Just as massive poverty in this country has become intolerable because it is no longer inevitable, so the gap between the rich nations and the poor nations is also rapidly becoming intolerable in the world of today because it too can be largely overcome through a deeper commitment to the pursuit of social justice for all men.

In an address to the Sixth World Order Study Conference in 1965, Barbara Ward declared that the 20 percent of the world's people who live in North America and Western Europe absorb 75 percent of the world's income, investment, and trade.[7] In 1960 the average per capita income in the United States was $2,800; in Europe, it was $1,079; in Latin America, $389; and in many countries in Africa and Asia, it ranged as low as $30 to $100. Despite efforts to reduce this disparity through various forms of economic aid, the chasm has continued to widen. More determined and realistic steps are needed to provide the capitalization necessary for the industrial development of the underdeveloped countries. Such appalling and growing differentials in standards of living between the rich nations and the poor nations have become the great "new threat" to world peace and world community in the mid-twentieth century.[8] In both the affluent and the underdeveloped countries the churches are caught up in this struggle, and the latter tend to view the gospel in terms of the special economic interests of their members.

B. SOCIAL STRATIFICATION AND THE CHURCHES

1. Church Membership

In order to understand the impact which social stratification has had upon the churches in this country, it is necessary to examine the relationships between the churches and the class structure at a number of different levels. To what extent, for example, is the membership of a particular denomination drawn from a single social class? To what extent does the leadership of the various denominations cut across class lines? Similarly, to what extent does the value orientation of a particular denomination reflect the special interests of a single status group? These same questions also need to be asked with regard to local churches.

Many careful studies have been made of religion and the class structure in a variety of American communities over the past three or four decades. Although they differ considerably in their detailed findings, they consistently show that membership and participation in specific religious bodies are closely related to the patterns of social stratification in various communities. Taken together these studies reveal a picture of the churches that differs sharply in many respects from the images as well as the norms that the churches hold concerning themselves.

In the first place, while each denomination tends to include some people drawn from almost every social level, each also tends to be identified on the whole with a particular social class.[9] Thus, the Protestant Episcopal, Congregational, Presbyterian, and Unitarian denominations tend to attract a larger proportion of upper- and upper-middle-class people than do other Protestant or Roman Catholic bodies. Methodists, Disciples of Christ, Lutherans, and Baptists tend to be drawn more largely from the middle to lower-middle social class range. Assembly of God, Pentecostal, and Holiness churches tend to be identified primarily with the lower classes, including the working class.

On the average, Protestants apparently still represent somewhat higher social class levels than Roman Catholics, although the difference between the two groups is becoming increasingly less pronounced.[10] It is clear, however, that the traditional, or main-line, Protestant denominations attract predominantly middle- and upper-class constituencies, whereas the membership of the newer, more largely sectarian groups is drawn chiefly from the lower classes. It is particularly difficult to generalize about the Baptists. Some Baptist bodies have a sizable proportion of middle-class membership; most, however, are drawn largely from the lower classes, including the working class or blue-collar group.

Among the rural population, farm owners and managers are more likely than tenants and laborers to be church members. In urban areas larger proportions of business, professional, and white-collar workers are affiliated with the churches than is true in the case of manual laborers.

Generalizations such as the foregoing, it should be emphasized, are subject to wide regional and community variation; and denominations cannot be ranked as always having the same position in relation to the class scale. Nevertheless, the general, over-all relationship of the various denominations to the patterns of social stratification is significant in view of the tendency of church bodies to exaggerate their own inclusiveness and equalitarianism.

Although the table on page 34 is based upon a division of the social continuum into three rather than five classes, it provides a valuable summary of the relationship between church affiliation and social class position in the United States, as measured by a national sample of 12,019 members of the voting population. It should also be pointed out that the term "class" was defined in this particular tabulation in terms of *economic* stratification rather than in terms of a number of additional criteria. Interviewers in the polls upon which the data used in this analysis was based were instructed to classify each respondent in relation to the latter's own community rather than in relation to the country as a whole. The list is arranged according to the percentage of each denomination in the upper class. The corresponding figures for the national sample as a whole are given at the head of the table.

One of the most striking aspects that the table shows is the evidence that it provides of an almost exactly parallel stratification in the constituencies of the Roman Catholic and Baptist churches. Each of these groups appears to draw approximately two thirds of its members from the lower economic stratum.

SOCIAL CLASS PROFILES OF AMERICAN RELIGIOUS GROUPS

	Class			
Denomination	Upper	Middle	Lower	Number
National Sample	13.1%	30.7%	56.2%	12,019
Christian Scientist	24.8	36.5	38.7	137
Episcopal	24.1	33.7	42.2	590
Congregational	23.9	42.6	33.5	376
Presbyterian	21.9	40.0	38.1	961
Jewish	21.8	32.0	46.2	537
Reformed	19.1	31.3	49.6	131
Methodist	12.7	35.6	51.7	2,100
Lutheran	10.9	36.1	53.0	723
Christian	10.0	35.4	54.6	370
Protestant (small bodies)	10.0	27.3	62.7	888
Roman Catholic	8.7	24.7	66.6	2,390
Baptist	8.0	24.0	68.0	1,381
Mormon	5.1	28.6	66.3	175
No Preference	13.3	26.0	60.7	466
Protestant (undesignated)	12.4	24.1	63.5	460
Atheist, Agnostic	33.3	46.7	20.0	15
No Answer or Don't Know	11.0	29.5	59.5	319

From Nicholas J. Demerath III, *Social Class in American Protestantism* (Rand McNally & Company, 1965), p. 2.

However, when allowance is made for the fact that the Baptist churches are not represented in this *voting* sample on a comparable basis with the other groups because of the large number of nonvoting Negroes in their membership, especially in the South, it is probable that they have a larger percentage of their constituency in the lower economic stratum than does the Roman Catholic Church.

It has been widely assumed that Roman Catholics are generally considerably below Protestants in terms of their comparative socioeconomic status. The foregoing analysis indicates, however, that this differential is not so great as has been commonly assumed. This finding is also confirmed by other studies. Relying upon data collected in two polls taken by the National Opinion Research Center of the University of Chicago in 1953 and 1955, Donald J. Bogue concluded that Roman Catholicism and Protestantism tended to have quite similar constituencies insofar as occupational composition is concerned, the main difference being that the former had a slight excess of urban working-class persons, whereas the latter had a larger proportion of farmers.[11]

Ranking the different religious bodies on a " high," " median," and " low " income scale, Bogue made the following classification: [12]

High Income	Median Income	Low Income
Jewish	Catholic	Baptist
Episcopal	Lutheran	Small Protestant
Presbyterian	No Religion	Sects
	Methodist	

When the various religious bodies were ranked with respect to the average educational level achieved by their constituencies, the result was as follows: [13]

Episcopal
Jewish
Presbyterian
Methodist
Other Protestant
Lutheran
No Religion
Roman Catholic
Baptist

Jewish, Episcopal, and Roman Catholic groups had exceptionally high concentrations of their memberships in standard metropolitan areas. Whereas only about one half of the total sample of households were located in such areas, 98 percent of the Jewish, 78 percent of the Episcopal, and 74 percent of the heads of Roman Catholic households lived in metropolitan centers. Baptists, in particular, among the larger Protestant bodies, were concentrated in nonmetropolitan areas (52.8 percent) and smaller (less than 1 million inhabitants) metropolitan areas (31.7 percent). Methodists showed a similar, though less pronounced, tendency to be concentrated in these same areas (49.4 percent in nonmetropolitan and 29.0 percent in smaller metropolitan areas). Presbyterians, on the other hand, were somewhat more likely to be found in metropolitan (62.7 percent) than in nonmetropolitan (37.2 percent) areas.[14]

While the foregoing analyses deal generally with the class characteristics of predominantly white denominations, other studies make it clear that among Negroes church affiliation is also associated with class identification in much the same way that it is among whites. The Episcopal, Congregational, and Presbyterian churches tend, for example, to attract upper-class Negroes. There is also some tendency on the part of upper-class Negroes to join the Roman Catholic Church. The membership of the Baptist and Methodist denominations is drawn typically from the middle classes. The numerous sects, cults, and storefront churches derive their memberships largely from the lower classes. That the total number of Negro church members belonging to these latter groups is comparatively small is indicated, however, by the fact that the five largest Negro denominations are either Baptist or Methodist and that these bodies reported a total membership of about 10,000,000 in 1960. While this figure is undoubtedly much too large, it indicates the relative strength of these bodies in comparison with the smaller sects and cults.[15]

Thus far, we have been analyzing the relationship between denominational groups as a whole and the class structure. When, on the other hand, we turn our attention to local congregations, we find that the class lines are even more sharply drawn here than they are in the case of the over-all denominational bodies. Members of the same social class tend to live in the same residential areas and go to the same neighborhood church of their particular denomination. There are, of course, many exceptions to this general pattern of church membership, but the exceptions occur more frequently in respect to the place of residence than to the class alignments of a specific congregation. The large downtown church with a famous minister may, for example, attract upper- and middle-class members who have moved to more desirable residential areas, but such a church generally does not draw many members from the inner city. The prevailing pattern followed by the major Protestant denominations, however, has been for churches in deteriorating sections of the city to move to the suburbs or to the more stable residential areas and abandon the inner city to the sects, the cults, and the storefront churches. Since the residents of a particular suburb tend to belong to the same general social class, the churches of suburbia almost inevitably become fellowships that are divided along class lines.

But the close identification of local churches with single socioeconomic groups is not limited to the suburbs. Many churches of the major Protestant denominations are found in most sections of the city except the central core. Such congregations also reflect similar patterns of socioeconomic stratification and isolation.

What Gibson Winter refers to as " exodus " of the traditional Protestant churches to the suburban and satellite sections of the metropolitan areas has resulted in two major changes in the memberships of their respective denominations.[16] In the first place, there has been an increasing identification of the latter with the middle classes, and, in the second place, there has been a radical change in the occupational character of the memberships of these denominations as a whole. Not only has the proportion of the rural population itself rapidly declined during recent decades, but traditional Protestant denominations have not continued to hold their onetime rural members once the latter have moved to the cities. Rather, as we have noted, such groups as the Methodists, the Presbyterians, and the Baptists have abandoned the central city, where these rural migrants are concentrated, to the sects and storefront churches.

Like their more affluent counterparts in the suburbs, the sects and storefront churches that spring up in the inner city also fall into captivity to their socioeconomic environment. In this case, however, it is bondage to the prevailing economic interests, values, and ideologies of those groups which live in the blighted sections of the city. The members of these churches tend to be unskilled manual laborers and lead a marginal economic existence. They are isolated from the remainder of the metropolitan community in their church identification — both at the denominational and at the local church levels — as well as in almost every other aspect of their cultural life. Under such circumstances people tend to turn to religion as a way of escape from the frustrations of daily life, and they tend to view the churches as being set against the world of culture, which appears to be hostile and evil. To people who are caught in these conditions religion has appeal because it offers consolation, hope, emotional release, and the promise of otherworldly salvation.

In summary, due to the processes of industrialization and urbanization together with the accompanying changes that these have brought in the class structure, the memberships of urban churches have come to be increasingly concentrated in single social classes. As a result, local churches have become increasingly isolated from the real life of the city as a whole. To the extent that they have become class-oriented and isolated, they not only reflect but also actively foster the social cleavages, the fragmentation of community, and the increasing secularization that are characteristic of urban life.

Finally, there is a third level of institutional church life that is affected by the tendency of both denominations and local congregations to be identified with particular classes, namely, the ecumenical movement. The National Council of the Churches of Christ in the U.S.A., for example, is constituted primarily of those denominations in which the middle and upper classes are dominant. Not only have such relatively new churches of the lower classes as the Pentecostal, Holiness, and storefront groups refused to join this body, but the Southern Baptist Convention, whose membership is drawn largely from the lower economic strata, has also remained aloof from it. Hence, while the National Council is more inclusive than many of its constituent bodies, it also appears to be predominantly oriented toward the middle and upper classes, not only in its membership but more especially in its leadership.

Despite its own particular class bias, however, the National Council of Churches serves a mediating and moderating role in Protestantism insofar as the divisive effects of the class structure are concerned. Accordingly, it is criticized — frequently from within — for being too closely identified with the conservative interests of the privileged classes in its pronouncements on economic matters; yet, at the same time, it is also accused of being socialistic and communist-infiltrated by members of the right-wing groups within its constituent denominations as well as by the theologically and socially conservative National Association of Evangelicals.

In many respects the Protestant ecumenical body in which the American middle-class structure and value system are least dominant is the World Council of Churches. As its name implies, this body includes denominations that are scattered all over the world. Many of its members are located in countries in which the average per capita income is extremely low — $30 to $100 per year — and in which a middle class is almost non-existent. In such a situation there is frequently a far greater social and economic gap between the upper and lower classes — especially in the countries of Asia, Africa, and South America — than is found in the United States. Under such circumstances the older, more traditional churches in these lands tend to represent the privileged and conservative classes whereas the younger national churches have a broader base among the masses and tend to be more closely identified with their revolutionary social aims.

In view of the great economic, political, and social differences among Christians in different parts of the world, it is one of the major strengths of the World Council of Churches that it provides an inclusive framework in which the competing self-interests and ethnocentrism of each of its constituent groups are subjected to criticism and partial correction by its fellow members. But even here the ideal of a church that effectively transcends class is not so much a reality that has been achieved as a goal to which the church is committed.

2. Church Leadership

Turning from a consideration of the membership to that of the leadership and value orientation of the churches, we find that the influence of class alignments is even more pronounced in the case of the latter. In 1928, Jerome Davis investigated the social composition of the governing boards of 387 Protestant churches representing seven denominations. In this study Davis found that " on the whole the membership of the boards of control is made up overwhelmingly of the favored classes." [17] The privileged status of the leadership of the church boards, he believed, resulted in an essentially conservative viewpoint on the part of the churches, a strengthening of the *status quo,* and resistance to social change.

This problem has not received much attention from researchers since Davis' study. However, there seems to be very little basis for supposing that the general tendency of the churches to select their leaders from among their more well-to-do members has changed much since that time. Lay delegates to the national governing bodies as well as the leading officials of the local churches are likely to be chosen from the higher status occupation, education, and income members of the congregation. Business proprietors, people from the upper levels of management, successful salesmen, lawyers, physicians, and educators — as well as their wives, who represent the same social classes — are far more likely to be chosen for leadership positions in the local church and as delegates to the denominational conventions than are policemen, laborers, union leaders, and farmers. Moreover, when leaders are in the blue-collar occupations, they are generally skilled craftsmen rather than unskilled workers.

It was reported at the Triennial Convention of the Protestant Episcopal Church in 1955, for example, that while manual workers might be found in some vestries, they were "rarely in diocesan conventions and almost never in the General Convention." [18] In view of the relatively lower-class status associated with membership in The Methodist Church as compared with membership in the Episcopal Church, it is even more striking that there were only four farmers and six laboring people among a total of 718 delegates at the 1952 General Conference of The Methodist Church.[19] Similarly, only 7.7 percent of all clerical and lay delegates to the 1960 General Conference of The Methodist Church had incomes below $6,000, whereas 44.7 percent of all Methodist pastors and lay leaders in local parishes had incomes that fell below $6,000.[20] At the other end of the scale, 61 percent of the total delegates reported incomes of $10,000 or more, whereas only 26.5 percent of all Methodist pastors and lay leaders in local parishes reported salaries in this income bracket.

Following the 1963 Triennial Assembly of the National Council of Churches, the Bureau of Research and Survey of the NCC analyzed the characteristics of the delegates and visitors to that Assembly. A total of 260 voting representatives, including 30 alternates, and 540 nonvoting consultants and visitors responded to the questionnaire mailed out by the Bureau of Research and Survey. An analysis of these returns showed that a total of 77 percent of the 260 delegates belonged to the professional and managerial occupations; 13.1 percent consisted of persons not included "in the labor force" such as students, housewives, and retired persons; and the remaining 9.9 percent did not give their occupations. In contrast to the 77 percent of the delegates who belonged to the professional and managerial groups, only 22 percent of the total labor force in the United States as a whole falls into these categories. Most significantly, the remaining 78 percent of the labor force — including white- and blue-collar workers in addition to service personnel and farm laborers — failed to be represented among the responding delegates; and only 9 of the 540 responding visitors to the Assembly fell into these categories.[21] It is true that the preponderance of professional and managerial occupational groups at this meeting is explained in part by the fact that 65 percent of the delegate respondents and 60 percent of the visitors were ordained. Nevertheless, approximately one third of the delegates and visitors were laymen, and these were drawn almost entirely from the upper status occupational groups.

A similar picture emerged when the income level of the respondents was analyzed. While the median family income in the United States in 1963 was $6,140, only 6 percent of the 260 responding delegates to the 1963 Triennial Assembly had annual family incomes of $6,000 or less; and only 15 percent had corresponding incomes of $6,000 to $10,000. Almost one third of the delegates — 32 percent — had annual family incomes of $10,000 to $15,000; and 23.2 percent had corresponding incomes of more than $15,000.[22]

Such class stratification in both the clerical and the lay leadership of the churches poses a serious problem for institutions that are committed to serving all the members of society without regard to sex, age, race, education, and social or economic position. It is obvious that the business and professional people who comprise the overwhelming majority of the lay leadership in the major Protestant denominations are desperately needed. Their talents and experience in assuming responsibility in other fields are indispensable for the churches. But the fact remains that a more accurate cross section of the total membership of the churches should be represented in leadership roles, both at the level of the local church and at the level of state and national policy-making bodies.

Despite all that has been said in the foregoing pages about the class alignments of the various religious groups, the churches, taken as a whole, are still the most inclusive voluntary organizations in our society. This is especially true at the denominational and ecumenical levels, but it is also true of many local congregations. It seems evident, therefore, that those policy-making and administrative bodies which are officially designated to represent the churches and speak for them ought to represent the membership as a whole and not just segments of that membership — and frequently only a minority at that.

This relative exclusion of the lower classes from the governing bodies of the churches constitutes a serious obstacle to these bodies in their effort to reach all members of society. In the first place, the churches tend to become identified with the values of the middle and upper classes. It is commonly recognized that these groups tend to be more conservative than the poverty-ridden and economically deprived segments of society. Since the former are more satisfied than the latter with the *status quo,* they tend to be more resistant to social change. Hence, in a period of great social turmoil and transition — both in rural and urban areas and on the domestic scene as well as in the world at large — it is difficult for churches of the privileged classes to understand and deal effectively with the basic problems that they meet in the larger communities where they are located. It is extremely difficult, for example, for a middle-class church council in a transitional section of a city to re-orient the program of a church in such a way as to meet the needs of an increasingly lower-income neighborhood. Because its values are different, it is unable to comprehend the special problems, goals, and needs of the socially depressed groups to whom it seeks to minister.

Similarly, churches of the middle and upper classes located in insulated suburbs or in protected pockets in the city have little understanding of the social problems of the city as a whole — juvenile delinquency, crime, alcoholism, drug addiction, and slums. They tend to interpret problems such as these in moralistic, individualistic terms and fail to recognize the extent to which they are associated with social conditions over which the deprived groups in society have little or no control.

It must, of course, be recognized that the problem of preparing the churches to minister more effectively to the communities in which they are set cannot be solved merely by making their leadership more representative of a true cross section of their membership. The problem is much deeper than this, for the churches themselves are also oriented primarily toward the middle and upper classes both in their value creeds and in their membership. Even the members of the churches that are drawn from the lower socioeconomic strata frequently accept the values of the more privileged groups as normative and aspire toward them. But the recruitment and effective involvement of leaders drawn from all economic, educational, and occupational levels in the churches would be a sign of greater equality and freedom than presently exist; and they would also provide a check upon the tendency of each group to absolutize its own social interests and goals.

What is needed for the achievement of a larger measure of genuine community, both in the churches and in society as a whole, is the discovery of common values, goals, and loyalties that transcend the barriers created by different social classes. As we shall see, the churches are committed to the realization of just such a community in their own life based upon a common faith in the Lordship of Christ. Moreover, they also witness to God's will that all men should live together in a universal community based upon a recognition of the relationship that all men bear to him. But it is clear that the kind of community to which they point can become a reality — in spiritual depth as well as in overt inclusiveness — only to the extent to which the churches themselves are freed from bondage to the special values of the privileged classes or, for that matter, of any classes.

3. Church Literature

The middle- and upper-class orientation of the Protestant churches is also strongly reflected in their denominational literature, including both church school and general publications. David W. Barry points out, for example, that the educational materials used by the major denominations are generally directed toward pupils who live in single-family houses in middle- or upper-middle-class neighborhoods.[23] The households are composed of two parents and two or three children. Typically, the father is a professional or business man who enjoys greater than average security. The surrounding neighborhood is relatively homogeneous, quiet, and attractive. The people who live in such neighborhoods are well-mannered and friendly. There is a considerable amount of community spirit evidenced in a variety of civic activities. The main problems faced by the children are those involved in learning how to get along with other children of similar circumstances and acquiring the conventional patterns of social and moral behavior. It is assumed that the readers are white, but they should learn to get along with Negroes and Orientals because these are also God's children. It is also assumed that the readers will complete high school, go to college to prepare for a career in business or one of the professions, get married, and, on the whole, be successful leaders in their communities.

As Barry points out, the kind of family that is generally presupposed by church school literature is far from typical of American families as a whole. Indeed, most children probably come from households that do not consist of two parents and two or three children. Most do not have fathers who are professional or business people, nor do they live in such attractive, homogeneous, friendly neighborhoods. The basic problems of most children are not those of adjusting to friendly environments so much as those posed by the struggle for acceptance both by their families and by society, by the struggle for recognition, and by competition in the effort to gain adequate educational and job opportunities. Literature teaching children to be nice to Negroes and members of other minority groups is obviously *not* written *for* members of minority groups. Similarly, lesson materials that are programmed for youth and young people are clearly intended primarily for students in high school and college. Yet a large percentage of our youth drop out of school before receiving a high school diploma, and the majority of young people between eighteen and twenty-two years of age are not in college.

Effective education involves identification with the interests and values of the persons one is attempting to reach. As we have seen, denominations are much more inclusive classwise than are most local churches; hence, the need for educational materials with broad appeal is particularly urgent at the denominational level. Literature that is aimed primarily at the middle- and upper-class members of the churches fails to reach a large portion — ranging from about one third to one half — of the membership of every major denomination.

The implications of the privileged-class orientation of Christian education materials are even more disturbing when the latter are considered in relation to the total population of the United States and particularly of the world at large. If these publications seem unrelated to the life and experiences of large segments of the membership of the churches, they are even more irrelevant to the life of the nonchurched. Hence, the traditional denominations inevitably cut themselves off from an effective ministry to members of the lower classes outside the churches through their failure to become identified with the needs and goals of the socially disinherited. More seriously still, insofar as the religious literature of the churches insulates their members from large areas of human need, insofar as it shelters them from the *de facto* racial and ethnic pluralism of society, and insofar as it gives religious sanction to the prevailing values and attitudes of the middle and upper classes, it distorts the universal message of the gospel into a form of culture religion and deepens the existing class cleavages both within the churches and in society as a whole.

The most striking failure of the Protestant churches to meet the needs of economically depressed groups is seen in the flight of these churches from the inner city. A large proportion of the rural migrants to the central city were formerly members of the middle-class denominations; but since the churches that belong to the traditional denominations have moved to the sub-urbs, the incoming migrants have either become detached from organized religion or joined the sectarian, storefront churches that have sprung up in the deteriorating sections of the city. As the result of their flight to the suburbs, the main-line denomi-nations have failed to minister to the metropolitan area as a whole, thus cutting themselves off from a potential member-ship perhaps twice their present size,[24] and, equally impor-tant, they have isolated themselves from the basic issues and problems of the city as an inclusive community.

C. THE DILEMMA OF THE CHURCHES

Our purpose in the present chapter has been to call atten-tion to an aspect of the life of the churches that is disturbingly inconsistent with their understanding of themselves and their mission, especially insofar as Protestantism is concerned. Ro-man Catholicism tends to rationalize the class structure in terms of natural law. Thus, it is considered natural that men should be ranked hierarchically in accordance with the func-tions they perform in society. In keeping with this view, Ro-man Catholic parishes tend to be deliberately structured so as to conform to existing residential areas of the city. The one-class parish is looked upon as a natural adaptation of the church to the social and ecological structure of the city, and the program of a particular church is purposively adapted to the specific class characteristics of the parish that it is designed to serve. Protestant leaders, on the other hand, are much more reluctant to recognize the reality of social stratification both in secular society and also within the churches.[25] Protestant churches are organized along congregational rather than territorial lines, and their ministers tend to be quite defensive about the tendency of local churches to be identified with particular social classes. As a result, the Protestant clergy are not generally aware of the significance of class stratification in determining the patterns of church membership, and, on the whole, they appear to be less successful than Roman Catholic priests in adapting the programs of local churches to the particular needs of local congregations and local residential communities.

Just as some kind of social stratification is probably inevitable in any complex society, so it is probably inevitable that the social structure that prevails in society as a whole will manifest itself in the churches in various ways and to various degrees. The problem of class and social status is one of the continuing problems with which Christians in all days and ages have to wrestle. Just as complete equality in the political area is never fully achieved either in a democracy or in a communist state, so it also eludes the churches since they are composed of people who differ in native abilities, values, education, and income.

Yet the church is the one voluntary institution in society that is committed to the service of all men without regard to these relatively accidental or secondary characteristics. When it is true to itself, it must always feel a tension between the norm to which it is committed and the existing institutional churches insofar as the latter are class-oriented and exclusive. It is not that the values that the middle- and upper-class churches pursue are bad or evil per se. Education, economic security, comfortable homes, attractive neighborhoods, and vacations are goods rather than evils. The problem, as far as the membership of the churches is concerned, is not that some people have access to these things; rather, it is that most of the world's people are deprived of them, and even of the barest necessities of life. As a consequence of this fact, the people who possess these goods are separated from the people who do not possess them, and thus the community that all men share with each other under God is effectively denied. Moreover, insofar as the churches of the privileged groups sanction the *status quo*, they help to perpetuate the divisions and the underlying social injustices of which the less privileged classes are the primary victims.

Theologically understood, the temptation of class-oriented churches is to substitute an idol — a god of a particular class — for the God of Christian faith, who is the Lord of all socio-economic groups and loves all men equally. Since class divisions based upon exclusive loyalties are always threatening the integrity of the churches, the latter are continually summoned to repentance for the erection of man-made barriers to fellowship and for their failure to extend their ministry to all peoples of the earth, both at home and abroad. For the churches are called to proclaim the coming of a Kingdom that is not only "beyond caste" but also beyond class; moreover, such a message can be proclaimed with power only as it is made manifest in the life of the churches themselves.

II

A FELLOWSHIP OF RACE

Although the cleavage of the churches along class lines may well prove to be a more formidable barrier to Christian fellowship in the long run than the division of these bodies along racial lines, the latter nevertheless presently constitutes a more pervasive, more absolute, and more flagrant denial of brotherhood than the former. Not only do racial divisions affect more aspects of church life — particularly at the level of the local congregation — than class divisions; but also, due to the fluid character of the class structure in our society, class lines can be crossed much more easily than racial lines.

Moreover, since World War II a number of events, both domestic and international, have focused world attention upon the depth and the pervasiveness of racial discrimination in the United States. This period has been marked not only by the growth of the civil rights movement in this country but also, more fundamentally, by the worldwide revolt of nonwhite peoples against white domination in every form. The colored peoples of the earth far outnumber the whites. The newly emerging nations of Africa and Asia are seeking freedom, equality, and human dignity. Most of them are neither democratic in their political commitments nor Christian in their religious heritage; and they cannot be expected to take either democracy or Christianity seriously so long as both appear as instruments of white domination. Addressing the Sixth World Order Study Conference in St. Louis in 1965, Dr. Absalom L. Vilakazi, Professor of African Studies at American University, warned the churches: "Discrimination against the Negro in this country is an affront to the man of color anywhere in the world, and when practiced by the churches it gives religious sanction to a practice which is, by every standard, unchristian, barbaric, and contrary to all the democratic principles for which this country stands. To the Africans, all the breast-beating and angry outbursts against South African apartheid are a colossal pose and deception so long as the American churches condone and practice racial discrimination!"

The primary purpose of the present chapter is to examine the extent to which, and the ways in which, the churches have both condoned and practiced racial discrimination. In the first place, attention will be given to the growth of racial barriers in the churches, including both the rise of separate Negro denominations and the formation of racial divisions within the predominantly white denominations. Secondly, we shall attempt to evaluate the progress that has been made toward the elimination of segregation and discrimination in the churches since World War II. Finally, we shall examine the relation of the churches to the struggle for civil rights and to the freedom movement generally.

A. THE RISE OF RACIAL BARRIERS IN THE CHURCHES

When we examine the patterns of race relations in the churches in relation to society as a whole, it becomes clear that here too, just as in the case of class cleavages, the churches have not simply reflected the fragmented character of community life. On the contrary, they have contributed — and continue to contribute — to the deepening of these divisions both in society as a whole and in themselves in a number of important respects. It is important that this aspect of the churches' involvement in the prevailing patterns of segregation and discrimination be made clear; for there is a widespread tendency even on the part of those churches which are publicly committed to complete equality and brotherhood to assume that they themselves are simply the victims of the prevailing sociocultural forces and that they, therefore, do not share the responsibility for these evils, either in themselves or in society at large. Since such churches tend to excuse their own participation in these practices as being due to circumstances beyond their control, they generally do not recognize either the need for repentance or the possibility of any significant, creative action on their part. This conception of the churches as passive institutions which merely reflect dominant social patterns is extremely unrealistic. It fails to take into account the dynamic and interesting character not only of cultural institutions themselves but also of the underlying human relationships upon which they are based. Such a view ignores the creative role of beliefs and value systems — of ultimate convictions about God, the universe, and man's nature and destiny — upon human action. Moreover, it rests upon an inaccurate and superficial historical understanding of the rise of segregated churches in this country, both in the North and in the South.

In order to understand the involvement of the churches in the development as well as the deepening of racial divisions in our society as a whole, it is necessary to recognize that segregation appeared within the churches, both in the North and in the South, at least as early as it occurred in secular society.[1] It is frequently pointed out that Negroes and whites usually worshiped together — almost universally in the South and also to a large extent in the North — from colonial times down to the Civil War; but the reasons why Negroes eventually came to establish separate congregations and denominations are not generally understood. Moreover, it is not sufficiently recognized that, with the exception of the institution of slavery in the South, racial lines were much less rigidly drawn in American life down to the beginning of the present century than they have subsequently been. Yet it was during this period of relative freedom in relationships between the races in society at large that the major divisions of the churches along racial lines occurred, both at the level of the local congregation and at the level of denominational bodies.

A careful analysis of the gradual development and deepening of Negro segregation in American life makes it clear that the churches, far from being innocent victims of a pattern of race relations that was firmly established in society generally, were actively involved in the formation and strengthening of these barriers in a number of important ways. Thus, Prof. C. Vann Woodward has shown that the systematized patterns of racial segregation that have characterized recent life in the southern United States took shape in the closing decade of the nineteenth and the opening years of the twentieth century.[2] Contrary to popular opinion, legally enforced segregation and disfranchisement were not the immediate and necessary consequence of the withdrawal of Federal troops from the South in 1877, for these practices did not arise during the years immediately following the Reconstruction. It was more than a decade after the end of the Reconstruction period before the first southern state adopted a Jim Crow law, and more than two decades before Virginia, North Carolina, and South Carolina passed similar legislation. Prior to 1900 the Jim Crow laws adopted by most southern states applied only to passengers aboard trains. The right of Negroes to vote was vigorously defended by southerners during this period, and large numbers of Negroes continued to vote in most parts of the South for at least twenty years after Reconstruction.

It was not until the first two decades of the present century that racial segregation experienced such mushroom growth that it became universal in the South. Through the combined effects of a large number of state laws, municipal ordinances, and extralegal methods of discrimination, Negroes were excluded from such public places as theaters, water fountains, toilets, waiting rooms, and parks; they were barred from many types of employment; and they were restricted to segregated residential areas.

Yet it was during the period when relationships between the

races were relatively fluid in the South — in the years immediately following the Civil War — that the churches in that region came to be divided along racial lines. The question naturally arises as to why the earlier pattern of common organization and joint worship was replaced by separate churches and denominations. The answer to this question reveals the depth of the racial divisions in our present-day churches and, in particular, focuses attention on some of the more subtle barriers to full acceptance that are frequently present even within the framework of racially inclusive churches.

It is sometimes supposed that these early examples of integrated church membership and worship reveal a larger measure of Christian brotherhood and fellowship in the churches at that time than there is at present. It has been suggested, for example, that the racial divisions in the churches could be solved by going back to the kind of inclusiveness that prevailed in the churches under slavery. But even a cursory examination of the rise of all-Negro churches and denominations makes it clear that the earlier inclusiveness was not based either on equality or on brotherhood; hence, it contained the seeds of its own dissolution.

In the South, for example, the unity of the races in common worship rested primarily upon prudential considerations. At first, many masters resisted any effort to convert their slaves to Christianity on the grounds that conversion would make them less efficient and more rebellious and that it would also destroy the masters' right to keep them in slavery. In order to gain permission to carry their missionary message to the Negroes, the churches generally adopted the position that conversion and baptism did not automatically require their liberation from bondage. Many churchmen also argued that conversion of the slaves and common worship with their masters would greatly improve relationships between the two. Despite the efforts of the churches, however, widespread opposition to the evangelization of the slaves continued. Where missionary activities were permitted, the owners insisted upon common worship out of fear that exclusively Negro churches might become centers for conspiracy or at least for the preaching of doctrines that would make the slaves dissatisfied with their condition.

In this way, the white masters sought to assuage their consciences by providing an opportunity for the salvation of the Negroes' souls while at the same time they protected themselves against the danger of insurrection. Moreover, they were able to accomplish all this controlled evangelism within the setting of a master-slave relationship which, because it was paternalistic, robbed the Negro of his personality by treating him as a *thing* to be possessed and dominated. Thus, even though there was outward religious unity of the races in common worship, in spirit this unity reflected the aristocratic spirit of secular society whose highest ideal was that of the *noblesse oblige* rather than Christian brotherhood.

It is not surprising, therefore, that from the Civil War onward, the Negro members of the southern churches " voluntarily " withdrew from the mixed denominations in large numbers. Stimulated by a new sense of freedom and motivated by the desire to have their own organizations and leadership and to escape the embarrassments of unequal treatment (segregation in galleries, for example) in the mixed denominations, the Negro members of the Methodist Episcopal Church, South, the Cumberland Presbyterian Church, and three Baptist groups withdrew from their parent bodies and either joined already existent Negro denominations or formed additional independent groups. In 1860, the Methodist Episcopal Church, South, had 207,766 Negro members; but by 1866 this number had been reduced to 78,742, largely through losses to the African Methodist Episcopal Church and the African Methodist Episcopal Church, Zion. In 1866 the General Conference of the Southern Methodist Church gave the remaining Negro members permission to organize an independent body. As a result, the Colored Methodist Episcopal Church was formed in 1870, and almost all the Negroes in the Southern Methodist Church withdrew to join the new denomination. By far the largest of all the Negro denominations arose out of the separation of Negro from white Baptists in the years immediately following the Civil War. This separation, which began with the formation of Negro state conventions in the South, culminated in the organization of the National Baptist Convention in 1880. Similar schisms occurred in the Cumberland Presbyterian, the Primitive Baptist, and the Free Will Baptist churches. Where the withdrawal and separation of Negroes from the formerly mixed churches did not issue in the formation of new denominations, it almost always resulted in the formation of all-Negro and all-white congregations and, generally, also in the establishment of segregated patterns of church government.

When one similarly examines the growth of discrimination against the Negro in the North, one finds that here too divisions based upon racial identity developed in the churches simultaneously with, and in some instances earlier than, their appearance in secular society. Sometimes the whites excluded the Negroes from the all-white churches, but more often it was the latter who took the initiative and formed independent bodies in order to escape from the limitations and inequalities to which they were subjected in the mixed churches. Ironically, due to the fact that the institution of slavery did not exist in the North, segregation of Negroes both in separate congregations and in independent denominations took place earlier in the North than it did in the South. Yet the reasons for its appearance in both instances were essentially the same. In both cases the Negro received unequal treatment in the predominantly white churches, and in each instance he wanted a larger share in the leadership and control of ecclesiastical affairs than was open to him in the mixed bodies. In the North, however, at least from the Revolutionary period onward the Negro was free to establish separate churches, whereas in the South he was generally not permitted to do so until after his emancipation.

Independent Negro congregations thus began to be formed in the North shortly after the Revolutionary War. At first these local churches tended to remain affiliated with their older parent organizations, but eventually the former began to form separate denominations for pretty much the same reasons that they had withdrawn originally from mixed congregations. The African Methodist Episcopal Church, which was organized as a distinct denomination in 1816, grew out of an earlier secession of Negroes from St. George's Methodist Episcopal Church in Philadelphia in 1787. The African Methodist Episcopal Zion Church, which became an independent sect in 1821, was similarly built around a group of Negroes who had withdrawn from the John Street Methodist Episcopal Church of New York in 1796. Although the Methodist Episcopal Church did not become divided into separate Negro and white denominations, as its counterpart in the South had done, it did permit the establishment of separate annual conferences for Negro ministers. Like the Methodist Episcopal Church, the Protestant Episcopal Church avoided a split along racial lines, but it eventually yielded to the struggle of Negro missionary districts for freedom from control by white dioceses and provided for the appointment of Negro suffragan bishops to supervise the work of Negro churches.

As the result of the various schisms and separations that had taken place along racial lines, north and south, prior to the 1926 religious census, 88 percent of the Negro church members at that time were segregated in Negro denominations; and the great majority of the remainder were placed into Negro conferences in which they were, for all practical purposes, separated from their white brethren.

In retrospect, two aspects of the development of segregated forms of worship and ecclesiastical organization stand out in sharp relief and reveal the depth of the division between the races even in the churches. In the first place, while it is true that Negroes, in both the North and the South, have generally taken the initiative in the formation of separate churches, denominations, and even conferences, it is clear that the responsibility for this voluntary action on their part rests with their white brethren, who by their attitudes and unequal treatment of the Negroes caused the latter to seek a greater measure of freedom and dignity in separate churches. Moreover, in the second place, this withdrawal of the Negro from the mixed churches and denominations was, under the circumstances, the best alternative available. Brotherhood was impossible on the basis of inequality, and independence seemed necessary as a condition for gaining equality. At the time when the various schisms were taking place, many leaders of both races shared the conviction that the religious welfare of the Negroes could best be provided for through independent churches. The subsequent development of these churches as the basic social institution in the Negro community — because of their contribution not only to the religious life but also to education, morality, the creation of a sense of dignity and racial solidarity, and the development of indigenous leadership — has vindicated the wisdom, under the circumstances, of establishing separate Negro churches and denominations. It should never be forgotten, however, that the white Christians were responsible for the creation of the circumstances that made this step desirable and even inevitable.

Although attention has been focused here upon the rise of separate Negro congregations and denominations in the South and in the North, it should be noted that the churches have also been divided along other racial and ethnic lines in those sections of the country in which other racial and cultural minorities — for example, Orientals, Mexicans, various European ethnic groups, American Indians, Puerto Ricans, and Cuban refugees — are found. Due to the increasing mobility of the population generally and particularly to the large-scale migration of Negroes from the rural South to the industrial centers of the North and, more recently, of the West, many predominantly white Protestant communities and churches are being faced — often for the first time — with problems of discrimination in employment, in housing, and in worship. Sometimes the churches have defended these cleavages in the name of religion; more often, they have simply reflected and reinforced these divisions in their own life and permitted the underlying forms of prejudice and discrimination to go unchallenged.

B. SEGREGATION IN THE CHURCHES: 1945–1960

1. The Statistical Picture at the End of World War II

A number of important statistical studies of racial segregation in the churches have been made in recent years. Taken together, they give some indication of the extent to which the development of separate Negro churches had proceeded prior to World War II and also the degree to which the racial patterns of church membership have changed since that time.

Let us look first, therefore, at the racial pattern that existed in Protestantism at the end of the Second World War. Relying upon figures drawn largely from 1943–1944, Frank S. Loescher estimated in 1945 that 8,300,000 of the 14,000,000 Negroes in the United States belonged to some Christian church.[3] Of these, approximately 8,000,000 were Protestants and 300,000 were Roman Catholics. Out of the 8,000,000 Protestants, approximately 7,500,000 — or almost 94 percent — were in separate Negro denominations. Only 500,000 — just slightly more than 6 percent — were in predominantly white denominations. The Methodist Church contained 60 percent — 330,600 — of this latter group, but placed them in a separate jurisdiction. Like the Methodists, the Disciples of Christ also placed the Negro churches of that denomination in a separate organization, viz., the National Missionary Convention, which although not racial in theory proved to be so in practice. Although these were the only two predominantly white denominations in which Negro churches were segregated at the national level, most Negro Presbyterian and Congregational churches were placed in separate regional and local bodies — synods, presbyteries, and associations — in the South. Thus, the Convention of the South, consisting of 210 all-Negro Congregational Christian churches and including 5 in New York City and 1 in New Jersey, was organized as late as 1950; 22 separate Negro congregations outside of the South, however, were organically related to their own local associations and state conferences.[4] In a word, almost all Negro Protestants, including those in the mixed, predominantly white denominations, were in organizations of their own; and there was little opportunity for contact with white Christians in a religious context except in occasional ministerial associations, on national boards and agencies of the mixed denominations, and in such interdenominational bodies as the Federal Council of Churches.[5]

At the level of local church membership, Loescher estimated that less than 1 percent of the local white Protestant churches included any Negro members.[6] Moreover, where such interracial memberships did occur, they were limited for the most part to communities where only a few Negroes lived and where the latter had already been integrated into other community institutions. According to Loescher, the total number of Negro Protestants participating in racially inclusive worship services in local white congregations was probably not more than 8,000, or about .1 percent of the total number of Negro Protestants.[7] Significantly, a survey of almost 18,000 churches in six major denominations failed to disclose a single white church with a mixed membership in an area undergoing transition in its racial constituency.[8]

While the statistics used by Loescher were incomplete and not entirely typical of Protestantism in the United States as a whole, they nevertheless provide the best indication available concerning the prevailing pattern of Negro-white relations in Protestantism at the end of World War II.[9] Moreover, the results of a number of other related studies make it clear that the picture drawn by Loescher was, on the whole, remarkably accurate. In some respects he perhaps presented an unduly optimistic picture of the amount of integration that had taken place at the level of the local congregation throughout the country as a whole. At any rate, the discovery of 290 predomi-

their congregations had some form of Negro-white integration. Responses of 182 Unitarian churches to a questionnaire in 1956 indicated that almost 40 percent of these had Negro members.

In that same year the Disciples of Christ reported a survey of 7,000 local churches which revealed that 464 local congregations in forty states — almost 23 percent of the 2,051 churches replying — were racially mixed. Twenty-one of those having at least one Negro member were located in the South.[13] At about the same time, David Loth and Harold Fleming reported instances of some 130 local churches located in twenty-three northern and western states that had included Negroes either as members or as participants between May, 1954, and May, 1956; they also found at least 10 churches located in the South that had accepted Negroes.[14] Whereas Dwight Culver had found only about 100 white Methodist churches with one or more Negro members in 1946, at least 92 Methodist churches in the Ohio and Los Angeles Episcopal Areas alone were reported to be interracial in 1959.[15]

Summarizing the extent to which local churches had become racially mixed by 1960, J. Oscar Lee estimated that "possibly 10 percent" of the Protestant churches had members of more than one race at that time.[16] This figure, it should be noted, included all Protestant churches having any form of racially mixed membership. Hence, it can not be compared with the results of Loescher's study in the mid-'40s. Nevertheless, it did indicate — along with a number of denominational studies — that the Protestant churches were moving, more rapidly than previously expected, in the direction of integration at the level of the local congregation.

A second major change in the racial pattern of Protestantism at the level of the local church has begun to take place in the transitional areas of the city. This development is closely related to the first, but it deserves special attention since this is the crucial point at which a significant change in the racial character of the local congregation is most likely to take place if no artificial barriers to membership are imposed. Negroes

nantly white local churches with Negro participants — out of an original sample of 17,900 churches in six major denominations — was greeted with surprise as an "extraordinary revelation" of the extent to which white Protestant churches had become racially inclusive!

More realistically, however, Loescher's study made it quite clear that the number of Negro Protestants participating in predominantly white churches in this country in 1945 was almost microscopic. Even in those instances where there were a few Negro members in white churches, there was little evidence of real freedom and participation on the part of the Negroes in the total life and leadership of the congregation. On the whole, such churches were biracial rather than interracial or integrated. Equally significant was the fact that there was little difference in this regard between northern and southern churches; between northern, southern, and national denominations; or between churches with centralized and those with congregational forms of ecclesiastical polity.

2. Cracks in the Wall of Segregation: 1945–ca. 1960

Relationships between the races have been altered in many basic and far-reaching ways in American society, especially since World War II. The question naturally arises, therefore, concerning the relationship of the churches to the changes that have taken place in secular society generally in this regard. Essentially, this question is twofold. In the first place, it is a question of internal reform: to what extent have the churches themselves overcome the racial barriers that had been erected in their own midst? Secondly, it is a question about the involvement of the churches in the struggle for social justice. We turn now to the first of these questions; the second will occupy our attention later in the present chapter.

In attempting to assess the changes that have taken place in the churches since Loescher's study, it is necessary to examine the changes that have taken place at three different levels — namely, the over-all division of Negro and white Protestants in separate denominations, changes at the level of the local church, and, finally, changes in the organizational structures of predominantly white denominations.

Insofar as the first of these patterns is concerned, the over-all division of Negro and white Protestants in separate denominations has remained substantially unchanged since the end of the Second World War. In 1960, there were a total of 18,871,831 Negroes living in the United States. Although accurate figures are not available, it was estimated that the five largest Negro denominations [10] had approximately 10,000,000 members in 1960. In contrast, there were an estimated 600,000 Negro Protestants in predominantly white denominations — approximately 366,000 of this number being in The Methodist Church, primarily in the Central Jurisdiction — and an estimated 596,000 Negro Roman Catholics. The most striking change in this regard is represented by the fact that the number of Negro Roman Catholics had almost doubled in the period between World War II and 1960. As far as Protestantism is concerned, the outstanding fact is that the overwhelming proportion — still about 94 percent — of the Negro Protestants remained in Negro denominations and had few religious contacts with white Protestants even of the same denominational family. At this level Protestantism continued — and apparently still continues — to be as racially divided as it was in 1945.

When one turns to the level of the local churches, however, it is clear that a number of important developments began to take place during this period. Moreover, each of these new trends gained momentum in the '60s. In the first place, there was a significant trend toward greater racial inclusiveness at the level of the local congregation.

Between 1950 and 1954 a study was made of three denominations — the United Lutheran Church, the Congregational Christian Churches, and the Presbyterian Church in the U.S.A.[11] A total of 13,597 questionnaires were mailed out to local churches in these denominations, and 4,810 were returned. Of this latter number, 1,331 — about 28 percent of those reply-

ing and over 9 percent of the total sample — re[...] mixture either in their membership or in some c[...] activity. Although it is probable that the figure o[...] far more typical of the three denominations as a[...] the larger one, even this represents a substantial in[...] number of racially inclusive churches in the deca[...] the Loescher study. Surprisingly, 110 of these racia[...] churches were located in the Southeast, and Negro[...] volved in 45 of these instances.

A more intensive study of 405 of the mixed ch[...] vealed that minority participants comprised 2.7 per[...] total membership of this smaller group. Significantly,[...] ported that only 26 persons out of a total of 237,476[...] in these churches had withdrawn because of the acce[...] members from minority groups. In view of the widesp[...] that the transition from an " all white " to an inclusi[...] bership policy would be accompanied by a split in the[...] lar congregation or at least by a large-scale withdr[...] members, the finding that only one in nine thousand[...] involved in such transitions had withdrawn for this rea[...] impressive; moreover, the net effect of such withdraw[...] reported to be beneficial to the churches involved in t[...] their spiritual enrichment.

A subsequent study of the racial practices of local Con[...] tional Christian Churches in metropolitan areas was re[...] in 1958.[12] Using data furnished in interviews by offici[...] 1,054 such churches in every section of the United States,[...] man H. Long found that 26.6 percent of these included [...] bers drawn from more than one racial or cultural group [...] 73.4 percent had members of only one group. Approxim[...] one half of the " mixed " churches — 12.1 percent of the [...] sample — represented predominantly white congregations [...] at least one Negro member. An equal number of w[...] churches included at least one Oriental, one Spanish-speak[...] person, or one Indian American.

The American Baptists reported in 1956 that 21 percent[...]

and other minority groups are concentrated in the inner city; as their numbers increase, they expand into adjacent areas occupied by whites. As has already been noted, the prevailing pattern has been for the whites to move out of such transitional areas to the suburbs. As the members of the middle-class white congregations have moved out to the suburbs, they have generally sold the buildings that they have left behind to incoming minority groups and built new ones on the fringes of the city; moreover, those churches which were unable to relocate in the suburbs have — almost without exception up until the end of World War II — served only their traditional white memberships and discouraged nonwhites both from becoming members and from participating in their programs. So much did this pattern prevail down to World War II that, as we have seen, Loescher failed to find in 1945 a single predominantly white church with an open or mixed membership in a transitional area.

Subsequently a large number of such churches have appeared. In 1950, S. Garry Oniki reported on a study of some twenty mixed Protestant churches and religious fellowships, most of which were located in transitional or interracial urban areas.[17] While no statistics are presently available to indicate the total number of interracial churches in transitional, downtown, and other interracial areas, there is mounting evidence that the flight of white Protestant churches to the suburbs has greatly slowed down in the last few years and that the number of integrated urban churches is increasing rapidly.

A third significant development at the level of the local congregation during this period was a growing tendency on the part of many white churches, particularly in the South, to be inclusive in worship even while refusing to be open in membership. Under the pressure of "kneel-ins" as well as their own national governing bodies and social action agencies, many white congregations were faced with the necessity of reexamining their traditional segregationist policies. They were forced to recognize the hypocrisy of publicly welcoming anyone who wished to come to worship while at the same time turning Negroes away. Under such circumstances, many white Protestants began to think seriously for the first time about the nature of the church, and many churches took an *initial* step toward the breaking down of racial barriers when they accepted Negroes in their regular services of worship without discrimination. Although this step in itself constituted only the beginning of a pilgrimage toward brotherhood, it was significant insofar as it constituted a recognition of the fact that the existence of racial barriers to common worship is alien to the nature of the church.

In addition to the foregoing changes at the level of the local congregation, a number of denominations had taken significant initial steps during this period toward the elimination of racial barriers from their over-all organizational structures as well as from certain church-related institutions. This trend has also been accelerated since 1960. For example, the all-Negro synod and all but three Negro presbyteries had been eliminated from the Presbyterian Church U.S. by the early '60s. All the diocesan conventions of the Protestant Episcopal Church had also become desegregated by that time. Similarly, in The Methodist Church pressure mounted at the national level during the '50s and early '60s for the elimination of the all-Negro Central Jurisdiction through the transference of the churches in this body to the other geographically defined jurisdictions. Shortly after the 1964 General Conference of The Methodist Church, two Negro bishops were given supervision over predominantly white constituencies in that body. By the early '60s, also, there were four Negro bishops of the Protestant Episcopal Church, one of whom was serving as the Suffragan Bishop of Massachusetts.

It is still true, however, that many barriers to racial equality continue to exist in most of the predominantly white denominations at nearly every level of their organizational structures. This is true both of the major Protestant groups and also of the Roman Catholic Church. Although the Roman Catholic Church has been more successful than the Protestant bodies generally in achieving racial inclusiveness at the level of the local congregation, the latter have taken the lead in breaking down racial barriers at the leadership levels in this country. Although segregation had been abolished in all Roman Catholic parishes and although there were approximately 130 Negro priests in this country at the time, the first appointment of a Negro Roman Catholic bishop was made in 1965.

C. THE GAP BETWEEN TOKENISM AND BROTHERHOOD

Despite the progress toward racial inclusiveness that has been made in the churches since the end of World War II, the membership and worship patterns of the vast majority of Protestant churches in the United States are still segregated. Inclusiveness in worship, the welcoming of two or three Negro families into the membership of a large white church in a white residential area, and even the integration of the administrative governing bodies, boards, and agencies of the denominations represent only very limited expressions of brotherhood. They may, indeed, reflect just as great a denial of equality as that which existed before the earlier divisions of the churches along racial lines took place.

It has been noted above that, almost without exception, the first white Protestant churches to adopt open membership policies were those which were located in white residential areas in which at most only a very few members of a minority group lived. Often there was no nonwhite church to which the latter could go. Under such circumstances the whites accepted the non-Caucasians in a paternalistic spirit but were not threatened in their control of church affairs. As we have seen, predominantly white churches in racially changing residential areas have been much slower to lower their racial bars to membership and participation.

But in a fundamental sense, it is only churches in changing or in nonsegregated residential areas that have a real possibility of becoming genuinely interracial in the sense that members of all constituent groups are incorporated into the life and leadership of the congregations on the basis of equality. Even in those sections of the country that are outside of the South, residential areas are largely segregated and inclusive white churches normally attract only a handful of nonwhites. In 1957 a survey conducted by The United Presbyterian Church in the U.S.A. showed that it was virtually impossible for approximately 90 percent of the churches of that denomination to become integrated because they were located in communities in which no Negro families were then living.[18] In view of such facts as these, it seems doubtful that white suburbanites are much different in their racial attitudes from whites who live in transitional urban areas, for the former have the power to — and do — control the influx of Negroes through zoning ordinances and the policies and codes of real estate developers, builders, and mortgage companies. Protestants obviously share the responsibility for such restrictive policies, and white suburban churches are in fact protected by them. A number of forces, e.g., the development of more tolerant racial attitudes on the part of the white population, the growing economic strength of the Negro middle class, the issuance by President Kennedy of an executive order banning discrimination in federal housing programs, the Civil Rights Act of 1964, and the Economic Opportunity Amendments of 1965 are collaborating to reduce discrimination in housing, but the process promises to be slow. Only as such a change occurs, however, are churches likely to become genuinely interracial even if the overt bars to inclusive membership and the more subtle forms of inequality within the churches themselves are removed.

When the removal of racial barriers in the churches is compared with similar changes that have taken place in secular society, it is obvious that the former, in the main, reflect prior advances in society at large. The church has followed rather than led the secular institutions in this regard; and it promises, moreover, to be the last institution in American society to eliminate segregation from its own life. Indeed, comparing the progress that it has made toward racial inclusiveness since 1945 with that which has been made in the armed services, in sports organizations, in education, in organized labor, and in the political life of the nation, it is difficult to escape the conclusion that, on the whole, the church has lost ground even during this period.[19]

The single most important change that has taken place in the white churches in the area of race relations since the Second World War has been the growing consensus that racial segregation is incompatible with the nature of the church. While this is only an initial step toward the achievement of genuine inclusiveness, it does constitute a real and necessary beginning for large numbers of white church members. Just as it has been difficult for many white persons who were taught that segregated schools and public facilities could be " separate but equal " to learn that the latter cannot be equal if they are forced to be separate, so it has been, and is, difficult for white Protestants who have been taught that racial segregation in the churches represents the will of God to understand why the exclusion of Negroes constitutes a betrayal of the church and a denial of Christian brotherhood.

Beyond the acknowledgment of their guilt, there has been a deepening commitment by the churches to the elimination of segregation from every aspect of church life. The leadership of the major denominations, particularly at the national level, is united in its commitment to this effort. But the path from commitment to fulfillment is a difficult road. The predominantly white churches will be tempted to settle for superficial organizational changes and token integration in the place of genuine equality and brotherhood. They are eager to get rid of the symbol of segregation, but many are unwilling to make the adjustments that must be made if integration is to be more than an empty gesture for the benefit of their own public images. If this happens, Negro Protestants will not only lose the advantages they formerly had in the segregated units of these denominations, but they will also become even more dependent upon the whites and suffer even greater inequities than they did in their segregated status.

1. The Default of Leadership by the White Churches

In view of the great concern with racial discrimination since the '30s, it is difficult to realize that prior to that time relatively little attention was being given to this problem by predominantly white groups and organizations in this country, including the churches. There were many injustices to Negroes — lynching, subjection to the terroristic tactics of the Ku Klux Klan in the '20s, segregation in the armed services, segregation in the churches, discrimination by industry and the unions, widespread unemployment, and gross inequalities in housing, education, and medical care. But in the main it was the Negro leaders who protested against these forms of discrimination and called for specific action in these areas.

Although they continued to contribute substantial funds to missionary and benevolent enterprises among Negroes, prior to 1930 the white denominations seldom addressed themselves to the need for reform in the basic institutions of society in order to get rid of racial discrimination. Thus, for example, in his analysis of the official denominational pronouncements on social issues in this country in the period 1908–1929, F. Ernest Johnson found only six that dealt with race relations, and these were limited primarily to condemnations of lynching and mob violence.[20] Johnson did find, however, a large number of such statements by the Federal Council of Churches and other denominational agencies; moreover, the Federal Council went farther than the individual denominations and called for equality of opportunity, adequate services, and equal treatment for the Negro.

During the depression period of the '30s the number of official denominational pronouncements on race relations increased greatly, but usually these were couched in vague generalities and dealt specifically with only the grossest forms of injustice, particularly lynching. The more controversial and basic issue of economic discrimination was almost completely avoided. More significantly, the churches showed little awareness of discrimination in their own organizational life and practice. Only two denominations, the Northern Baptists and the Congregational Christians, declared their opposition "to all forced segregation."

Since the beginning of World War II a number of important steps have been taken by the Federal Government to bring about greater racial equality. Among these have been the establishment in 1941 by executive order of a Fair Employment Practices Committee and the desegregation of the armed services. Since the war, attacks upon discrimination both through the enactment of civil rights legislation and through the federal courts have effected the breakdown of legalized racial barriers in such major areas of civil life as interstate transportation, restrictive covenants, institutions of higher education, public parks, voting, the selection of juries, and, increasingly, public schools, employment, and housing.

Shortly after the war, in 1946, the Federal Council of Churches denounced "the pattern of segregation in race relations as unnecessary and undesirable and a violation of the gospel of love and human brotherhood." The Council called upon its constituent members to take similar action and to work for "a nonsegregated church and a nonsegregated society." This statement of the Federal Council has subsequently been endorsed by most of the leading Protestant denominations in this country, and there has been a growing awareness of the need for self-examination on their part. As a result of this latter process, significant steps have been taken by many of these groups, particularly at the national and state organizational levels. Some of these steps have already been noted. In general, the lowering of racial barriers in various church-controlled agencies, such as parochial schools, denominational colleges and hospitals, has followed rather than preceded similar changes in corresponding secular institutions in the same geographical areas. In 1957, for example, only 55 out of 188 Protestant institutions of higher learning in the South were biracial, although 105 of 206 state colleges and universities were desegregated at that time, as were 35 of 45 such Roman Catholic schools. By 1964 the number of Protestant campuses that had become racially inclusive in the South had increased significantly, but such schools continued to lag behind the state-supported institutions in this regard.[21] However, since 1965 increased economic pressure from the Federal Government has greatly accelerated the desegregation both of the public schools and of denominational colleges in the South.

Probably the most dramatic evidence that the churches have followed the leadership of secular groups was that provided by their response to the decision of the United States Supreme Court in 1954 outlawing segregation in the public schools. Though most of the churches had not called for such action, and indeed frequently had not integrated their own church-related schools and colleges, in the months immediately following this decision most of the major religious bodies commended it as being both democratic and Christian. They saw in it a challenge not only to assist in the implementation of this decision in local communities throughout the land but also to renew their efforts to rid their own institutions of any remaining forms of discrimination.

Despite the failure of the white churches to provide leadership in the struggle for racial equality both in themselves and in society at large, there have been notable exceptions to this general pattern, as evidenced by the intense opposition that the latter have aroused. This opposition has been focused upon outspoken ministers, the social action agencies of a number of denominations, and groups associated with the National Council of Churches. For example, an estimated two hundred or more clergymen in the South lost their pulpits in the five-year period 1959–1964 because they took a stand declaring the race problem to be a moral issue that required a Christian response of justice and brotherhood.[22] Many courageous laymen have also been victims of harassment, economic reprisals, and violence because of the stand they have taken for racial justice on the basis of their faith. For many years women's organizations, in particular, have been actively working to overcome racial barriers in the churches and to secure greater social justice. The National Council of Churches has aroused similarly strong opposition among many groups in different sections of the country because of its stand against segregation and other forms of racial discrimination.

2. The Negro Church

In comparison with the white churches, the Negro churches have been much more actively involved in the struggle for racial equality and brotherhood. As the freest institution in the entire community, the Negro church, especially in the South, has long provided the building space that has served as the center of operations for groups — including interracial and religious ones — working for racial justice. In addition, much of the leadership in secular groups devoted to fighting segregation and discrimination has been drawn from within the Negro churches. Moreover, while the Negro church has been a segregated institution it has not itself been a *segregating* body. Most predominantly Negro churches do not in fact include any white members, but the former do not exclude the latter; and, indeed, the great majority of Negro churches would welcome white persons to their services and to their memberships.

But if the Negro church has been less exclusive in its racial attitudes and practices than the white church, the former has not escaped the same basic temptation with which the white church has been confronted, namely, the temptation for the church to accommodate itself to the prevailing patterns of culture. Thus, throughout most of its history the Negro church in the South has been accommodationist and escapist in its relationship to the system of segregation.

Although it did a great deal during this period to alleviate the burdens and injustices of life under the prevailing caste system both by its focus upon the otherworldly aspects of faith which promised justice in the hereafter and by the development of educational and social organizations aimed at the improvement of the Negro community itself, the Negro church did little to challenge the underlying system of segregation.[23] The leaders — clergy and laymen alike — within the Negro church who felt called to work for changes in this basic pattern of race relations were forced to find other institutions such as the NAACP and the National Urban League through which to work. In this respect their situation was similar to that of liberal white Protestants, who also found it necessary to work through agencies and institutions outside of the white churches.

Beginning with the Montgomery bus boycott (1955–1956) led by Martin Luther King, Jr., and the subsequent formation of the Southern Christian Leadership Conference, however, the Negro church has played an increasingly important role in the civil rights movement. Negro ministers have more and more provided the leadership for direct action attacks upon various forms of segregation, and the Negro churches have given strong support and assistance to such movements as the student-led lunch counter demonstrations, selective buying campaigns, the 1963 March on Washington, school desegregation, voter registration campaigns, and civil rights legislation in Congress.[24] As the Negro revolution has mounted and more militant action groups have gained strength during the '60s, the importance of the Negro church in the over-all struggle for racial justice has been increasingly recognized by white Americans generally. Not only has the Negro church determined the moral tone of the civil rights movement in the South since the Montgomery bus boycott, but its impact upon the national movement as a whole is evidenced by the fact that King emerged as the single most influential leader of the 1963 March on Washington. Since that time he and the Southern Christian Leadership Conference have been actively involved in the

civil rights movement in other sections of the country, particularly in the North. King's award of the 1964 Nobel Peace Prize
was an outstanding tribute to his leadership and indirectly to
the role of the Negro church in the quest for racial justice. Although King derived the method of nonviolent resistance from
Gandhi, he made it an instrument of Christian love in the quest
for social justice and reconciliation; and the philosophy of non-
violence has found its widest and deepest acceptance in the
Negro churches where the ground has been prepared for it by
the preaching of such Christian themes as love, reconciliation,
and redemptive suffering as well as the dignity and equality of
all men.

E. INVOLVEMENT IN THE STRUGGLE FOR HUMAN RIGHTS: 1963 ff.

Prior to 1963 the social action agencies of the churches had
limited their involvement in the civil rights movement largely
to the promotion of educational programs about race relations.
Officially these groups had not committed themselves to direct
action in this field, although they had on occasion supported
direct action groups such as those engaged in sit-ins, protest
demonstrations, and freedom rides. There had, however, been
a number of voluntary Christian groups — such as the Roman
Catholic Interracial Council and the Episcopal Society for Cultural and Racial Unity — that had participated in various forms
of direct action on a limited basis. But by the summer of 1963,
the civil rights movement had reached a new and critical stage.
It had gained a large base of mass support, and the ineffective-
ness of indirect action in bringing about any basic changes in
the status of the Negro was generally recognized. Hence,
groups such as the SCLC, CORE, and SNCC turned increasingly to direct action — protest demonstrations and voter-regis-
tration campaigns — in order to dramatize the plight of the Negro and marshal political and economic power to effect certain
fundamental changes that are needed in the political and economic life of the nation if equality and freedom are to become
realities for all citizens.

In response to the mounting tempo of the civil rights movement and the crisis that it had precipitated in our national life,
symbolized by the ruthless and brutal suppression of protest
demonstrations in Birmingham in the spring of 1963, the National Council of Churches established a Commission on Religion and Race in June of that year and directed it to move
directly into the center of the civil rights struggle.[25] This commission was instructed to engage in a twofold ministry of reconciliation and action aimed at the achievement of social justice.

Almost immediately after its formation, the Commission on
Religion and Race, along with the Roman Catholic Interracial
Council and the Synagogue Council of America, joined with
seven other civil rights and labor organizations in sponsoring
the March on Washington. This demonstration, involving some
40,000 white persons out of a total of about 250,000 marchers,
represented the first major involvement of the churches in direct action in the civil rights movement. Following this historic
march, the churches continued to work with other groups or-
ganizing support for the civil rights bill, which was passed in
1964. Indeed, the churches were credited by such leaders as
Senators Hubert Humphrey and Richard Russell with providing the crucial support needed to secure the passage of this
legislation.

Subsequently, the churches have continued to become involved in the broadened struggle for human rights through direct action programs, both in the South and in the North. They
have served as coordinating agencies for the freedom movement in northern cities, and in 1965 they helped rally nationwide support of the clergy and the churches for the Selma-
Montgomery march, in which a total of some 5,000 clergy of
all faiths participated at various stages. In the summer of 1965
the Commission on Religion and Race trained workers for the
COFO-sponsored (Council of Federated Organizations) Summer Project in Mississippi, and since that time it has cooper-
ated with the World Council of Churches in supporting the
Delta Ministry.[26] The churches were also instrumental in or-

ganizing support for the Economic Opportunity Amendments
of 1965, aimed at the elimination of discrimination in employment and the provision of specialized training for persons who
lack the necessary skills for employment in modern automated
jobs.

Because of their deepening involvement in the freedom
struggle the churches have been given a new opportunity to
play an important role in the development of this movement
and a new opportunity to recover their relevance to the daily
lives of large masses of people to whom they have seemed irrelevant and hypocritical. In order to do so, however, they
must serve both as agencies of reconciliation and as prophets
of social justice.

There are signs that the churches have reached a turning
point and made a new commitment to the struggle for freedom
and equality, but this change has taken place largely at the
leadership levels of the ecumenical movement and denominational structures. The real battle for genuine freedom, meaningful equality, and true brotherhood lies ahead, and it will be
waged at the grass-roots level of the local community and the
local church. Like the ecumenical movement, the struggle for
human freedom can achieve depth only as it permeates the life
of the local congregation. The real test of the struggle for human dignity and equality will come as local communities face
up to issues such as segregation in residential areas, token desegregation in the public schools, racially exclusive membership policies of local churches, and the more subtle barriers to
the deeper levels of community in each of these areas.

F. THE DEPTH OF THE RACIAL PROBLEM IN THE CHURCHES

There are many reasons for the failure of the churches to
provide moral leadership in the struggle against racial discrimination. Frequently the denominational leadership has failed to
give adequate support to individual ministers who have attempted to deal constructively with controversial issues at the
grass-roots level. On the basis of their study of the clergy in

the desegregation crisis in Little Rock, Arkansas, Ernest Q. Campbell and Thomas F. Pettigrew concluded that what is needed is a greater balance between the prophetic task and the organizational concerns of the denominations, so that the social critic or prophet is given importance similar to that which is now given to the " organization man " and the priest.[27] It is both unfair and hypocritical for a minister to be penalized in his denominational relationships for his efforts to implement the pronounced teachings of his own denomination on controversial issues. Moreover, it is impossible for either an individual minister or a local congregation to speak with authority on issues of social justice in the name of the church so long as the denominations to which they belong give only lip service to this part of the church's ministry and reserve their full support for programs involving organizational expansion.

Other critics of the churches emphasize the need for changes in the geographical structure of the parish so that the local pastoral unit would become more representative of the total community. Since Protestant congregations tend to be drawn from economically and racially homogeneous residential areas, the former tend to reflect the divisions of secular society in both of these respects. What is needed, it is argued, is a restructuring of the parish to include within the same fellowship people from different economic, occupational, and racial groups, thus making the local church truly inclusive.

In addition, it is generally recognized that the laity must be given a larger role in the total ministry of the church if it is to recover its relevance to contemporary life. Radical changes are also needed in the institutional form of the churches, in the patterns of worship and forms of theological expression, and in the traditional conception of the ministry. But the basic reason for the failure of the churches, including both local congregations and denominational leadership, to support a prophetic ministry lies in the failure of Protestants to understand the meaning of the Christian faith and, more particularly, the nature and mission of the church.

In the past the churches in this country have, on the whole, practiced racial segregation and accommodated themselves to it from generation to generation. They have, wittingly or unwittingly, participated in the development and defense of such racist doctrines as segregation, white supremacy, and nativism in the name of Christian faith. In so doing they have substituted a racially distorted form of the gospel for the true faith and thus provided the final justification for discrimination and inequality. This is the deepest betrayal of the churches, and it is at this point that their repentance must begin. While some have proclaimed the racist heresy openly, others have permitted it to go unchallenged in the community at large if not in the churches themselves.

In a word, the race problem is, at bottom, a conflict of faiths in the church itself. The reality and the threat of racism are still present in the churches and also in society and the world at large. In the midst of this conflict and tension the church is summoned to point men, by prophetic word and reconciling deed, to the universal community for which all are created, symbolized by the Kingdom of God. Viewed in the light of this norm, all those cleavages that still separate men from one another by denying their common humanity, whether in the churches or in secular society, stand under the judgment of God. Protestants, however, can never fully comprehend the depth of their involvement in the guilt of the churches so long as they are dominated by atomistic and minister-centered conceptions of the church and by individualistic conceptions of morality. Moreover, as long as these conceptions prevail the witness of the churches in the area of race relations will be lacking in authority, and it will also be ineffective and socially irrelevant. Basically what is needed, therefore, is a deeper understanding of the nature and mission of the church, of who constitutes the church, and of where the church exists. We shall attempt to answer these questions in the subsequent sections — Parts Two and Three — of this book.

III

RELIGIOUS PLURALISM
AND THE CHURCHES

A third aspect of the crisis faced by the churches is associated with the passage of this country from a form of Protestant establishment to religious pluralism. Not only have Roman Catholicism and Judaism come to be accepted as fully American forms of religion, but also our society is now well on the way to becoming officially a secular state. Insofar as public policy is concerned, the state is becoming increasingly neutral toward every form of religious belief, including humanism, agnosticism, and atheism as well as the traditional forms of Protestantism, Roman Catholicism, and Judaism.

The emergence of religious pluralism has forced the churches to recognize the extent to which they had come to substitute an idolatrous form of American culture-religion for faith in the universal, transcendent God of Biblical faith. As this culture-religion has become increasingly disestablished, the churches have had to consider anew their relationship to the state in the light of the radical freedom of man proclaimed in the gospel. Thus they have gained a new understanding of the nature of religious freedom and the importance of such freedom for living, authentic faith.

As contemporary society becomes increasingly pluralistic and secular, the churches are faced with the necessity of developing new forms of strategy in order to recover their relevance to modern life. Not only must they seek a deeper understanding of the historical forms of Christian faith, but they must also find new ways of communicating this faith by relating it more directly to man's life in secular culture, where contemporary man "lives and moves and has his being." Pluralism represents a challenge to the churches to take faith seriously — to live and act by faith rather than on the basis of cultural and religious conformity. It also represents a challenge for the churches to take secular man seriously, in his freedom and responsibility, by confronting him with the possibility of faith as a personal act of trust and commitment of the whole self to that universal Power and Will upon which all men are finally dependent.

In the present chapter we shall attempt to do two things. First, we shall trace briefly the major steps in the development of pluralism in the United States; and, secondly, we shall consider some of the major implications of this emergent pluralism for the churches.

The election of President John F. Kennedy in 1960 was widely acclaimed at that time as the event that marked the transition of this country from an officially Protestant to a religiously pluralistic society. As subsequent developments have shown, however, this transition was by no means completed with the election of a Roman Catholic President. Rather, this event, as important as it was, is in reality best understood as a major landmark on the road to a fully developed pluralism. It marked our achievement as a nation of a fuller measure of religious liberty and also our attainment of a more mature understanding of our ethnic and religious diversity.

A number of events since 1960 — particularly a series of decisions of the United States Supreme Court and the growing ecumenical movement as reflected in the Second Vatican Council — have called forth a great deal of discussion concerning the meaning and implications of religious pluralism. What the results of this discussion will be is not yet clear. But there is urgent need that the churches seek to understand the changes that have taken place in the religious composition of

American society over the past century and a half, together with the implications of these developments both for religious freedom and for church-state relationships.

A. THE DISESTABLISHMENT OF THE CHURCHES

One of the most striking and at the same time least understood ironies of American religious history is the fact that, despite our heritage of religious freedom, Protestantism has in effect had the status of a state church down to quite recent times. According to the prevailing myth of church-state relations in this country, the original colonies were settled by refugees from religious persecution in Europe and, because of the persecution that they had suffered, they adopted a policy of religious liberty in the new world. But such was not the case; and, indeed, when a policy of religious liberty eventually gained general acceptance in the early years of the new republic, it did so largely on the basis of expediency and compromise rather than on the basis of commitment to freedom of religion as a principle. Moreover, in actual practice the principle of freedom of religion has been qualified in certain important respects since the beginning of our national existence, and the demand to give it fuller expression in our political life presents to the churches one of their most serious challenges.

A brief glance at church-state relations in the colonial period is illuminating in this regard. Congregationalism, modeled generally upon the theocracy of Calvin's Geneva, became the established religion of all the New England colonies except Rhode Island. The Church of England was the state church of Virginia and the Carolinas throughout the pre-Revolutionary period, and during a considerable portion of this time it was also the established church in Maryland and Georgia. In New York and New Jersey, as well as in Maryland and Georgia, the official religion changed at least once during this period. In New York the Dutch Reformed Church and the Anglicans competed for domination, and, similarly, in New Jersey the Presbyterians and Anglicans alternately shared control. In Maryland,

Cecil Calvert (also known as Lord Baltimore), a Roman Catholic, established a policy of broad religious toleration for all orthodox Christians. Indeed, the Act of Toleration, adopted in 1649, gave Maryland a more liberal policy in religious matters than existed at that time in any of the other colonies except Rhode Island and Pennsylvania. Following the English revolution of 1688, however, the colony passed out of Roman Catholic control; a royal government was instituted, and the Church of England was established, with a resulting curtailment of religious freedom.

The only three colonies that did not have some form of state church during the colonial period were Pennsylvania, Delaware (originally part of the province of Pennsylvania), and Rhode Island. Moreover, it was only in these "free colonies" that non-Christians were accorded substantial liberty of conscience. Yet even in Pennsylvania this liberty was qualified, because of pressure from the home government, by the imposition of essentially Protestant religious tests for officeholding; and in Delaware full liberty of conscience was granted only to persons confessing belief in Almighty God. In Rhode Island, on the other hand, full freedom of conscience was extended to all, including by implication atheists as well as theists, in its charter of 1663, which continued in force down to 1842 when it was replaced by a similarly liberal state constitution. Thus, although neither Pennsylvania nor Delaware had an established church, Rhode Island alone provided for complete freedom of conscience, and it is for this reason that Anson Phelps Stokes calls it the "home of American religious freedom." [1]

Despite the fact that most of the colonies in pre-Revolutionary America had some form of state church, it is important to note that most had achieved a considerable measure of religious liberty — or at least toleration — by the end of the colonial period. In general, the proprietary middle and southern colonies were composed of more religiously and nationally diverse groups than the colonies of New England; and it was largely for this reason that the former were, on the whole, ahead of the latter in developing religious freedom. In each section, however, as William Warren Sweet points out, the widespread achievement of toleration was due more largely to a variety of circumstances that existed in this period than to any widespread commitment to a theologically based principle of religious liberty.[2] Chief among these circumstances were the following: the religious diversity of the population in the various colonies, the background of religious persecution in Europe, the unchurched character of the great majority of the population toward the close of the colonial period, and — in the case of the proprietary colonies — the need to attract settlers in order to assure their economic success. It should not be forgotten, however, that these circumstantial factors were supported by the genuinely liberal ideas of men such as William Penn and Roger Williams, who believed in liberty of conscience as a matter of conviction; by the example of toleration in Roman Catholic Maryland; and, indirectly, by the influence of the Great Awakening with its emphasis upon voluntarism in matters of religion.

By the end of the Revolutionary period, sentiment in favor of religious freedom had become so strong that the great majority of delegates to the Constitutional Convention of 1787 not only believed that there should be legal separation of church and state at the level of the new Federal Government, but they also believed that a similar pattern would gradually prevail in the various states. By this time the Great Awakening, which had begun in New England in 1734, had given increased impetus to such Protestant groups as the Methodists, the Baptists, and the Presbyterians in their support of religious liberty. In addition, the cause of separation also received strong support in the latter half of the eighteenth century from the impact of rationalistic conceptions of religion associated with the Enlightenment and exemplified in deism, Unitarianism, and Freemasonry. Thomas Jefferson and Benjamin Franklin, for example, were essentially Unitarian in their religious beliefs; and Thomas Paine, who through his writings did a great deal to advance the cause of religious liberty as well as American independence, was a deist.

As Thomas G. Sanders points out,[3] the alliance of the Protestant sectarian revivalist groups and the rationalist forces for the common purpose of achieving separation of church and state was a pragmatic union. Yet it was essentially this combination of forces, together with the inability of either the Congregationalists or the Anglicans to secure their own establishment as a national state church, which made possible our constitutional provisions for the separation of church and state in particular and for religious liberty generally.

The guarantee of freedom of religion contained in the federal Constitution consists of two basic provisions. The first of these is included in Article VI, Section 3, of the original Constitution. It stipulates that "no religious test shall ever be required as a qualification to any office or public trust under the United States." According to this specification, no person shall ever be excluded from any public office because of any particular religious belief that he holds. Although the foregoing prohibition of any religious test of office constituted the only safeguard to religious liberty contained in the original Constitution, there was an immediate demand that the former be supplemented by a more explicit guarantee of freedom of religion. Hence, the First Amendment, which was included in the Bill of Rights, provided that " Congress shall make no law respecting an establishment of religion, or prohibiting the free exercise thereof." This Amendment meant that no single denomination could be given preferential status or government support at the national level either through the levying of taxes or through the requirement of attendance at its services. It also meant that Congress could not give such support to all of the denominations any more than to a single one, since this too would be a form of establishment.

Viewed in the light of the dominant pattern of state churches both in Europe and in colonial America, the provisions for religious liberty contained in the federal Constitution marked a decisive turning point in the struggle for religious freedom. They constituted our commitment as a nation to full freedom of religion rather than to the far more limited principle of toleration. Moreover, as we shall see, this commitment in itself marked a major step toward the achievement of a religiously pluralistic society, the full implications of which we are just now beginning to comprehend.

In his well-known study of religious liberty, M. Searle Bates, commenting upon the status of religious freedom in the early years of the new republic, wrote in 1945 that the federal Constitution together with the Bill of Rights " secured full freedom of religion in terms of individual rights." [4] While recognizing that some of the states still had established churches, Bates concluded, " The total picture was one of full freedom for the individual and for religious groups of all types, including those not of the Christian family." [5]

Protestants, in particular, have generally shared Bates's tendency to romanticize the religious liberty that we have had in this country from the beginning. It is true that " full freedom of religion in terms of individual rights " is " secured " in the Constitution in the sense that the former is recognized as normative. Moreover, the Constitution does provide a legal framework in which the quest for a full expression of religious freedom can be pursued and safeguarded. Nevertheless, the actual achievement and preservation of such liberty — like other forms of freedom — involves a continuous struggle and demands constant vigilance. The tendency to assume that all groups in the United States have enjoyed full freedom of religion from the beginning reflects a basically Protestant bias in the reading of American religious history.

Attention has already been called to the fact that the constitutional prohibition of an established church did not apply to the various states that constituted the new republic. Thus the pattern of state churches persisted in a number of the states well into the nineteenth century. Connecticut continued to support its Congregational churches until 1818 by means of taxes which were applied to clergy stipends. A similar situation prevailed in New Hampshire down until 1819. But it was not until 1833 that a state constitutional amendment terminating the establishment of Congregationalism in Massachusetts was finally adopted, thus bringing to an end the long tradition of legally established state churches in this country. Even so, however, some civil disabilities continued against Roman Catholics, particularly in regard to officeholding; and in one or two states Jews were not legally eligible to hold certain public offices.[6]

The struggle for disestablishment in the various states met with a great deal of resistance from those groups which benefited from state support in one form or another. But once the battle for separation of church and state was won, even such staunch defenders of establishment as Lyman Beecher of Connecticut recognized that the shift to voluntarism and self-support was good for the Congregational churches themselves. This too was an important milestone on the road to religious pluralism.

B. THE GROWTH OF RELIGIOUS PLURALISM

Although only about 5 percent of the total population of the colonies at the time they won their independence belonged to any church, it has been generally assumed throughout our history that the United States has been a Christian nation and, more particularly, a Protestant nation. At the same time it has been almost universally assumed, at least up until World War II, that all groups have enjoyed complete freedom of religion in this country from 1789 onward. As a people we have only recently begun to recognize that these two assumptions involve a basic inconsistency. If we are, indeed, basically a Protestant nation insofar as our *corporate* policy in the fields of education and law is concerned, then non-Protestant groups do not have full freedom to participate in our national life.

When both these assumptions are examined carefully, it becomes clear not only that they are inconsistent but also that both are false. Both do contain elements of truth, but both falsify the actual relationships of the churches to our national life that have prevailed in this country in the past. Moreover, both are closely related; and, from a Protestant point of view, both reflect serious misunderstandings of the nature of the church and of the proper relationship of the churches to the state.

The true status of religious liberty in post-Revolutionary America is obscured by the fact that only a small portion of the population at that time consisted of Roman Catholics and Jews. In a total population of approximately 3,500,000 in 1776 there were only about 25,000 Roman Catholics and 6,000 Jews. Thus, while only about 5 percent of the total population belonged to any church in 1776, the vast majority of this number belonged to various Protestant groups, and the latter had an influence far beyond their proportionate size in the formation of the new republic.[7] Protestantism had generally been the established religion in the colonies, including Maryland following the English revolution of 1688; and this pattern continued in a number of the original states well into the nineteenth century. Although many of the founding fathers — for example, Washington, Franklin, Jefferson, Madison, and George Mason — held quite liberal religious beliefs, they generally believed that sound democratic government and the welfare of the country as a whole depended to a large extent upon the support of religious faith.

In a variety of ways our public officials from George Washington to the present have acknowledged belief in a Supreme Being; national and state legislative sessions have customarily been opened with prayer; and general assistance has been given to the cause of religion through the enactment of Sabbath laws, the provision for chaplains in the armed services, and the granting of tax exemptions to religious bodies. Hence, given the position of dominance that Protestantism has in fact held throughout our entire history, it is not surprising that Americans have generally assumed that this is a Protestant nation, nor is it surprising that, on the whole, they have been insensitive to the extent to which Protestants have enjoyed special privileges as adherents of the favored religion.

In his book *From State Church to Pluralism*, Franklin H. Littell identifies two major movements that have largely determined the shape of religious life in America over the last hundred and fifty years, viz., mass evangelism and large-scale Roman Catholic and Jewish immigration.[8] Both these forces have profoundly influenced the growth of pluralism in this country.

The first of these movements — mass evangelism — had its roots in the Great Awakening in the first half of the eighteenth century. Because of its emphasis upon voluntarism in religion, the Great Awakening played an important role in preparing the ground for the separation of church and state in the federal Constitution, and this same emphasis in Protestant revivalist groups has operated to maintain the institutional separation of church and state down to the present. As has been noted, this in itself has been an important contribution to the development of pluralism in our national life.

Yet, on the other hand, insofar as the emphasis in mass evangelism has been upon the numerical growth in church membership and upon the external manifestations of religion (church membership, church attendance, and the ceremonial public aspects of religion), mass conversionism has helped produce a religion of conformity which runs counter to genuine religious liberty. The widespread practice of mass evangelism over the span of a century and a half has resulted in a spectacular increase in the percentage of the total population belonging to some organized religious body. As the table on page 90 shows, this figure had risen from an estimated 5 percent in 1776 to an estimated 64.4 percent in 1964.

Ironically, this growth in institutionalized religion — and of Protestantism in particular — has led to the secularization of the churches, and this in turn has fostered a continuation of the image of the United States as essentially a Protestant nation despite the fact that even as late as 1940 less than one half of the total population belonged to any organized religious body

TABLE [9]

1776	5%	1920	43%
1800	6.9%	1930	47%
1850	16%	1940	49%
1880	20%	1950	57%
1890	22%	1960	63.6%
1900	36%	1964	64.4%
1910	43%		

and only about 28 percent of the population belonged to Protestant churches.

The other major factor in the shaping of modern American religious life — large-scale Roman Catholic and Jewish immigration — has contributed more directly to the growth of religious pluralism in the broader sense of liberty for all religious groups to participate fully and equally in the public life of the nation. Whereas the voluntarism of revivalism led to a demand for the legal separation of church and state on the basis of a quasi-established Protestantism, the influx of large numbers of Roman Catholics and Jews led to the demand that the concepts of religious liberty be broadened so that Roman Catholics and Jews might enter into the mainstream of American life on an equal basis with Protestants.

As noted above, there were only about 25,000 Roman Catholics in the colonies at the time of the Revolution. Following this period, however, the Roman Catholic element of the population increased steadily due to the impact of revivalism on the frontier; a more adequate provision of spiritual supervision for the Roman Catholic constituency, made possible by the influx of priests from France and Ireland; the establishment of the Northwest Territory; and the acquisition of the Louisiana Purchase. By 1815 there were perhaps 90,000 Roman Catholics in the new republic.

After about 1830 the Roman Catholic portion of the population began to increase dramatically as the result of successive waves of immigrants from Europe. In the period between 1830 and the Civil War the number of Roman Catholics grew from an estimated 600,000 to 3,500,000. By 1880 this figure had risen to 6,400,000; by 1920, to 20,000,000; and by 1960, to 42,100,000. In 1964 the Roman Catholic Church reported a total of 45,640,-000 members, thus comprising 23.9 percent of the total population of this country, as compared with a total of 68,300,000 Protestants (35.9 percent of the population).[10]

There has been a similar but less spectacular growth in the Jewish segment of the population, due primarily to immigration from Germany and Central Europe between 1830 and 1850 and similar immigration from Russia between 1880 and the passing of restrictive immigration laws in the early 1920's. In the two decades following 1830 some 60,000 Jews arrived in this country; and in the years between 1880 and 1914 an estimated 2,000,000 immigrated to America. By 1964 the total reported membership in the combined Jewish congregations in this country stood at 5,600,000 (2.9 percent of the total population).

Faced with the problem of being accepted into the mainstream of American life, many of the second-generation immigrants abandoned the ethnic churches to which their forebears had belonged in Europe. But these groups soon discovered that the rejection of all religious ties impeded rather than aided the process of Americanization.[11] Hence, they have subsequently turned again to their traditional churches and synagogues in an effort to find — or establish — their identity as Americans. The impact of mass evangelism has been such that religion had become part of the American democratic creed. But the pressures toward conformity to religion still operated in an over-all context of individualism, competition, and an acceptance of separation of church and state. By mid-twentieth century, we were no longer a Protestant country, Herberg discovered; rather, we had become a nation with three equally acceptable forms of religious identity: Protestantism, Roman Catholicism, and Judaism.

This development was not achieved, however, without a

struggle. Just as there had been opposition to toleration and disestablishment in the colonies and in post-Revolutionary America, there was also strong opposition to any further movement of the nation toward pluralism through Roman Catholic immigration in particular. In part, this opposition rested upon a mythical and romantic conception of early American history; in part, it rested upon a desire to preserve the *status quo*. In any event, nativist sentiments began to appear even before the end of the eighteenth century, and numerous anti-Roman Catholic groups were organized beginning in the 1830's. Among the earlier of such groups were the Protestant Reformation Society (founded in 1836) and the American and Foreign Christian Union (founded in 1849). The Know-Nothing Party spread rapidly in the '50s and threatened to sweep the nation in the Presidential election of 1856. As reorganized in the twentieth century, the Ku Klux Klan has been strongly anti-Roman Catholic, anti-Semitic, and anti-immigrationist as well as anti-Negro. About 1925 the membership in the Klan reached a peak of between four and five million.

Since that time nativism has appeared sporadically in a variety of forms, including the opposition to Governor Alfred E. Smith in the Presidential election of 1927, subsequent revivals of the Ku Klux Klan, the rise of White Citizens Councils in the South beginning in 1954, and the emergence of the "radical right" in the Presidential campaign of 1964.

But just as disestablishment and separation of church and state won the day in the early period of our national life, so a developing pluralism has on the whole triumphed over nativism. The election of a Roman Catholic President in 1960 was a victory over nativism. It symbolized, in an unprecedented way, the full acceptance of Roman Catholics into the public life of the nation. It marked a new stage in the religious maturity of the country as a whole. It did not, however, mean that the transition to pluralism was complete, especially insofar as the full acceptance of other religious and humanistic groups are concerned. Rather, its primary significance lay in the fact that it marked the beginning of a confrontation, both by the nation and by the churches, with the realities of the *de facto* pluralism of American religious life. Such a confrontation has been long overdue, and the willingness to accept it represents a gain both for political freedom and for the integrity of the churches.

C. FACING THE REALITIES OF PLURALISM

Regardless of whether they like it or not, the churches are faced with the realities of a pluralistic society. If they are going to be relevant to the formation of public policy in increasingly large areas of modern life, they must first of all accept this religious diversity and seek to understand it. However, there are two main obstacles that prevent Protestant churches from dealing realistically with this contemporary religious situation in the United States. We have already examined one of these, namely, the widespread assumption that this country has always been an essentially Christian (Protestant) nation. As we have seen, this view is the product of an erroneous reading of American history. It represents a nostalgic longing for a mythical past, and as such it prevents a realistic understanding of present-day problems of church and state. The second obstacle that hinders the churches from facing up to the realities of pluralism is their fear of losing the traditional privileges and support that they have received due to the quasi-establishment of Protestantism. As a nation we have, therefore, only begun to wrestle with the legal, moral, and theological implications of this emergent pluralism; hence, it is impossible to tell what the full effects of this transition will be either upon the institutional churches themselves or upon the public life of the nation. Nevertheless, it may be helpful to consider three implications of religious pluralism that are receiving growing attention and a considerable area of agreement, particularly in Protestant circles.

1. A Secular Society

In the first place, religious pluralism implies — indeed, presupposes — a secular society. The latter idea represents, of course, a much more radical conception of pluralism than that described by Herberg when he spoke of Protestantism, Roman Catholicism, and Judaism as three equally acceptable forms of American religion. All three of these religious traditions have a great deal in common: belief in the same God, a common conception of the nature and destiny of man, and a generally common morality. All three are opposed to secularism, atheism, and agnosticism. Hence, neither Roman Catholicism nor Judaism poses a real threat to the effort to preserve the image of the United States as a religious (Judeo-Christian) nation. But a secular society, whatever else it may be, is one that " explicitly refuses to commit itself as a whole to any particular view of the nature of the universe and the place of man in it." [12]

At this point it is necessary to distinguish clearly between two closely related words: " secular " and " secularist " (cf. secularism). A pluralistic society is secular, but it is not secularist; for a secularist society is one in which secularism as an antitheistic conception of reality has become the official world view. Secularism has its own distinctive dogmas which its adherents seek to impose upon society as a whole through the public institutions. Hence, a secularist society would be just as much opposed to authentic pluralism as any other form of establishment.[13]

A secular society, on the other hand, refuses to adopt any particular world view. It recognizes the right of groups that hold radically different conceptions of the ultimate nature of man and the universe to participate fully and freely in the civil community. Such a society is unlikely to be religiously homogeneous, and it does not seek to become so through its public policy. Rather, it seeks to maintain its unity through the discovery and pursuit of common aims derived from the common humanity shared by all its members.

Insofar as pluralism implies a secular society, then, it means that Buddhists, Muslims, secularists, humanists, agnostics, and atheists are to be accepted on a level of equality in our public life along with Protestants, Roman Catholics, and Jews. This is the sense in which the United States Supreme Court has interpreted the constitutional guarantees of religious liberty in a number of recent decisions involving compulsory prayer and Bible-reading in the public schools, Sunday closing laws, public oaths, and the right to claim exemption from military service on grounds of conscience.

Viewed in terms of the positive values that it represents rather than exclusively in legal terms, the development of a secular society means a greater respect for the individual and for the smaller groups of which the community is composed. It means an enlargement of man's freedom and a fuller recognition of the importance of religious liberty. It means a greater respect for the integrity and responsibility of religious faith, for it recognizes the freedom of religion to stand in judgment upon society and to seek to transform the latter.

From the standpoint of a Protestant understanding of faith, a secular society is more nearly in accord with the will of God than one that in the name of Christianity seeks to impose a particular set of beliefs and practices upon the total community. More particularly, it is more in keeping with the will of God as this is disclosed in the incarnation, in the cross, in the New Testament understanding of the church as koinonia, and in the Biblical understanding of the way in which God actually deals with men in human history, both in judgment and in grace. To borrow a phrase from John Courtney Murray, the secular society is "written into the script of human history."[14] It is a prerequisite both for liberty and for vital faith.

2. The Need for Dialogue and Involvement

A second characteristic of a genuinely pluralistic society is that the latter provides a framework in which honest dialogue among the various religious traditions, including secularism, can best take place. It also provides a framework in which each particular group, whether religious or secularist, can participate in the shaping of public policy in a secular society on the basis of the democratic principles of equality and freedom.

In such a society no religious group would have any built-in advantage from the official culture; hence, each would be thrown back upon its own resources both in the areas of evangelism and religious education and in the effort to influence the formation of public policy. Each religious group would be driven to a deeper examination of its own heritage and of its own distinctive beliefs and values; thus, it would gain strength born of theological depth and historical perspective. Pluralism means that each tradition would be encouraged to maintain its own inner spiritual and moral integrity, for without such integrity it could not make its full contribution to society as a whole.

A pluralistic society thus creates both the possibility and the demand for a twofold dialogue on the part of the churches. On the one hand, it provides a greater opportunity for ecumenical dialogue of the various religious faiths with each other due to the greater equality of the different traditions; it also creates a greater demand for such *rapprochement* because of the religious and moral interests and goals that the churches and synagogues have in common. One illustration of the need for such dialogue and cooperation among Protestants, Roman Catholics, and Jews is found in the area of church-state relationships. Special consideration will be given to this issue momentarily as a third implication of pluralism.

In addition to ecumenical discussion among the churches themselves, however, a second kind of dialogue is urgently needed in a pluralistic society, namely, dialogue with humanist, secular-oriented, and even secularist groups. Openness to these groups is needed in part as an antidote to the pride, the vested interests, and the authoritarianism of the churches; it is also needed as an indispensable prerequisite for the relevance of the churches to the secular life of contemporary man. Moreover, such dialogue must go beyond the level of conversation in which ideas are simply exchanged; it must be based upon the existential involvement of the churches in the secular life of contemporary man — in his pursuit of economic, educational, and political goals; in his sense of meaninglessness, alienation, loneliness; and in his frustrations, dilemmas, and defeats. We shall return to this need for the churches to be involved in secular culture in the concluding section of our study.

There is, of course, no final guarantee that a pluralistic society will not degenerate into a secularist culture or that it will not develop a lowest-common-denominator faith. Herberg's analysis of the tendency of Protestantism, Roman Catholicism, and Judaism to degenerate into a common faith in democracy clearly illustrates this danger.[15] Insofar as the three faiths become transformed into a common culture-religion, the very possibility of a genuine pluralism is jeopardized; for the end result of this process is the emergence of a vague, generalized, man-centered faith in the values and loyalties that hold the civil community together. From the standpoint of historic Christianity and Judaism such a secularized faith is idolatrous; it represents a betrayal of the faith that gave rise to these traditions and which has been the source of their spiritual and moral power and renewal from the beginning. The point that needs to be emphasized here, however, is twofold. In the first place, every religious group — whether in a pluralistic society or in a culture where one religion is given official status — is tempted to refashion its faith into some form of culture-religion. But, in the second place, it is precisely for this reason that a pluralistic society provides a greater safeguard against this tendency, which is found in every group, than does any form of establishment.

3. Beyond Separationism

A third major implication of pluralism for the churches is the need for a reappraisal of the doctrine of separation of church and state. In the course of our national history this term has meant many different things to different groups. Moreover, sharply opposing groups have frequently joined in the defense of this principle for widely divergent and inconsistent reasons. Ironically, as Professor Sanders has shown, the principle of separationism provided the common ground upon which secularists and Protestant revivalists united to oppose any form of established church in the period when the Constitution was being drafted.

Although this particular alliance proved to be quite unstable and soon fell apart, there has been a recurrent tendency throughout our history for pietistic, individualistic Protestants to join forces with secularists in defending an absolute wall of separation between church and state against any assault by the Roman Catholic Church. Hence, Protestant separationism has often been associated with a strong anti-Roman Catholic polemic. This has been true, for example, of a variety of nativist groups which have appeared throughout the past century and a quarter. It has also been true — for quite different reasons — of Protestants and Other Americans United for Separation of Church and State, which was organized in 1948. Due to the emergence since World War II of such issues as the appointment of an ambassador to the Vatican and public financial support of religious schools, the Protestant churches generally have been forced to reexamine their traditional positions on church-state relations. As a result, they have become increasingly aware of the extent to which Protestant separationism has been based upon a militant anti-Roman Catholicism; and it has become increasingly clear that the effects of this polemic are equally as disastrous for Protestantism as for Roman Catholicism. Such anti-Roman Catholicism not only produces bigotry and further divides the Christian community, but it also inevitably plays into the hands of secularism. In the long run it results in a loss of genuine freedom of religion and thwarts the development of authentic pluralism.

Taken by itself, the principle of separationism implies a neg-

ative approach on the part of the churches to the state that is
inconsistent with the spirit of Protestantism as well as with the
American tradition of church-state relationships. Hence, it is
not surprising that this doctrine has come to imply the separation of religion from the political life of the nation and the re-
striction of the former to the private life of the individual.
When the principle of separationism is absolutized, it creates
a moral and spiritual vacuum into which doctrinaire forms of
secularism inevitably move. Thus, in the name of separation of
church and state, secularism itself becomes an antireligious
establishment.

In view of the increasing inroads of secularism in American
life and in view of the common problems confronting all the
major religious groups, many Protestants have come to recognize the need for a theological position that goes beyond separationism and is more positively related to the goals and aims
of Christian faith. Hence, there has been growing support for
what Sanders calls the "transformationist view" of church-
state relations. Biblically, this position is deeply rooted in the
Old Testament with its strong sense of divine sovereignty and
judgment, social responsibility, and historical involvement; theologically, it is strongly grounded in Calvinism, Puritanism,
and the social gospel. This view is represented in this country
by Reinhold Niebuhr, John C. Bennett, Kenneth Underwood,
William Muehl, and Paul Ramsey. It is also represented in a
number of denominations, including the United Church of
Christ, and in the National Council of Churches.

The transformationist approach to church-state problems re-
jects the tendency implicit in separationism to draw a sharp
distinction between the religious and political spheres of life;
it seeks, rather, to relate both spheres to the values and norms
of Christian faith. Instead of dealing indiscriminately with all
matters of church-state relations on the basis of a doctrinaire
appeal to a "wall of separation," transformationism seeks to
analyze specific problems on the basis of their objective merit
and in the light of presently existing circumstances. It recog-

nizes, for example, that American society, including both Roman Catholicism and Protestantism, has undergone significant changes over the last hundred and fifty years and that American Roman Catholicism is different in many respects from European Roman Catholicism. The transformationist approach to church-state relations implies a strong emphasis upon cooperation among Protestants, Roman Catholics, and Jews in their common effort to overcome the secularism of American life. Since these groups share so largely a common moral and spiritual heritage, it is possible for them to find a large area of "overlap," or consensus, in the pursuit of social justice and in the effort to influence the formation of public policy.[16] But the aim of this cooperation is not the formation of a lowest-common-denominator faith. On the contrary, its purpose is the renewal and enrichment of each tradition in a context of dialogue and in a common quest for social responsibility.

In summary, then, the transition of this country to a religiously pluralistic society implies the emergence of a secular society. Moreover, it presupposes the need for creative dialogue among the various faiths represented in the national community. Finally, it also constitutes a challenge to the churches to make clear the relevance of Christian faith for the public, political life of the nation instead of withdrawing behind a mythical wall of absolute separation of church and state.

PART TWO: THE BIBLICAL VIEW OF THE CHURCH AND THE WORLD

IV

THE FAITH OF ISRAEL

Up to the present point in our study, attention has been focused primarily upon the empirical characteristics of the churches viewed as social institutions. The first two chapters dealt with the extent to which divisions in the churches both reflect and deepen the class and racial divisions that exist in the community at large. A third chapter traced the growth of religious pluralism in this country and called attention to some of the implications of this pluralism for the churches in our post-Protestant society.

In contrast to the preceding portion of this study, which has been primarily descriptive in character, we turn now to an analysis of the church's understanding of itself as a community of faith. In this section we will be seeking a normative definition of the church in Biblical and theological terms. Finally, in Part Three, we shall consider some of the implications of this Biblical-theological understanding of the nature and mission of the church for the renewal of the churches in the present day and, particularly, for a recovery of their relevance to contemporary life.

A. THE FAITH OF ISRAEL AND THE FAITH OF THE CHURCH

It may seem strange to some that we should begin our consideration of the nature of the Christian church and its relationship to the world with an inquiry into the character of Hebrew faith as this is portrayed in the Old Testament. As Dietrich Bonhoeffer once remarked, Christians frequently try to come to the New Testament too quickly and too easily without first seeing it in relationship to the Old Testament. Such an attempt leads inevitably to a misunderstanding of Christian faith. The result of this effort to view the New Testament as complete within itself is particularly disastrous insofar as any adequate understanding of the relationship of Christian faith to culture is concerned, due both to the more individualistic conception of man and to the eschatological expectations that underlie the New Testament generally. In contrast, in the Old Testament much greater attention is given to the sovereignty and judgments of God within history; and there is a far more fully developed sense of man's social responsibility and of his involvement in history and culture. But it needs to be emphasized that these concepts, which are so largely associated with the Old Testament, are not rejected in the New; indeed, they are basically presupposed in the latter, even though attention is focused there upon the particular events surrounding the life, death, and resurrection of Jesus and the meaning of this unique Christ-event for the followers of Jesus who believed that the end of the present world order was near at hand.

From its beginning the church has understood itself as standing within the historically continuous drama of God's self-disclosure to man that runs from Abraham through Moses and the prophets to Jesus and the Christian church. Indeed, the New Testament is unanimous in proclaiming that God's promises to Israel had been fulfilled in the person of Jesus, whom it hailed as the long-awaited Messiah. Just as the Old Testament points beyond itself to the New, so the latter is incomprehensible apart from the former. It is for this reason that the books included in both the Old and the New Testaments have been accepted by the church as canonical and are included in the Christian Bible.

There are, of course, a great many important differences between the religious and moral teachings of the Old and New

Testaments. These differences are emphasized at many points in the New Testament itself. Theologically speaking, the decisive difference lies in the New Testament claim that Jesus of Nazareth was the Messiah, or the Christ. Yet, far from consti-tuting a rejection of Israel's faith in God, this Christian confes-sion of faith in Jesus as the Christ was in reality an affirmation that the God of Israel had disclosed himself in a unique, de-cisive way in the person of Jesus of Nazareth. As the author of The Letter to the Hebrews declared, "In many and various ways God spoke of old to our fathers by the prophets; but in these last days he has spoken to us by a Son, whom he ap-pointed the heir of all things, through whom also he created the world" (Heb. 1:1-2).

The contrast between the moral teachings of the Old and New Testaments is presented in equally sharp form at some points in the New Testament. In the Sermon on the Mount, for example, Jesus is represented as placing his requirements in sharp opposition to those which had been taught to "the men of old." Thus, Jesus says: "You have heard that it was said to the men of old, 'You shall not kill; and whoever kills shall be liable to judgment.' But I say to you that every one who is angry with his brother shall be liable to judgment; whoever in-sults his brother shall be liable to the council, and whoever says, 'You fool!' shall be liable to the hell of fire" (Matt. 5:21-22). And in place of the ancient law of vengeance, "an eye for an eye and a tooth for a tooth," Jesus places the new demand, "Do not resist one who is evil" (Matt. 5:38-39). Yet even here Jesus warns those who seek to justify the abrogation of the Ju-daic law on the basis of his teachings: "Think not that I have come to abolish the law and the prophets; I have come not to abolish them but to fulfil them" (Matt. 5:17). Moreover, the two commandments that he gave his followers represented a summary of the Mosaic law — a summary itself drawn almost verbally from the Old Testament: "And he [Jesus] said to him, 'You shall love the Lord your God with all your heart, and with all your soul, and with all your mind. This is the great and first commandment. And a second is like it, You shall love your neighbor as yourself. On these two commandments depend all the law and the prophets.'" (Matt. 22:37-40; cf. Deut. 6:5 and Lev. 19:18.) Similarly Paul, who understood the meaning of Christian liberty as fully as any writer in the New Testament, viewed the law of Israel as a directive pointing man beyond itself to the will of God. While Christian love (agape) breaks and shatters every form of bondage to this moral law, love nevertheless fulfills the intent — but not the letter — of the moral law of Israel (Gal. 5:14). Love transforms the law and uses it in the service of the neighbor.

In summary, then, this Biblical faith which reaches its fulfillment in Christ — neither Old Testament faith alone nor New Testament faith in abstraction from that of the Old — is the faith of the church. As Prof. G. Ernest Wright, the distinguished Old Testament scholar, declares:

> When the New Testament is separated from the Old, it is a superstructure hanging in midair, a small torso of a literature filled with presuppositions which can be misunderstood and perverted. Without the Old Testament there could be little conception of God's purposive work in and through history, which reaches its climax in Christ. . . . By itself the New Testament contains insufficient material for a doctrine of creation, of justice and the responsible society, and of man in relation to his world and people.[1]

No single conception of Christian faith can be adequately understood unless it is seen against the background of the Old Testament, but the insufficiency of the New Testament taken by itself becomes most apparent when one begins to consider the social relevance of Christian faith — its relevance to life in community, its relevance to culture, and its relationship to the world. When the underlying faith of the Old Testament is forgotten, the church tends to turn its gaze inward upon itself and to become narcissistic and idolatrous. Such idolatry takes many forms — a tendency to focus upon the experience of forgiveness as the totality of the gospel, the preservation and defense of itself as an ark of salvation for the pious, the claiming of salvation as the exclusive possession of Christians, the substitution of love for Jesus in the place of love for God, and the worship of Christ either as the one God or as a second deity in the place of the God to whom Christ pointed men and whom he revealed.[2] Whenever these or any other form of idolatry replace the God of Biblical faith in the witness of the church, the church inevitably becomes irrelevant to large segments of man's life in culture, for its God is too small to be the Creator of all and the Sovereign over all. Understood at its deepest level, therefore, the crisis in the contemporary church arises out of its preoccupation with itself, out of its narrow loyalties, and out of its unfaithfulness to the God of the nations whose Kingdom symbolizes a universal reign of love and righteousness. It is this God, the ultimate reality with which both individuals and nations must finally reckon, who is revealed by Christ to be love in his creation and in his judgments.

B. ISRAEL AS A COVENANT COMMUNITY

In the previous section of this chapter we have dealt with the question of the relationship of the faith of Israel to that of the New Testament church. Despite all the differences between the two, there is from the standpoint of the Christian church a basic unity between the Old and the New Testaments, so that the faith of the former is in the deepest sense fulfilled in the good news of the gospel. This unity, as we have seen, arises out of the fact that both Testaments are built around a common theme: namely, the self-disclosure of God to man in word and deed in history. Both are concerned with the revelatory acts of God through which he has made his will known to man.

Not only does this conception of the revelatory action of God serve as the unifying element that binds the entire Bible together into one inseparable whole; it is also the theme that gives unity to the great variety of religious beliefs and traditions in the Old Testament as well as to the widely different interpretations of the meaning of Christian faith and morality in the various parts of the New Testament. In the present interpretation of the faith of Israel — as in our earlier references to " New Testament faith " and " Biblical faith " — we have chosen to emphasize the unity in the Biblical understanding of God and of man's relationship to God instead of focusing upon the obvious differences that are to be found between the various parts of the Bible. Such a conception of unity does not imply, however, that there is any systematic body of beliefs that were always accepted as normative by the Hebrews throughout the Old Testament period; nor does it imply that there is any such body of beliefs that can be identified as " the Christian faith " or as " New Testament faith " in the sense that it is universally accepted by all of the writers of the New Testament. Rather, the unifying principle which gives the Biblical account of revelation its inner unity is a principle that emerges, or becomes manifest, in the course of the continual unfolding of the drama of God's mighty acts. The unity between the earlier and the later accounts — whether within the Old Testament or in the Bible as a whole — is a unity that is discerned by those to whom God's later revelatory acts are addressed. In a sense this unity is implicit in the faith of Abraham; but clearly it is not explicit there, for Abraham's faith was quite different in content from that of Moses or Isaiah or the Evangelists or Paul. But the unity is discerned by the later writers, who see their religious history as part of a rich, diverse pattern of God's dealings with men in a common community of faith. This unity is recognized even though God was known by different names at different times in the Old Testament period and even though the concept of monotheism probably did not appear until the seventh century B.C.; similarly, it is recognized in the New Testament even while the latter declares that God's revelation of himself in and through Jesus of Nazareth represents the climax of his historical self-disclosure and indeed constitutes the decisive revelation for Christians.

Similarly, in the present day large numbers of Protestant and Orthodox Christians with widely different denominational backgrounds are discovering a unity that transcends their special theological traditions and institutional histories in the ecumenical movement. Likewise, Protestant, Orthodox, and Roman Catholic Christians are discovering a fundamental kinship of faith among themselves — and also with Jews — even though such groups continue to differ greatly among themselves with regard to many important theological beliefs. Indeed, it is increasingly recognized that such unity emerges most clearly when the differences between the various confessions are cherished and when dialogue takes place across these traditional and confessional lines rather than when unity is sought through the reduction of the various theologies and traditions to a lowest common denominator.

One of the most significant keys for understanding the unity implicit in the Old Testament, and indeed in the Bible as a whole, is that of the covenant. Throughout her history, even when the term itself was not used, Israel understood her special relationship to Yahweh essentially in terms of a covenant which he had freely and graciously established with her. The creation of this relationship was not due to any special merit on the part of Israel — or of any particular group or tribe of Israelites; rather, it was due entirely to God's grace in electing her and choosing her from among all of the nations of the earth for the working out of his purposes. In the course of her spiritual pilgrimage this concept underwent a great deal of development in the Old Testament. Indeed, Yahweh is represented as having made a series of covenants with Israel through a number of prominent tribal, national, and religious leaders such as Abraham, Noah, Moses, Joshua, David, and Ezra. The Mosaic covenant was renewed under King Josiah, and Jeremiah foresaw a time when the Lord would make a new covenant with his people — a covenant written not upon tables of stone but upon the heart (Jer. 31:31-33). At first the covenant was conceived in more nationalistic and exclusive terms, but in the course of her historical and spiritual development, Israel came to see that Yahweh's grace and mercy extended to all peoples and that he had chosen her to be his messenger to declare his salvation to the nations.

While there are important minor differences within each group, the covenants contained in the Old Testament are of two major types.[3] In the first place, there are those in which only God is bound by any obligation. Included in this group are the covenants that Yahweh made with Abraham, Noah, and David. In the case of Abraham, Yahweh promised that he would be the father of many nations and that the Land of Canaan would be given to him and his descendants as an everlasting possession. Hence, as originally understood, circumcision was not an obligation but rather a " sign of the covenant" (Gen. 17:11), like the rainbow of Gen., ch. 9. The purpose of this rite was to serve as a concrete indication that Yahweh had made the covenant with Abraham and also to identify those who should participate in the fulfillment of its promises. Those males who did not keep this sign would be excluded from the Israelite community. Even more clearly in the covenants with Noah and David, it is Yahweh alone who is bound by the promises that he would never again destroy all living creatures with a flood and that he would preserve the Davidic line and spare the kingdom of David forever.

The second main type of covenant in the Old Testament is that in which Israel is also bound to God by certain specified obligations. The Mosaic covenant (Ex. 20:1-17) is by far the most important example of this kind of bond between Yahweh and his people. Other illustrations include the covenant of Joshua (Josh., ch. 24), the reform of Josiah (II Kings 23:2-3), and the covenant of Ezra (Neh., chs. 9; 10), all of which apparently represent renewals of the Mosaic covenant in some form. New light has recently been thrown upon this particular form of Israel's covenant relationship to Yahweh by the analysis of international treaties among the Hittites in the period from about 1400 to 1200 B.C.[4] These treaties were also of two types:

parity and suzerainty. The former of these consisted of a treaty between equal powers and involved a reciprocal covenantal agreement intended for the mutual benefit of both parties. The suzerainty type of treaty, on the other hand, was a form of covenant between a suzerain — the overlord or ruler over many lesser kings within a vast empire — and a vassal. According to this kind of treaty, the more powerful suzerain established a covenant with a vassal. Such a treaty offered the vassal protection and security, and the vassal in turn was placed under obligation to obey the commands of the suzerain. This kind of agreement did not in any way limit the sovereignty of the superior ruler. Moreover, it was not considered fundamentally as an arbitrary assertion of power or even as a coerced treaty; rather, it was a treaty offered by a generous and benevolent superior, and the vassal's motivation for obedience to the latter was gratitude.

A close comparison of the Sinaitic covenant with this particular form of Hittite suzerainty treaty makes it clear that the latter was appropriated by Moses shortly after the exodus from Egypt to provide the *form* for expressing Israel's faith. In the Abrahamic covenant Yahweh had, out of sheer grace, bound himself to fulfill certain promises to Israel. In the Mosaic covenant, on the other hand, Yahweh bound Israel to keep the commandments contained in the Decalogue. He gave Israel the covenant, but his sovereignty was not limited by it. As the prophets subsequently declared, he had freely established the relationship and he was free to terminate it if he chose. Moreover, the bestowal of the covenant was preceded by the reminder that the Author of the Decalogue was the one who had delivered Israel out of bondage (Ex. 20:1-2). Like the Abrahamic covenant, therefore, the Mosaic covenant was basically a manifestation of divine grace; but the latter, unlike the former, included a set of obligations that the recipients of the covenant pledged themselves to fulfill. The covenant with Abraham was marked by the sign of circumcision; the covenant that was given at Sinai was sealed by a blood sacrifice which symbolized the participation of both Yahweh and the people in the establishment of the covenant.

The ceremony marking the making and sealing of the Mosaic covenant is described in Ex., ch. 24. Moses built an altar at the foot of Mt. Sinai and set up twelve pillars to represent the twelve tribes of Israel. Animals were then sacrificed to Yahweh. Half the blood of these animals was thrown against the altar as a symbol of Yahweh's participation in the rite, and the other half was collected in basins. Moses then read to the people " the book of the covenant." After they had pledged themselves to accept and obey Yahweh's demands, Moses sprinkled the remaining blood upon the people, saying, " Behold the blood of the covenant which the Lord has made with you in accordance with all these words " (Ex. 24:8). The sacrificial blood not only confirmed the people in the vows that they had made, but it also symbolized the binding nature of the covenant and the close relationship that was established between Israel and Yahweh since the same blood was dashed against the altar as was sprinkled upon the people.

In view of the role the Mosaic covenant has played both in the subsequent development of Judaism and in Christianity, it is important to examine briefly some of the reasons for its importance. In the first place, it marked the emergence of Israel as a people. Prior to the events that took place at Sinai, the Hebrews had been a loosely organized coalition of tribes. Politically speaking, they continued to be a loosely organized association of semiautonomous tribes throughout the period of the Judges; but, religiously speaking, they became molded into a people through their participation in a common covenant at Sinai. Through this experience a number of hitherto separate tribes with diverse traditions and expectations for the future became conscious of their unique historical destiny as a single " people of Yahweh," as the Israel of God.[5] It was the single action of God toward them all in choosing them, in delivering them from bondage, and in granting them the covenant that gave them their essential unity as a people bound to the will of

Yahweh. Frequently in the Old Testament the covenant relationship is summarized in the saying, "I will be your God and
you shall be my people." Before the Hebrews were bound together by the divine action in the establishment of the covenant, they had been no people. It was the establishment of this
relationship that gave them their identity as a people.

In the second place, the covenant at Sinai made it quite clear
— in utter contrast to the Hittite political treaties — that Israel's
primary loyalty was to Yahweh and not to any national state.
The Israelites were bound to God and to the keeping of a series
of moral obligations in relation to their fellowmen. Israel was
not yet a nation; it was primarily a community of faith. When
the people came together in obedience to the call of God, they
came as an "assembly" or as a "congregation" — groups that
have primarily a religious rather than a political connotation. It
is true that the religion of Israel did provide a strong stimulus
toward the creation of an independent nation, but from the
beginning this goal was subordinated to obedience to the divine
will and the fulfillment of Israel's destiny as a religious people
of God. Temporal blessing was made conditional upon obedience to the previously announced moral demands of Yahweh,
and calamity was promised as the consequence for disobedience. Both individuals and the community were confronted
with the moral requirements of God. The Decalogue represented the will of a gracious and good Deity, but it nevertheless marked a recognition of the fact that the divine will is
absolutely sovereign over both the private and the community
life.

In the third place, the Mosaic covenant performed the essential function of giving form and structure to the social life of
the community. The demands of the covenant were not addressed to a collection of individuals considered merely as individuals apart from their participation in the public life of the
community. On the contrary, they constituted a requirement
that the total life of Israel be made obedient to the divine commandments and that the political and economic structures of

the community exemplify and foster such obedience. The Mosaic covenant, in short, was addressed to individuals-in-community, not to individuals apart from their relationships to society. It was a covenant that God made with the people as a community that he had brought into being. It could not be kept as a cultic form of worship or by the priests in behalf of the people; rather, if it was to be kept at all, it had to be kept by the community itself in terms of its corporate life.

It should be noted in this connection, in the fourth place, that in its original form the Mosaic covenant did not include the lengthy codes of law that are found in various parts of the Old Testament. Rather, it probably consisted essentially of the Ten Commandments in Ex. 20:1-17. In Hebrew these are frequently referred to as "the Ten Words." It is likely that in their present form even these have, in some cases, been expanded in the process of transmitting them from generation to generation. It was evidently assumed in the earliest period that these commandments would continually need to be interpreted and applied in the light of changing historical and social conditions. Hence the Decalogue provided only a framework for understanding the divine will. It did not attempt to say in what manner God was to be worshiped, how the Sabbath was to be observed, or how one's parents were to be honored. The task of working out the implications of such commandments for the daily life of each generation was left to the covenant community itself. The purpose of the Decalogue was to establish a charter of freedom, not to provide a code of laws which would tell men in advance precisely what Yahweh required of them in every situation.

Finally, the Mosaic conception of the covenant supplemented rather than replaced the conception that underlay the covenant with Abraham. In both instances God is understood first of all as Israel's Savior. Israel's first knowledge of him took the form of gospel or grace — that is, of "good news" of what God had done for her, rather than of law — that is, of demands which he had placed upon her. It was recognized in the Mosaic covenant, however, that God is righteous will and that the revelation of his love for man places a claim upon men to fulfill the divine will in their relationships to each other. In both cases, the covenant was offered quite apart from any special merit on Israel's part; but in the Mosaic covenant the continued enjoyment of Yahweh's blessings was made contingent upon obedience to his will. Moreover, as we have seen, Israel had reached a much higher level of social development by the time of the exodus; as a result a more profound understanding of the social nature of human existence is reflected in the Sinaitic covenant.

Thus, with the Mosaic covenant a second fundamental theme was introduced into the Biblical understanding of the relationship between God and man, namely, the theme of law, along with the earlier theme of divine grace. Henceforth, both these dimensions of the divine-human relationship are in constant tension throughout the Bible just as they are in our present-day experience as Christians.

It is true, of course, that the demand for Israel to obey the commands of Yahweh in her total life soon led to an effort to define the will of God in a number of codes of law. These codes tended to become substitutes for the living relationship of man with God presupposed by the covenant. The earliest such body of legislation, frequently called " the Book of the Covenant," is found in Ex., chs. 21 to 23, and probably comes from the ninth century. It was followed in the seventh century by the Deuteronomic Code (Deut., chs. 12 to 16) and in the sixth century by the Holiness Code (Lev., chs. 17 to 26). The effort to identify the will of God with specific legal codes reached its peak in the time of Ezra in the fifth century, when the religious traditions that had been collected and preserved in the Pentateuch were identified with the " law of Moses " which had been delivered by God to Moses on Mt. Sinai (Neh., chs. 9; 10). From the time of Ezra onward, these traditions were equated with the will of God, and the covenant was understood primarily in terms of this law. As divine law, the Pentateuch became the sacred Torah — or teachings — which constituted the foundation upon which Judaism as a rigidly defined way of life was subsequently built in the post-Old Testament period.

Despite the legalistic distortion of the covenant concept in the centuries that followed the institution of the Mosaic covenant at Mt. Sinai, from that moment onward Israel was never able to escape the understanding of her relationship to God that had been reflected in that event. Hence, of the two main conceptions of the covenant — the one associated with Abraham and David and the other with Moses — it is the latter that became dominant in Israel and the early church, even though both traditions were combined in various ways in post-Mosaic times and both found expression in the New Testament. The Mosaic covenant combined the recognition of the primacy of God's grace in his relationship to man, with a recognition of the inescapable obligations that rest upon man as a free moral being made in the image of God and destined to live in community.

At times the concept of the covenant became so distorted that the term itself was dropped in order to avoid misunderstanding. The Major Prophets of the eighth to the sixth centuries, for example, seldom used the word " covenant." In the popular thought of this period, it had come to be understood as an unconditional promise of divine protection and favor for Israel. The personal quality of the divine-human relationship, the moral character of the divine will, and the conditional nature of the promise of future blessing — all of which were implicit in the Mosaic covenant — had fallen into eclipse. Due to the prevailing misconception of the covenant, these elements in Israel's faith could not be recovered by appeal to the concept itself but only by the use of other symbols. Hence, the prophets such as Amos, Isaiah, Micah, and Hosea turned to the symbols of sonship, marriage, kinship, judgment, lordship, and sovereignty to describe Yahweh's relationship to Israel and what he required of her, namely, trust, loyalty, justice, integrity, and love.

Seen in this light, the prophetic silence with regard to the covenant concept itself stemmed out of a deep understanding of the meaning of the underlying relationship. It was, of course, impossible to capture the inner meaning of that relationship in any code of law. But, since the covenant community as a whole stood under the sovereignty and judgment of God, it was always necessary for it to attempt to make its corporate life an expression of the divine will in each succeeding generation. As the Mosaic covenant presupposed and as the prophets clearly discerned, this task was one that could never be finally accomplished, but it was nevertheless an inescapable demand. Jeremiah looked for a day when the tension between the gospel of divine grace and the law as the divine will for human conduct would be overcome. Thus he spoke of a time when God would make a new covenant with Israel and the law would be written upon men's hearts (Jer. 31:33). In that day the children of Israel would freely do God's will because they desired to do so in their hearts. In that day both the Law and the Prophets would be fulfilled through the renewal of the covenant community itself. Until that time the tension between gospel and law would remain, but neither could be jettisoned or forgotten without falsifying the righteousness of God, in whom love and justice are united.

Implicit in the tension that we have observed between gospel and law in the covenant concept was also the tension between the future and the present. The fundamental conviction underlying all Biblical thought about man's relationship to God is the faith that God is sovereign and that he is just. He is sovereign over the present and over the future; he will accomplish his purposes; and his loving-kindness toward man will endure forever. His justice, the later Old Testament writers came to see, consists essentially in his mercy and forgiveness rather than in justice conceived of as rewards or punishments. But he is faithful, and he is sovereign. Therefore, he will fulfill the promise of the covenant.

At first Israel looked for the fulfillment of this promise of salvation in the present historical order. Even the prophets expected the establishment of a new age upon earth rather than an eschatological Kingdom beyond man's present sociotemporal order of existence. In the period following the Babylonian captivity, however, Israel's hope for national restoration continued to be defeated; moreover, despite the efforts of the prophets, the lawgivers, and the sages, evil and corruption continued to persist even in the covenant community itself as well as in the world at large. Under such circumstances the later writers of the apocalyptic literature, represented in the Old Testament by The Book of Daniel, declared that the new age could come into being through the intervention of God himself. He would destroy the old world in a great catastrophic act of judgment and institute the new age. This event would be accompanied by the resurrection of the dead, who would appear together with the living at the Last Judgment, after which the righteous would receive their eternal reward and the wicked would be punished or destroyed. Evil would be completely overcome, and the whole earth would be transformed. In a dark and evil day, this apocalyptic vision gave eloquent testimony to Israel's faith in the sovereignty and goodness of God and in the final triumph of his righteousness.

While this treatment of the covenant as an expression of Israel's faith has of necessity been limited to a brief sketch of some of the major elements included in this concept, it is hoped that enough has been said to indicate the manner in which this symbol constitutes an integral bond between the two Testaments and why it was possible for the church in the New Testament to conceive of itself as a new covenant community. Before turning to a consideration of the faith of the church in the New Testament, however, it is important that we examine more fully the conception of God that underlies the covenant and constitutes the unifying element in Israel's faith, even when other symbols such as sonship, marriage, judgment, and lordship are used. For it is this underlying conception of God at the center of Israel's faith that binds the two Testaments together; and it is this that caused the early Christians to understand themselves as the New Israel which had been called into being by the God of the patriarchs, of Moses, and of the prophets — the same God who had revealed himself in Jesus of Nazareth.

C. RADICAL MONOTHEISM

The primary focus of the Old Testament — and indeed of the Bible as a whole — is upon God's self-disclosure through his mighty acts and upon man's response to the God who addresses him in and through his revelatory deeds. Thus, Biblical faith is historical in the sense that it finds the locus of God's self-disclosure in history rather than in some abstract, speculative system of ideas. This does not mean, however, that the Biblical writers were attempting to write what we might today call scientific history, for their primary purpose was to interpret the significance of historical events rather than to provide a disinterested, objective account of the events themselves. They assumed the historicity of the events that they reported, but these events were ultimately important only because of the inner meaning they conveyed concerning man's relationship to God, the Sovereign over men and history.

Quite naturally, the Biblical narrators described the events they reported in terms of their own understandings of nature, of the individual, of society, and of God. Event and interpretation went hand in hand, and the writers did not draw any sharp distinction between these two aspects of history. The historical happening or occurrence of an event was important, for it was the medium of revelation; but the deepest significance of the event lay in its inner meaning — that is, in its disclosure of the will and purpose of the Power behind all temporal events. Thus the Bible is a historical book in that it is grounded in the historical experience of a people who understood all its history as being significant because it was related to one God who is sovereign over history; but its approach to history is existential rather than scientific in that it is primarily concerned with the ultimate meaning of events rather than with their external forms and objective details.

From the perspective of Biblical faith, then, history is the sphere of divine action and human response. Biblical faith begins with revelation. It begins with Israel's effort to understand her existence and destiny in the light of that Power upon which she recognizes herself to be finally dependent, both in her origin and in her ultimate destiny. The Bible is an account — a record and an interpretation — of the acts of God through which he has revealed himself to a particular people. Such a view of history presupposes freedom for both God and man, but this presupposition itself was necessitated by Israel's experience and her encounter with a Reality that was given. For in her encounter with this Reality, Israel always recognized herself to be finite and dependent upon a Power and a Will that was prior to her own existence and her own will. Moreover, from the beginning she encountered this Power as sovereign and free in its relationship to her. And since it was sovereign and free whereas she was finite and dependent, Israel could finally know it only as it revealed itself to her.

Viewed in Biblical terms, revelation is an experience or event in which man acknowledges that he is confronted in the totality of his being by a Power upon which he is finally dependent. Moreover, in the Bible, this Power is understood ultimately as personal, righteous Will. Man cannot fully understand or explain this Will or why it has chosen to reveal itself to him; but neither can he ignore it or explain it away. In his confrontation with this Will, man is apprehended at the deepest level of his being. He is faced with the inescapable decision of affirming or denying his existence at its deepest level, namely, that of authentic selfhood. For that Reality which is disclosed in revelation is the Power and the Will that has called man into being and is sovereign over man's future, including his final end. Hence, in the moment of revelation, man is summoned to commit himself to this Power, to trust in it, and to be loyal to it.

Man has done nothing — and indeed can do nothing — to merit the divine favor, but the decision that he is summoned to make determines the kind of self that he will be henceforth. In this sense, faith is essentially a gift, unmerited and free, but it involves a commitment of the self to the object of faith as that which gives the self its final meaning and value. The very possibility of faith is a gift, but the actualization of faith involves man's response, first of all, of trust and, secondarily, of fidelity to that Power and that Will which has disclosed itself to him in personal terms.

The story of Israel's faith is the story of the emergence and deepening understanding of monotheism. Biblical scholars are uncertain as to when this concept first appeared among the Hebrews. However, its first explicit formulations in the writings of the Old Testament come from the seventh century B.C.[6] Some scholars believe that Moses was a monotheist; but, since there is no clear evidence that he denied the existence of all gods except Yahweh, it seems preferable to speak of the religion of Moses as monolatry. Yet, in a sense, the monotheism of the later period was implicit in the Mosaic religion, with its demand for absolute loyalty to Yahweh, its belief that he was independent of geographic locality and able to control nature, and its confidence that he could accomplish his purpose at any time and in any place. Moreover, the First Commandment of the Decalogue forbade the Israelites to worship any other deities; and the Second Commandment forbade them to make any graven image or likeness of any created thing lest they fall into idolatry (Ex. 20:3-4).

As we have already seen, the Hebrews first understood God primarily as the giver of salvation — as the One who had revealed himself to Abram and promised him a blessing and an inheritance; as the One who had elected Israel from among all the peoples of the earth, delivered her out of bondage in Egypt, and established a covenant with her. But as Israel subsequently sought to understand the totality of her life — her sufferings and defeats as well as her prosperity and triumphs — all in relationship to Yahweh, her perception of the divine will deepened. With increasing clarity she came to understand her relationship to Yahweh in a threefold way. Yahweh's will toward her was one, for he was one and he had shown himself to be merciful and loyal to Israel. Yet, as she sought to comprehend the meaning of her fortunes among the nations and as she wrestled with the meaning of suffering, both of the wicked and of the innocent, she recognized a threefold pattern in the divine will: creation, judgment, and reconciliation.

Although these patterns of divine action were perceived to be different in man's subjective experience, they nevertheless had an inner unity which came to be most adequately understood — in the later Old Testament and particularly in the New — as sovereign love. Sometimes this love was encountered primarily as forgiveness, as liberation, and as reconciliation with God; sometimes it was encountered primarily as the creative ground of all finite existence; and, again, it was experienced as judgment upon man's pride and rebellion against the Creator. Yet, amid all the variety of Yahweh's dealings with Israel, his intent and his will were perceived to be ultimately one even though man can never fully comprehend the purposes of God. If any one of these aspects of God's relationship to man is lost sight of, the meaning of the other two is distorted and the God of the Bible is replaced by an idol — that is, by an object of faith that is too small, too anthropocentric, or too sentimental to give meaning to all human life and history.

In its most fully developed form the faith of Israel represented faith in one God who is the living Lord of the whole created order and who is related to all men as their Creator, their Judge, and their Redeemer. This is the heart of the Old Testament faith in God, and it constitutes the basic, underlying unity between the Old and the New Testaments. In his life and teaching Jesus stood within this faith of Israel, prayed to the God of Israel, and pointed men to this God as their Heavenly Father. Thus, he represents a continuation of this faith while at the same time his life, death, and resurrection constitute for Christians a still deeper revelation of the love of God than had been given prior to his coming.

It has been noted above that the history of Israel's faith is the history of the emergence and deepening of her understanding of monotheism. It is the story of a spiritual pilgrimage through which the prophetic leaders of Israel came to understand the totality of human life — and, indeed, of all existence — in relationship to one ultimate Power conceived of as personal, righteous will. It is this Power and this Will which is the ultimate source both of being and of value. All other beings derive their existence from this Will and have their final value in relationship to it. It is this Power and this Will that Biblical faith declares to be love in all of its action toward man. Moreover, because God is sovereign over all that he has made and because he is righteous Will, he demands radical obedience to his will.

H. Richard Niebuhr used the term "radical monotheism" to describe this prophetic faith.[7] Niebuhr recognized that radical monotheistic faith is something that is given to men more as "a hope and a goal" than as an achievement.[8] In her own life Israel never fully exemplified this radical trust and radical obedience to Yahweh. Her own life and worship were continually corrupted by disobedience and idolatry. But this idolatry and disobedience did not disprove the prophetic perception of the transcendence and unity of the divine will. Indeed, the former confirmed the latter. For the radically monotheistic faith of the prophets enabled them to understand the sufferings and punishments of Israel as part of a consistent pattern of divine action. Beyond the exclusiveness of Jewish nationalism and beyond the ceremonialism of popular piety, they pointed Israel to the God of the nations who demanded justice and righteousness of all men. Faith in this living God caused the prophets to recognize the divine judgment upon Israel for her idolatry and her unfaithfulness in keeping her covenant. But behind Israel's suffering and punishments the prophets saw the will of the Creator working out his purposes for his people, and they glimpsed the saving will of God even in the midst of his chastisements.

Ultimately Deutero-Isaiah came to apprehend the purpose of God in radically universalistic terms. He perceived that the God of Israel was none other than the Creator and the Savior of all peoples, and this God had chosen Israel not for her own glory but to be his messenger in bringing the knowledge of the one God to the ends of the earth. Seen in the light of this faith, the popular religion of the day often appeared as the enemy of true faith. Instead of bringing men into the presence of the living Lord, it served as an escape from God and kept them from his presence. Seen in the light of this faith, popular religion was polytheistic and idolatrous. Such gods, the prophets declared, were dead; but in their place radical, monotheistic faith pointed men to the universal Power and Will that undergirds and sustains all things. This Power — from which all things come, in which all things cohere, and in whose will alone all are able to find fulfillment — and this Power alone is the Lord of " heaven and earth "; he alone is worthy of worship. This Power is the Center of existence, the ultimate source of all being and value, for all finite beings derive both their existence and their value from him.

As we have already seen, the later Biblical writers generally understood this divine will as being continually revealed to man in a unified but threefold pattern of creation, judgment, and reconciliation. Moreover, these are the traditional categories that Christians have continued to use to describe the will and purpose of God. However, these concepts are not usually understood in a radical way; hence our faith tends to be polytheistic and idolatrous rather than monotheistic. Our loyalties are divided among many finite centers of value instead of being united in a single, final loyalty to the universal Center of being and value. It is the genius of the prophetic faith of Israel that it points men always beyond popular religion and indeed beyond every religious form and symbol to the living God who inhabits eternity. It confesses faith in this universal Power and ultimately declares its will toward man to be love. But this love is made manifest among men in a threefold way. Since these concepts are so central for an understanding of the nature of God in Biblical terms, it is important that we examine briefly each of these modes of divine action.[9]

1. *God as Creator.* Although the Hebrews at first understood God primarily as the giver of salvation — as the One who had elected Israel, delivered her out of bondage in Egypt, and given her the covenant — the most fundamental conviction about God to which they were eventually led was the belief that he is the Creator. As the Hebrews sought to understand the totality of their life in relation to the God who had chosen them and made of them a people, they came to perceive that the Redeemer of Israel was also the Creator of the heavens and the earth and that beside him there were no other gods at all (Isa. 42:5; 45:5). The sovereign mercy and power of Yahweh in revealing himself to Israel and electing her to be his people, his faithfulness in fulfilling his promises, and even Israel's defeats by her enemies could be understood only if the God of her fathers was in fact sovereign over the nations and "maker of heaven and earth" (Gen. 14:22). By his mighty acts the God of Israel had revealed himself through history and through nature to be Lord of both. And since he had shown himself to be sovereign over all, faith declared him to be the Creator of all.

The Biblical doctrine of God as the Creator, it should be noted, was not intended as a scientific theory or account of how the world came into existence. On the contrary, its purpose is to affirm the conviction, born of faith, that all temporal existence is grounded in the will of God: "In the beginning God created the heavens and the earth" (Gen. 1:1; cf. Ps. 19:1; Isa. 42:5; Job, chs. 38; 39). Everything that is outside of God is absolutely dependent, both for its existence and for its meaning, upon him, while he is dependent upon nothing outside of himself. Not only is God the source of all things, but he is the power that sustains all in being. He is also the source of that unity and order which characterize the universe and prevent it from becoming a chaos.

Faith in God as the Creator affirms the goodness of the entire created order: "And God saw everything that he had made, and behold, it was very good" (Gen. 1:31). All that exists has value to God and is fundamentally good. Evil is, therefore, not ultimate; rather, it represents a perversion, or distortion, of that which God has created and values. But at the same time, the concept of divine creation points to the absolute gap between God, the unconditioned and totally independent source of everything that is created, and his creation, including both nature and man. God alone is uncreated and infinite; all other beings are created and finite. The latter are good when they fulfill their appointed purpose in the larger order of creation, but they cannot be made the center of existence.

The Biblical doctrine of God as the Creator and Ruler of all things recognizes the ultimate mystery of creation and of God's purpose in creation and in history. His ways are not man's ways, and his thoughts are not man's thoughts. Yet, Biblical faith declares that he has partially revealed his nature and his purposes to man through his creative action in bringing the world of nature into being, in maintaining it in beauty and harmony, and in the establishment of the moral order that he has ordained. As we shall see, his purposes are also made known through his judgments and redemptive action; but apart from the final grounding of the latter in the will and power of the Creator, judgment and reconciliation would lose their ultimate meaning. Creation and salvation would lose the essential unity that the Bible declares them to have. Biblical monotheism would be replaced by an ultimate dualism, and Christ would cease to be the revealer of that Power through whom all things were made and in which they cohere (John 1:1-3; Col. 1:15-17; Heb. 1:2-3; Rev. 4:11). Power and love would be ultimately in conflict with each other, whereas Biblical faith affirms that the ultimate power in the universe is love.

Summarizing the meaning of "radical monotheism" as this idea has appeared in Western culture, H. Richard Niebuhr found its two great mottoes to be: "I am the Lord thy God: thou shalt have no other gods before me," and "Whatever is, is good." [10] The first of these mottoes comes from the Decalogue; the second is a restatement of the Biblical doctrine of creation. Taken together, they affirm the faith, in abstract and philosophical language, that the principle of being and the principle of value — the ground of existence and the ground of meaning — are identical; or, in religious language, that the Creator and the God of grace — power and love — are one.

2. *God as Judge.* The concept of God as Judge is implicit in the understanding of God both as sovereign and as righteous Will. In the preprophetic period, for example, the idea of divine judgment is particularly evident in the Mosaic covenant. Since God was related to Israel primarily as righteous Will, she could not disobey him and still receive the promises contained in the covenant. If God were not Judge, he would not be sovereign, and his purpose in the creation of man could be defeated with impunity.

Hence it is not by accident that the Creation narratives in Genesis are followed at once by an account of the Fall of man and of the " curse " that God placed upon him for his disobedience. When Adam disobeyed the command of the Creator, he immediately encountered him as his Judge. God said to Eve, " I will greatly multiply your pain in childbearing; in pain you shall bring forth children, yet your desire shall be for your husband, and he shall rule over you " (Gen. 3:16). And to Adam he said, " Because you have listened to the voice of your wife, and have eaten of the tree of which I commanded you, ' You shall not eat of it,' cursed is the ground because of you; in toil you shall eat of it all the days of your life " (Gen. 3:17). And the Lord drove Adam and Eve forth from the Garden of Eden. Taken together, the stories of the Creation and the Fall declare in unmistakable terms that man's Creator is also his Judge and that, although it is possible for man to live without God's blessing, it is nevertheless impossible for man to live without the divine judgment.

On the whole, the writers of the Old Testament understood the divine judgment as falling upon the collective life of Israel as well as upon individuals who disobeyed the commandments of God. In the Biblical view of man, the individual always exists in community with other individuals; hence, the consequences of his actions are shared by the community of which he is a part. In the Genesis account of the Fall, it is not simply Adam and Eve who are banished from the Garden of Eden, but because of their sin all their descendants are destined to live in a fallen world instead of a paradise of innocence and unbroken community with God. Similarly, in the Decalogue the injunction against idolatry is accompanied by a recognition of the unity between the generations in terms of the consequences of sin: " You shall not bow down to them or serve them; for I the Lord your God am a jealous God, visiting the iniquity of the fathers upon the children to the third and the fourth generation of those who hate me " (Ex. 20:5).

But it was the prophets of the eighth to the sixth centuries who discerned most clearly the judgments of God upon Israel as a nation. By that time, as noted above, the covenant had become popularly misunderstood as a divine promise of Israel's ultimate vindication over all her enemies. Amos, however, clearly perceived that Yahweh was independent of Israel's existence as a nation; moreover, Israel had not been chosen for special favor in the sense that she would no longer be measured by the standards of justice. On the contrary, Israel was like the Ethiopians to Yahweh (Amos 9:7). He had indeed freely chosen her from among all the nations of the earth, but he was not dependent upon her continued existence as a nation to achieve his sovereign ends.

The prophets saw God's judgments falling not only upon Israel, but also upon all peoples and all nations. Jeremiah saw God making " an indictment against the nations " and " entering into judgment with all flesh " (Jer. 25:31). And, in like manner, the Second Isaiah prophesied against Babylon: "You felt secure in your wickedness, you said, ' No one sees me '. . . . But evil shall come upon you, for which you cannot atone; disaster shall fall upon you, which you will not be able to expiate; and ruin shall come on you suddenly, of which you know nothing " (Isa. 47:10-11).

The judgments that the prophets saw God as meting out in

the calamities of history were primarily judgments against human pride. They followed inevitably upon man's refusal to acknowledge the finite character of his existence and the moral nature of the world in which he is placed. Hence, far from proving that God is either indifferent or weak, they confirmed the prophets' faith that he is both righteous and sovereign. They revealed the moral structure of the created order and the self-destructiveness of every effort to defy it.

It should be noted, however, that in its most fully developed form, the prophetic perception of a divine judgment in history did not imply that there is any simple or complete correlation between human evil and justice in history. It was evident from the experience both of individuals and of nations that the suffering of men is not strictly proportionate to the evil that they have done; moreover, the innocent frequently suffer along with the guilty. Job protested strongly against the smugness of those who sought to explain his suffering on the basis of some secret sin. The Second Isaiah recognized that Israel had received double for her sins while her evil oppressors had gone unpunished. Similarly, in the New Testament, Jesus rebuked his disciples for assuming that it was either because of his own sins or because of the sins of his parents that a certain man had been born blind: " It was not that this man sinned, or his parents, but that the works of God might be made manifest in him " (John 9:3).

Neither the Old nor the New Testament attempts to give a speculative answer to the question, Why do the innocent suffer? Since every speculative answer to the problem of evil is finally inadequate, the writers of the Bible do not attempt to explain its existence; rather, they seek to come to grips with evil and overcome it by drawing upon the resources of faith in the sovereignty and goodness of God. Evil and suffering cannot be fully understood by finite men, but neither can they be evaded. Much suffering can be understood in terms of just retribution, but there is enough that cannot be explained in these terms to warn men and nations against the proud assumption that the prosperity and blessings that they presently enjoy are proof of their superior virtue. The Lord uses even the ungodly nations — Assyria, Babylon, and Persia, for example — as his instruments to execute judgment, although they too will eventually also be brought low because of their pride, their idolatry, and the injustice that they have perpetrated.

Since the justice that men receive in history is only rough and incomplete, Israel's faith in the sovereignty of God who had revealed himself to be righteous led to the rise of a messianic hope. Although the latter took a variety of forms, some of which were strongly nationalistic, this hope was essentially an expression of the confidence that God's justice would be fully vindicated, if not within history at least at the end of history. In later Judaism and in the New Testament the fulfillment of this expectation was associated with an eschatological judgment. Immediately prior to Jesus' baptism, John the Baptist appeared in the valley of the River Jordan announcing the imminence of such a divine judgment and summoning men to repentance. Jesus also began his ministry in Galilee proclaiming, " The time is fulfilled, and the kingdom of God is at hand; repent, and believe in the gospel " (Mark 1:15). Again and again he spoke of the nearness of the Kingdom and of the consequences of the judgment associated with its advent. Belief in such a judgment was the corollary of belief in the sovereignty and righteousness of God. Belief in its coming meant belief that the purposes of God in Creation would be fulfilled in the establishment of his Kingdom. Since for Jesus the ruler of this Kingdom is man's Heavenly Father, the announcement of its advent was for him an occasion of joy.

3. *God as Redeemer.* The God of the Old Testament is frequently pictured in popular thought as a God of wrath in contrast to the God of love who is revealed in the New Testament. In actual fact, however, from the beginning of her history Israel understood Yahweh's relationship to her to be essentially a relationship of love rather than wrath. This love was manifest in Creation and more particularly in a special way in his dealings

with Israel. Through his mighty acts Yahweh had shown himself from the beginning to be Israel's Redeemer. As the knowledge of God deepened and as Israel's faith became more consciously monotheistic, the Second Isaiah declared that God's saving purpose extended to the ends of the earth and included all peoples.

In the Old Testament, as in the New, the purpose of God as Savior is inseparable from his purpose as Creator and Judge. The ultimate meaning of salvation lies in the fact that it is the Creator who forgives man's sin and guilt and restores him to fellowship with himself. Moreover, unless it is seen in the context of the divine judgment upon sin, the concept of salvation easily becomes sentimental and unbiblical. However, neither in the Old nor in the New Testament are God's judgments viewed as being merely, or even primarily, punitive in purpose. Even Amos, who of all the prophets perhaps stressed most exclusively the retributive character of Israel's punishment, held out the hope that, if Israel would repent, Yahweh might yet spare a remnant (Amos 5:14-15). But it was Hosea, Isaiah, Jeremiah, and Second Isaiah who perceived most clearly that the ultimate purpose of the divine judgment was not to destroy but to heal.

Thus, Hosea declared that Yahweh was acting through Israel's historical crises to free his people from bondage and restore them in freedom to himself. Yahweh's "wrath" was neither capricious nor vindictive; rather, it was what Luther later called a "strange" work of love. Its purpose was to free Israel from idolatry and pride. Just as Hosea continued to love Gomer after she had proved an unfaithful wife, so Yahweh remained steadfast in his love for Israel despite her infidelity. Through the divine judgments upon Israel, therefore, God was preparing her for a deeper understanding of his love and restoring her to the freedom of the covenant. "I will betroth you to me for ever; I will betroth you to me in righteousness and in justice, in steadfast love, and in mercy. I will betroth you to me in faithfulness. . . ." (Hos. 2:19-20.)

Similarly, Isaiah represented God as saying to Israel: "I will turn my hand against you and will smelt away your dross as with lye and remove all your alloy. . . . Afterward you shall be called the city of righteousness, the faithful city" (Isa. 1:25-26). And beyond the day of punishment Jeremiah foresaw a time when God would make a new covenant with Israel and Judah. This covenant would be based upon the forgiving love of God, the depths of which could be understood only after Israel and Judah had been made aware of their sin through the experience of the divine wrath. "But this is the covenant which I will make with the house of Israel after those days, says the Lord: I will put my law within them, and I will write it upon their hearts; and I will be their God, and they shall be my people. . . . I will forgive their iniquity, and I will remember their sin no more." (Jer. 31:33-34.)

Although the earlier prophets — particularly Hosea, Isaiah, and Jeremiah — had discovered a saving purpose on the part of God behind the national crises that had befallen Israel, they had understood this purpose primarily in terms of Israel's own salvation. They had viewed the disasters that she had experienced as chastisement for her own guilt and as a necessary means for her own salvation. The Second Isaiah, on the other hand, saw in Israel's defeat and captivity God's purpose of universal salvation. Her sufferings could be only partially understood as a divine punishment for her sin, for God is just and Israel had received double for her transgressions. But God had not deserted his people in the time of their captivity in Babylon. On the contrary, he had elected Israel to be his agent in bringing salvation to the Gentiles. She had been chosen, not for special privileges, but to be obedient even unto suffering and death that, by her witness to the redemptive purposes and power of God, she might be the means of bringing salvation to all peoples.

The description of the suffering servant in Second Isaiah (Isa. 42:1-4; 49:1-6; 50:4-9; and 52:13 to 53:12) represents the deepest insight into the meaning of suffering and the depth of

God's love in the Old Testament. While the expected Messiah was not usually identified with the suffering servant in Jewish thought, Christians have made this identification from earliest times. According to the Lucan narrative, Jesus opened his ministry in Nazareth by reading a passage from Isa., ch. 61, and announcing that "Today this scripture has been fulfilled in your hearing" (Luke 4:21). Although these verses may not have been originally intended as a description of the Servant of the Lord, many scholars believe that they were so understood in Jesus' day. Again and again Jesus described his ministry in terms that reflected the Servant poems. Speaking of his own work, he said, "For the Son of man came to seek and to save the lost" (Luke 19:10). He "came not to be served but to serve, and to give his life as a ransom for many" (Mark 10:45). In the fulfillment of his vocation he would have to "suffer many things, and be rejected by the elders and chief priests and scribes, and be killed" (Luke 9:22).

Looking back upon Jesus' death in the light of his teaching about God and about his own vocation, the early followers of Jesus saw in it the fullest disclosure of God's redemptive love. Because of his resurrection, they believed him to be the Messiah. But clearly he was not the kind of Messiah who had been generally expected. Instead of being a royal king, he was far more like the Servant of Yahweh who by his vicarious suffering had revealed the depth of God's love.

V

THE CHURCH IN THE NEW TESTAMENT

In the previous chapter we discussed the faith of Israel as a covenant community which had been called into being by God's self-disclosure of his will and purposes in and through history. Against this background we turn now to a consideration of the nature of the church as the latter was understood in the New Testament. Just as the Hebrews had been constituted into a people of God by their common experience of confrontation with Yahweh at Mt. Sinai, so the early Christians were constituted into a "new people of God" by their common confrontation with the new disclosure of God in Christ.

For the early Christians the self-disclosure of God in Christ became the decisive revelation of the nature and will of God. That event became the final norm of Christian faith, for it was acknowledged to be the ultimate standard by which all Christian understandings of God and of the divine will are finally measured. Yet, the confession of faith in Christ did not mean that in the church an entirely new faith had been substituted for the faith of Israel. Rather, it meant that the faith of Israel had been transformed by a new disclosure of the divine nature which had been mediated to the Christian community through the Christ-event, and most particularly by the radically new manifestation of the divine love (agape) in Christ. It meant a new understanding of the depth and universality of God's love symbolized by the cross; and it meant also a new understanding of the meaning of love among men. It meant a transformation of the popular Jewish conceptions of the Kingdom of God so that the latter was purged of all traces of nationalism and political messianism. It meant also a radical transformation of morality, particularly of the Jewish law. Yet even the law was not discarded; rather, it was transformed and brought under the judgment of love and the neighbor's need (Matt. 5:17; 22:34-40; Rom. 13:9; Gal. 5:14).

Many images or analogies are used in the New Testament to describe the nature of the church as a community of faith. In the present discussion we shall focus attention on three of the most important of these: the new covenant community, the body of Christ, and the koinonia.[1] Significantly, none of these images can be fully understood without a recognition of its implications for life in the world and for the responsibility of the church for the mundane needs of the neighbor in the world. Moreover, each of them focuses attention upon different aspects of the church's self-understanding; thus they serve to supplement and correct each other. For this reason, also, they need to be viewed together.

The analogy of the new covenant community emphasizes more clearly than either of the other two the deep rootage of the Christian community in the spiritual heritage of Israel. Hence, we turn to a consideration of this image first.

A. THE NEW COVENANT COMMUNITY

The most basic presupposition of the New Testament church consists of the conviction that in and through Jesus of Nazareth and subsequently through the church, God was fulfilling his promises to Israel. This conviction also underlay Jesus' interpretation of his own mission. Thus, according to Mark, he began his public ministry with the proclamation, "The time is fulfilled, and the kingdom of God is at hand; repent, and believe in the gospel" (Mark 1:15).

Although the specific term "Kingdom of God" is not used in the Old Testament, the idea itself is presupposed throughout. It was familiar to Jesus' contemporaries, and they — like

the prophets of old — believed that God himself would establish his Kingdom in power in the fullness of time. Jesus inherited this concept from Judaism, but he purged it of all its
nationalistic elements and transformed it into a universal reign
of God. In freeing it from its political connotation, he gave it a
new and deeper meaning. Significantly, however, it was an integral part of the religious heritage of Israel, and Jesus made it
the center of his own message.

Israel's faith in the final triumph of the Kingdom of God
found its most concrete expression in the messianic hope.
While the latter took a variety of forms in the Old Testament
and in later Judaism, essentially it represented the anticipation
of a new age in which God would subdue all the forces of evil
and establish a reign of righteousness which would endure forever. The advent of the Kingdom would be preceded by the
coming of the Messiah. It was generally assumed that this divine messenger would lead the Jews to triumph over all their
foes and restore the former kingdom of David. In its later
form, the messianic hope also included belief in a general resurrection of the dead and in a final judgment.

However strange it may seem, it is impossible to know with
certainty whether Jesus believed himself to be the Messiah.
The Evangelists, however, had come to believe that he had
fulfilled the messianic prophecy; hence, the Gospels were written in the light of this belief, and they reflect this faith. It is
also clear from the New Testament that during Jesus' lifetime
many people, including the disciples, believed him to be the
promised Deliverer; yet, it is equally clear that he failed to
fulfill the messianic role in any of its popular forms. As a result,
the hope that he would be the one who would "redeem Israel" (Luke 24:21) was shattered by his death.

Yet Jesus' death was not the end of the disciples' faith;
rather, it was a gateway to a deeper understanding of God's
will and purpose for humanity. For the astounding fact is that,
despite the failure of their hopes, the early Christians — in the
light of Jesus' life and especially in the light of his death and

resurrection — affirmed that he *was* indeed the Messiah, that is, the Christ. This miracle, which is the most surprising fact of all about the New Testament faith, is also the most incontrovertible of all! From the standpoint of this postresurrection faith the disciples and the Evangelists saw that the messianic character of Jesus' ministry had been contained implicitly in his words and deeds and that it had been made explicit by his death and resurrection; for through these events they had come to know the power and depth of the love of God in Christ which had not forsaken them but transformed them into new creatures and bound them together into a fellowship which even death could not overcome.

Like the belief that Jesus was the Messiah, the church also had its beginning in the resurrection faith. According to The Acts of the Apostles, the church came into being at Pentecost with the outpouring of the Holy Spirit. In the Lucan account of Pentecost the resurrection of Jesus, his exaltation, and the sending of the Holy Spirit are all inseparably bound together (Acts 2:32 ff.). The founding of the church was, thus, the work of the risen Lord, not that of Jesus during his ministry in the flesh. It is true, of course, that during his earthly ministry Jesus gathered a group of followers about himself, but they had remained within Judaism. It was only after his death and on the basis of the resurrection faith that the followers of Jesus gradually became separated from Judaism. This separation was the result of the distinctive character of the faith of the Christians, who declared that Jesus had been the Messiah and that God — even the God of the Jews — had exalted him as Lord and King. Indeed, the Christians could understand Jesus' mission only with the aid of concepts drawn from their Jewish heritage, no matter how inadequate the Jewish content of these symbols might be; and they continued to live in daily expectation of the coming of the Kingdom of God, in which the Jews also placed their hope.

Although the early Christian community was vividly aware of the distinctive character of its faith, it was at the same time also aware that its faith was deeply rooted in that of Israel. It is scarcely surprising, therefore, that from the beginning the first Christians thought of themselves as the true heirs of God's promises to Israel. They used terms drawn from Jewish religious circles to designate the community to which they belonged. For example, the Greek word *ekklēsia,* which is translated into English as "church," was used in Jewish religious literature before it was adopted in Christian circles.

The term *ekklēsia* appears one hundred and twelve times in the New Testament. It is used primarily in the letters of Paul, in The Acts, and in Revelation. It appears only twice in the Gospels, and both of these instances are found in Matthew. In general, in the New Testament the term *ekklēsia,* or church, refers to a community of believers that is gathered together by God's action in Christ.[2] This community belongs to God. It has been called into being by his action. He dwells in it, rules over it, and realizes his purposes through it. Moreover, the community of Christians existed as an *ekklēsia* prior to any specific assembly or gathering in local congregations. It came into being as a response of faith to God's action in Christ. By reason of their common faith in Christ, believers already had their oneness and that which gave them their identity as members of the *ekklēsia.* Thus, the author of The First Letter of Peter wrote: "But you are . . . God's own people, that you may declare the wonderful deeds of him who called you out of darkness into his marvelous light. Once you were no people but now you are God's people; once you had not received mercy but now you have received mercy" (I Peter 2:9-10). Yet this *ekklēsia* consisted of the very same community of believers who assembled for worship in various cities and villages — at Jerusalem, at Corinth, at Thessalonica, in Galatia, and throughout Asia Minor.

The church, however, was not only a community, or people, as Israel was also a "people." It was, indeed, the *true* Israel of God. The Old Israel had been disobedient and unfaithful to the covenant; therefore, God had gathered together a new people to be his witnesses. In part, this new people was a remnant of the faithful Jews, but it also included Gentiles. Its members might indeed be called the "sons of Abraham," but the true descendants of Abraham were not his posterity according to race; rather, they included all those believers, whether Jew or Gentile, who put their trust in God alone for their salvation. These were the true Israel, the new people of God, which had been brought into being by the reconciling work of God in Christ.

The church, therefore, was both a continuation and a consummation of the covenant community of Israel. Yet it was at the same time a *new* community of faith which had sprung from the gift of the Holy Spirit and the saving action of God in Christ. The purpose of God in the formation of this new community was to bring salvation to all peoples and races and nations. Through it he was fulfilling his promise to Abraham, namely, that through the latter's descendants all the nations of the earth would be blessed (Gen. 22:18; cf. Acts 3:25). Like Israel of old, the New Israel was called to be a faithful, merciful, and righteous people. But whereas the requirements of the Mosaic covenant had been written upon tablets of stone, the new covenant had been written upon the hearts of the believers (cf. II Cor. 3:3-6); and its only requirements were to love God with all one's heart, soul, mind, and strength and to love one's neighbor as oneself. Like Israel of old, and particularly like the suffering servant of Yahweh, the New Israel was called to witness to the reconciling work of God in Christ by proclaiming this gospel to all men and by becoming itself an agent of reconciliation in the world.

It is not surprising that the early church interpreted its mission among the nations largely in evangelistic terms, for throughout most of the New Testament period it was consciously an eschatological community which expected the end of the present age to come soon. Under such circumstances there seemed to be little time remaining for reforming an unjust social system, nor was such reform by human agents needed; for God himself was about to act to establish his reign of righteousness with power. Indeed, it had already begun to be made manifest in Jesus' own healing ministry and in the fruits of the Spirit in the church.

Gradually, however, the expectation of an immediate end to the present historical order was replaced by the expectation of a longer future. Against the background of this change, Paul and the Fourth Evangelist in particular sought to reformulate the basic meaning of Christian faith in existential rather than eschatological terms. For the delay of the end did not undercut the Christian faith; nor did it do so for the church as a whole. Indeed, Jesus had refused to set any exact date for the coming of the end, for only the Father knew the day and the hour when the Kingdom would come in its fullness. Belief that it would come soon had given an increased urgency to his call to repentance, but it had not basically determined his teaching about the ultimate dimensions of human existence. For while the full manifestation of the Kingdom had remained in the future in his teaching, Jesus had seen the new age breaking into history through his own ministry of exorcism and healing; and he had confronted his hearers with the necessity of making a decision for or against the Kingdom of God in the present moment.

For the Fourth Evangelist, the fundamental decision to which Jesus summoned men was not basically affected by the nearness of the final Day of Judgment. The summons to repentance is, essentially, a present call to faith and obedience; and the promise of the resurrection is the promise of a radically new quality of life in the here and now. Or, in the language of Paul, the promise of the gospel is the promise of a radical transformation of human existence which he describes in terms of the "new man," "new being," and life according to the Spirit. To be sure, God is still the Lord of history, Lord of its end as of its present and its beginning, and he will bring his purposes for the whole created order to fulfillment in his own time. But the call to repentance and the announcement of the divine grace are not affected by the nearness of the Kingdom; they are always relevant to man's present existence before God.

But there is also another reason why the New Testament evinces little specific concern with the cultural responsibilities of Christians; for, even though the future might be relatively long, it was still not possible under the circumstances either for the church or for Christians acting individually as citizens to exercise any significant influence upon political, social, and economic affairs. The social situation of the church in the first three centuries was far more similar to that which it faces in totalitarian countries today than to that faced by the churches in democratic countries such as the United States, where their members constitute a majority of the electorate and occupy almost all the public offices. Under such circumstances the development of a genuine social ethic was of little concern, if not impossible. Such an ethic would have been irrelevant to the life of the church in that day, and it would have been equally irrelevant as a pattern for responsible action in new sociocultural situations.

Implicit in the concept of the covenant community, however, was the basis for such a social concern once the relationship of the church to society had changed. It was implicit in the concept of one sovereign God who was related to men and communities as creator, judge, and reconciler. It was implicit in the concept of man-in-community and in the universal mission of Israel and the church. It was implicit in the admonition of Jesus that he had come not to abolish the Law and the Prophets but to fulfill them (Matt. 5:17). It was implicit in the concept of the Kingdom of God, to which the church pointed but with which the church could not be identified. It was implicit in the righteousness and love of God and in his demand for the radical obedience of the whole self in man's daily decisions in the present age.

B. THE BODY OF CHRIST

The most dynamic and in some respects the most fully developed metaphor that the New Testament uses to describe the church is that of " the body of Christ." From the time of Paul onward, this image has been one of the most important sources of the church's understanding of itself; and today it constitutes one of the major focal points of discussion of the nature of the church, both among Protestants and among Roman Catholics.

The image of the body of Christ is explicitly used only in the Pauline literature, although there are scattered and indirect allusions to it elsewhere. Indeed, the term itself occurs only in Romans, I and II Corinthians, Ephesians, and Colossians.[3] Even in these letters, however, the metaphor has a variety of meanings which reflect differences in the problems faced by the churches to which the several letters were written and also different stages in the development of Pauline thought. As a result, we shall not attempt to examine all these different usages of the term. Rather, we shall limit ourselves to a consideration of three major aspects of this metaphor which point, respectively, to the dependence of the church upon Christ, to the unity of the church, and to the relationship of the church to the world.[4]

Before turning to these specific meanings of the image of the church as the body of Christ, however, it will be helpful to call attention to the usage of the word " body " (*sōma*) in Greek thought. Paul wrote in Greek, and he appropriated this term as a tool for interpreting the nature of the church. In the New Testament period *sōma* was frequently used to mean " unity " and " wholeness." The primary emphasis was upon the unity and completeness of man in his own individual body; but the term had also come to be used in a figurative sense to refer to the entire cosmic order, which was conceived to be similar to the human body in its unity and wholeness. Hence, the basic meaning of the word referred to the individual body of man, and its secondary, figurative meaning referred to the larger unity — a people, a nation, or a cosmos — into which man and the whole cosmic order are incorporated.

Unlike Greek, the Hebrew language had no equivalent for the concept of " body." In the Old Testament man is spoken of, instead, as " flesh "; but " flesh " refers to the creatureliness, frailty, and mortality that each person shares with all men and with animals. Here the emphasis is upon man's creaturehood instead of his wholeness and upon the fact that he shares this creaturehood with all created things. Similarly, the Hebrew word for man, *adam*, refers primarily to mankind — to his common humanity — and only secondarily to man as an individual. Whereas Greek thought stressed the individuality of each person as a complete entity in himself, the Hebrews understood man primarily as a member of a community and as a creature who lives in constant dependence upon God.

While the word " body " appears numerous times in other parts of the New Testament, the metaphor of the church as the body of Christ, as we have already noted, appears explicitly only in the Pauline letters. The content of this latter phrase was largely shaped, at least insofar as Paul's undisputed letters are concerned, by Paul's discussions with his opponents at Corinth who tended to interpret Christianity in individualistic and spiritualistic terms. But the new content that Paul poured into the word " body " and the new context in which he used the term — *ekklēsia,* or church, as the " body of Christ " — were derived from his Jewish heritage and the earliest Christian tradition concerning the Last Supper. For not only was Paul deeply rooted in the Hebrew understanding of man, but also he had a profound understanding of the meaning of the Lord's Supper.

Although there was no word for " body " in Hebrew, such a term was current in Aramaic, which was the language spoken by Jesus. Thus, in Aramaic one word was used to designate " flesh " and another to designate " body." Moreover, the Aramaic equivalent for " body " included both the meaning of " physical body " and that of " self," or " ego." While the Gospels as we know them in the New Testament were written originally in Greek, it seems probable that Jesus used the Aramaic word for "body" in the institution of the Lord's Supper when he said, "This is my body" (Mark 14:22; Matt. 26:26; Luke 22:19; I Cor. 11:24). These words were followed by the familiar ones used with the giving of the wine: "This is my blood of the covenant, which is poured out for many" (Mark 14:24; cf. Matt. 26:28; Luke 22:17 ff.; I Cor. 11:25). In its earliest form (probably preserved in Mark 14:22), the first of these sayings emphasized the presence of the Lord at this Eucharistic meal, and the second — as all four accounts of the Lord's Supper agree — introduced the promise of a new covenant associated with the death of Jesus.

As the liturgy of the Eucharist developed, the saying about Jesus' body was also interpreted in the light of his death (I Cor. 11:24; Luke 22:19). Thus, taken together, the words of institution of the bread and wine meant that Jesus' body was the means by which he in his whole personality had lived, and was now about to lay down his life, for others; and his death was the sign of a new covenant which God had established with his people. Participation in the Lord's Supper meant participation in the death of Jesus' body on the cross for the sake of the church, and it meant sharing in the blessing — in the forgiveness, in the reconciliation, in the new life — which continues to flow from the whole Person of Christ in and through that event. In this sense, partaking of the cup is "participation in the blood of Christ," and the sharing in the Eucharistic bread is "participation in the body of Christ" (I Cor. 10:16).

When Paul encountered certain individualistic and spiritualistic conceptions of salvation in the Hellenistic world, he used the Greek term *sōma* (body) as a means of correcting these heretical views. In order to accomplish this purpose, however, it was necessary for him to transform the meaning of this term and use it as a vehicle, first, for proclaiming the believers' total dependence upon Christ and, secondly, for exhorting them to a life of mutual love and service.

Paul thus used this image, in the first place, to make clear the constant dependence of the church upon its crucified and risen Lord. This fact, indeed, was proclaimed in every celebration of the Eucharist (I Cor. 11:26). Participation in the Lord's Supper means participation in the whole personhood of Christ, including his life, death, and resurrection, together with the power and new life that flow from him. However, the individual believer does not participate in Christ primarily as an individual but rather, first of all, as a member of the church. The church is the body of Christ because as a whole it participates in his Person. Christ dwells in it as his body, and it in turn receives its life from him. The wholeness or completion of the individual believer, therefore, is to be found, not in oneself or even in an association of religious people, but in the relationship of the individual and the church to Christ.

Consideration of the relationship of the church to Christ in the sense of its total dependence upon him leads at once to the most practical implications for the daily life of its members. Two such implications are of particular importance for the present study — namely, the unity of the church and the consequences of this unity in the common life of the congregation. Paul had heard that the church at Corinth was divided into factions so that there was no unity and fellowship even in the celebration of the Lord's Supper (I Cor. 11:18-22). Each member of the church went his own way. Those who had plenty to eat let others go hungry. Some were even drunk on this occasion. As the result of these divisions, Paul wrote, the Corinthians did not in reality celebrate the Lord's Supper; they only ate a meal and were indeed worse off than if they had not come together in the first place.

Moreover, the church at Corinth was also torn with jealousy and strife occasioned by a variety of spiritual gifts — esoteric knowledge, speaking in tongues, the ability to prophesy, and the power to work miracles (I Cor., chs. 12 to 14). The dissension was most disruptive and demoralizing on occasions of public worship, when different members of the congregation claimed special status for themselves upon the basis of the particular gifts that they possessed. The invidiousness of such comparisons and the bedlam produced by the ostentatious display of such gifts made any genuine fellowship and worship impossible.

In an effort to meet this individualistic, spiritualistic conception of Christianity, Paul likened the members of the church to the members of the human body. Just as in the human body each member is important and needed to complete the whole, so it is in the church. The church is the body of Christ, and each believer was incorporated into this one body at baptism. All received the same Spirit when they were baptized, and the Spirit himself has bestowed a variety of gifts upon the different members of the church, apportioning "to each one individually as he wills." Hence, there is no occasion for boasting, for the one Spirit is the source of whatever gifts one may possess. Just as the human body has many members, and each member has a different function, so it is with the church as Christ's body. In the church there are many members, each with his particular gifts (for example, prophecy, healing, speaking in tongues) and special function (apostle, prophet, teacher, administrator, helper). Each gift has been given for the common good — that is, for the upbuilding of the church. All the members together are the body of Christ, and individually they are members of that body (I Cor. 12:27). Or, as Paul develops the same analogy in his letter to the Romans, " So we, though many, are one body in Christ, and individually members one of another " (Rom. 12:5).

The " spiritual gifts " are good when they are properly used for the mutual benefit and enrichment of the whole Christian fellowship, Paul declares. Indeed, he admonishes the Corinthians to " earnestly desire " them; but, even so, there is a " still more excellent way " of Christian life. Thus he comes to the magnificent description of Christian love in the thirteenth chapter of First Corinthians. Love, he writes, is far superior to speaking in tongues or prophecy. There are, in fact, three higher gifts: faith, hope, and love; these are the enduring and indispensable qualities of the body of Christ. Love is the bond that holds the body together. It is the "greatest" gift of the Spirit; it binds all believers together — whether Jew or Gentile, rich or poor, wise or unwise — into a single community of faith and mutual service.

As the body of Christ, the church is the visible form where faith is lived in a concrete way. Just as the love of God was made manifest in Jesus' earthly body, so the church is the visible form in which the living Christ continues to dwell. Just as Jesus gave his body for others, so the church is also called to give its life for others. Like its Lord, it is called to glorify God in its body through a life of love and service.

In his letters to the Corinthians and the Romans, Paul used the figure of the church as the body of Christ primarily to make clear the unity of the church and to challenge its members to a life of mutual love and service. Although he also spoke of the need for the whole body to serve the larger world, Paul used this image in these letters, for the most part, to describe the life of the local congregation. In Ephesians and Colossians, however, the primary emphasis is upon the relationship of Christ to the world at large and, indeed, to the whole cosmos. Here the missionary task of the church is connected with the image of the body of Christ, and the life of service to which the church is called is viewed primarily in terms of its mission to the nations and its vicarious suffering for mankind as a whole. As in the earlier letters, the image of the body of Christ is used to symbolize the absolute dependence of the church upon Christ and also its complete unity in him; but here the emphasis is upon the headship and sovereignty of Christ, not only over the church, but also over the whole created order (Eph. 4:1-16; Col. 1:18-20).

The specific schism that threatened the church at Ephesus was that between the Jewish Christians and the Gentile converts. This division, of course, was not new; it had indeed threatened the unity of the church from its beginning. It was one of the major problems that had faced Paul since he began his work as a missionary to the Gentiles. But, in any event, the problem persisted at Ephesus; and in his attempt to meet it the author of Ephesians picked up the image of the church as Christ's body and developed it in terms of its cosmic dimensions. Christ, he declared, had "broken down the dividing wall of hostility" between Jew and Gentile (Eph. 2:11-22). Jew and Gentile had been reconciled to God through the one event of Jesus' death on the cross. Through Christ, too, both had been made into a single new humanity, of which Christ is the head. Through him both have been joined together into one household of God; through him both have access in the same Spirit to the Father.

As head of the body, Christ is both distinct from the church and also inseparable from it. He is the power that vivifies the church, sustains it, guides it, and rules over it. But he is not only head of the church; he is also "head over all things" (Eph. 1:22). As the power through which all things were created and in which all things cohere (Col. 1:15-17), he is sovereign over all. The fullness of God dwelt in him, and all things were reconciled to God through him. Through his victory over the cosmic forces of evil, the church — and indeed, in principle, the entire world — has been delivered from these powers and is, therefore, no longer in bondage to them. At one and the same time Christ is head of the church, which is his body, and also head of all things.

The concept of Christ's universal headship implies that he is head over all men of every race and class and creed. On the one hand, all owe him obedience; and, on the other hand, his reconciling will extends to all. As Christ's body, the church is set in the midst of the world as a sign of the power of his reconciliation to free all men from every form of bondage and every power of evil. As his body, the church is to continue his ministry of reconciliation, participate in his sufferings, and above all abound in works of love and service. Insofar as it participates in Christ's victory over the powers of evil and receives its nourishment from him, it becomes a new humanity and the nucleus of a redeemed universe.

In the final stage of the development of this image in Ephesians and Colossians, the church is thus recognized as the body of Christ because of its obedience to its head. As his body, Christ sends the church into the world to share with him in his sacrificial suffering for all mankind. Indeed, it is only as it goes into the world in obedience to its Lord, and is willing, like him, to suffer for the world that the church does become the body of Christ.

C. THE KOINONIA

Like the image of the body of Christ, the concept of "koinonia" has a variety of meanings in the New Testament. The latter term, however, is more widely used throughout the New Testament than the analogy of the body of Christ. L. S. Thornton, for example, lists seventeen instances in which the noun *koinōnia* is used in a total of nine different writings in the New Testament.[5] In addition to the Pauline epistles, the word itself is found in The Acts, Hebrews, and I John. A number of cognate terms are also used in other places — including the Gospels, The Acts, the epistles, and Revelation — with much the same meanings as *koinōnia*.

In recent years there has been a veritable renaissance of the concept of koinonia in discussions of the nature of the church. The new interest in this idea is due in large part to the impact of social and political forces upon the churches and to the resulting breakdown of highly individualistic conceptions of the self, society, salvation, and the church. It is a concept that expresses the Christian view of life in community — a view that is at once opposed both to atomistic and to collectivist conceptions of the individual and society.

In a culture in which relationships among people have become increasingly depersonalized due to the impact of urbanization, technology, and industrialization, modern man has been driven to a quest for the rediscovery of community, in which his alienation both from himself, including his work, and from his fellowmen can be overcome. This quest for community has taken many forms in our day — for example, lodges, civic organizations, unions, managerial associations, civil rights organizations, patriotic societies, Communism, and a rising tide of nationalism since World War II. This same need for social identity has also contributed to the growth of organized religious groups in this country. Although this factor has clearly been only one among many in the recent growth of the churches, it does explain in part why the churches have enjoyed a sustained growth in membership in recent decades and also why they have become increasingly secularist in the sense of being organization-centered, pietistic, and culture-bound in their conceptions of values and morality.

Modern man in a depersonalized society seeks a sense of social belonging in the church, and he seeks it on the horizontal level of human togetherness or, at most, of human fellowship. He rightly perceives that the church holds out the promise of community and fully personal existence, but he fails to see that these are fruits of a different kind of relationship — namely, a fully personal relationship of man to his Creator; for the very possibility of personhood is grounded in the fact that man was created in the divine image and endowed with the capacity for selfhood. Human life can be truly personal and man can live in genuine community rather than a collective mass only because he has been created essentially a person rather than a thing in his ultimate relationships to the Source and Center of all human existence. The church, therefore, holds out the promise of authentic community insofar as it points men to God as the center of all human community and insofar as it exemplifies the reality of this community in its corporate life as the body of Christ.

In view of the great contemporary interest in the concept of koinonia and also in view of the significance that this idea has in the New Testament, we turn now to an examination of this metaphor to see what implications it may have for an understanding of the church as a prophetic community. In the first place, it will be helpful to note briefly some of the ways in which the term is used in the New Testament.[6] On the one hand, it is sometimes used in specific relationship to different Persons of the Trinity. Thus, Paul uses the term in two places in specific reference to the Spirit. In II Cor. 13:14 it is part of a benediction: "The grace of the Lord Jesus Christ and the love of God and the *koinōnia* [fellowship] of the Holy Spirit be with you all"; and in Phil. 2:1 it constitutes a ground of appeal to Christian faith and living. But in I Cor. 1:9 Paul speaks of Christians as being "called into the *koinōnia* [fellowship] of . . . Jesus Christ." And the writer of The First Letter of John declares that "our *koinōnia* is with the Father and with his Son Jesus Christ" (I John 1:3).

On the other hand, the term is frequently used to refer to almsgiving and the distribution of money. In Rom. 15:26 and II Cor. 9:13, Paul calls the collections that he gathered in the Gentile churches for the poverty-stricken Christians at Jerusalem a *koinōnia*, thus indicating that the former were an expression of the common life that Jews and Gentiles shared in Christ. The term is also used in Gal. 2:9 and I John 1:3 to signify the fellowship that believers have with one another. Elsewhere Paul used *koinōnia* in yet another sense in reference to the Lord's Supper: "The cup of blessing which we bless, is it not a *koinōnia* [participation] in the blood of Christ? The bread which we break, is it not a *koinōnia* [participation] in the body of Christ?" (I Cor. 10:16).

While there are additional shades of meaning associated with the usage of *koinōnia* in other passages in the New Testament, the foregoing examples are representative; moreover, they point to a common core of meaning which the term connoted in the early church. The fundamental idea expressed by *koinōnia* is that of "having *something* in common with *someone.*"[7] *Koinōnia* thus includes both the idea of *participation* and that of *association,* even though at times the main emphasis may fall upon one of these to the practical exclusion of the other. Moreover — and this is the most fundamental point of all — in the New Testament this participation and this association always have a religious or theological connotation.

Although this Greek noun is frequently translated into English, both in popular parlance and by some theologians, as " fellowship " in the sense of social association or togetherness, it should be noted that such a translation is grossly inadequate. Indeed, the present-day connotation of the term " fellowship " is such that it almost completely misses the meaning of *koinōnia* as it is used in the New Testament. Other English words that come closer to being adequate renderings of the Greek are " sharing," " joint possession," and " holding in common." [8]

In view of what has been said thus far, it is clear that the distinctive meaning of *koinōnia* in the New Testament is determined by the fact that the term is always used in a religious or theological context. The basic meaning of the church as koinonia is that of a fellowship of believers with one another based upon a common fellowship that they share with God — whether the Father, the Son, or the Holy Spirit. As members of the " body of Christ," the members of the church are joined in koinonia, both with Christ and with each other. The fellowship that believers have with God is primary; their fellowship with one another is derivative. The latter is a fruit of the former and derives its distinctive quality from the former. The relationship between these two dimensions of koinonia is clearly and succinctly expressed in I John 1:3: " That which we have seen and heard we proclaim also to you, so that you may have fellowship with us." But only through faith is it possible to enter into the true fellowship of the church; for " our fellowship," the author continues, " is with the Father and with his Son Jesus Christ."

Although *koinōnia* is sometimes used in relation to the Father (I John 1:3) and to the Son (e.g., I Cor. 1:9; 10:16; I John 1:3), it is characteristically associated with the Spirit, especially in the writings of Paul. The images of the church as the new covenant community and as the body of Christ, on the

other hand, are linked primarily with God the Father and with
Christ the Son, respectively. Thus, as Creator and Sovereign,
God the Father chose Israel and he has also chosen the church
to live in a covenant relationship with himself. He has called
them to be holy and obedient and merciful. In a similar way,
the figure of the body of Christ is associated particularly with
the Son. It signifies that, just as the whole will and purpose of
God were manifest in Christ, so the whole will and purpose of
Christ are to be manifest in his body, that is, in the church.
Similarly, the description of the church as koinonia is linked
in a special way to the Spirit. This latter association is especially clear in Paul's letters when these are considered as a
whole and when those passages in which he speaks of the gifts
of the Spirit are taken into account. Although Paul also speaks
of *koinōnia* in relation to Christ (e.g., I Cor. 1:9; 10:16), he
generally describes the common life that believers share with
one another as the fruit or the work of the Spirit.

The fact that Paul characteristically associates the koinonia
quality of life in the church with the Spirit does not imply,
however, that Paul had a fully developed doctrine of the Trinity or that he always distinguished precisely between the various forms of God's relationship to man. On the contrary, he
sometimes spoke interchangeably of God, Lord, and Spirit
(I Cor. 12:4-6; cf. I Cor. 3:16; II Cor. 3:17-18). Paul was primarily interested in describing three spheres, or forms, of God's
action, and he was scarcely concerned at all with the metaphysical question of how God, Christ, and the Spirit are related to one another. God is one. It is the Father who has reconciled the world unto himself in Christ, and it is also he who
is present to the church in the form of the Spirit. Christ and
the Spirit are one and the same according to Paul, but he uses
the designation " Spirit " to describe the way and the manner
in which the risen Lord is present and active in the church.

As we have previously noted, the gift of the Spirit is bestowed at baptism and marks the incorporation of the believer
into the body of Christ. The Spirit is the source of those special

gifts which are given to individual believers for the upbuilding of the church as a whole (I Cor. 12:4; Rom. 12:6-8). He is the source of those spiritual — or, more accurately, "charismatic" — graces and virtues which characterize the Christian life. These gifts are the expression of faith and love in the daily life of those in whom the Spirit dwells. They include "joy, peace, patience, kindness, goodness, faithfulness, gentleness, [and] self-control" (Gal. 5:22-23); but by far the most important of all such gifts is agape (love) (I Cor. 13:13). This love is to characterize the whole corporate life of the church as well as the lives of its individual members. The norm and source of this love is the divine love for man revealed in Christ and continuously "poured" into the hearts of believers "through the Holy Spirit" (Rom. 5:5). As Professor Nelson points out, apart from God's love, the whole "Biblical concept of koinōnia is completely unintelligible." [9]

In the New Testament the meaning of the church as koinonia is expressed most fully in the Sacrament of the Lord's Supper (I Cor. 10:16). In partaking of the cup and the bread, Christians participate in the blood and body of Christ. It is supremely in the celebration of the Eucharist that Christians have fellowship (communion) with him in his whole personhood — his mind and will, his total personality — as expressed in his incarnation, life, death, and resurrection, all symbolized by his body and blood. All who participate in this fellowship with Christ are united in a common act of worship; and through him all are joined together in a common fellowship with one another. Essentially, this fellowship is indivisible. There is only one head of the church, one Spirit who dwells in the church, one faith and one Baptism; hence, there can be only one koinonia, one body, one church. And just as the koinonia of the church is expressed most fully by the common participation in the Lord's Supper, so it is most poignantly and obviously denied by the refusal of fellowship at the Communion table (cf. I Cor. 11:17-27; Gal. 3:28).

But the New Testament makes it clear that this koinonia,

which comes to its fullest expression in the Lord's Supper and which is symbolized by this Sacrament, is to characterize the whole common life of the church and the daily life of its members in their relationships with one another. Those who live by the Spirit should also walk by the Spirit (Gal. 5:16, 25). Believers have been set free from bondage to the Jewish law, but they are called to be servants of one another, to love their neighbors as themselves, to "bear one another's burdens, and so fulfil the law of Christ" (Gal. 6:2; cf. ch. 5:13, 14). They are to be obedient to the Spirit and to Christ in all things. Their freedom is the freedom of those who are bound ultimately only by the law of love. But this obedience and this love are not spiritual in the abstract sense of being unrelated to the specific demands of concrete, human relationships. On the contrary, Christians are to show forth their faith and love not only in the relationships of husbands and wives and of parents and children but also in the manner in which they settle their differences among themselves in relation to courts of law. They are to overcome evil with good. They are to show love even to their enemies, not only by praying for the latter, but also by giving them food if they are hungry and drink if they thirst (Rom. 12:20).

These illustrations, drawn largely from Paul, are sufficient to make it clear that the church was to be a koinonia in its daily life as well as in its worship. They could be multiplied from the writings of the same apostle. Moreover, they are unequivocally and unanimously supported by all the remainder of the New Testament teaching about the church. In *The Cost of Discipleship,* Dietrich Bonhoeffer was a faithful interpreter of the whole New Testament witness at this point when he wrote: "To allow a baptized brother to take part in the worship of the church, but to refuse to have anything to do with him in everyday life, is to subject him to abuse and contempt. . . . And if we grant the baptized brother the right to the gifts of salvation, but refuse him the gifts necessary to earthly life or knowingly leave him in material need and distress, we are holding up the gifts of salvation to ridicule and behaving as liars." [10]

But what are the implications of understanding the church as koinonia for relationships, on the one hand, of believers with people who have not been baptized, and on the other hand, of the church to culture? Here again, as in the cases of the other images of the church that we have considered, it is evident that neither Paul nor the other writers of the New Testament devoted much attention specifically to these questions in their discussions of the meaning of koinonia. In view of the situation faced by the congregations at Corinth or Rome or in Galatia, it is not surprising that Paul, for example, should speak primarily of the faith and internal life of the church as it was taking form in an alien and hostile society. These congregations had control over their own internal life in a way in which they did not have control over political and economic institutions. The most obvious and pressing need was to build up the churches as the body of Christ, to nurture the new converts in the distinctiveness of the new faith, and to guide them to maturity as measured by the "mind of Christ." [11] Such growth and building up of the body was possible only if the faith of the church was active in love, transforming the daily relationships of its members and creating genuine koinonia. Humanly speaking, the possibilities of faith and love are greatest within the context of a supporting community of shared faith and mutual love and forgiveness.

But Paul was quite aware that the church was not an end in itself. The whole purpose of the building up of the body of Christ was that the church might proclaim the message of reconciliation and that Christians might become Christ's ambassadors, or agents, through whom God made his appeal to the world (II Cor. 5:18-20). As a community that had been reconciled to God, the church was to be itself a reconciling community in the world. In part, its mission was to proclaim the message of reconciliation that God had wrought in Christ; but, in part, it was also to continue Christ's reconciling work in the world by participating in his sufferings (Col. 1:24), by returning good for evil, and by being a koinonia which subjected itself in all things to Christ, who is not only its head but also the head over all things, both in heaven and upon earth.

Whether the church is understood as koinonia or as the body of Christ or as the new covenant community, it is called, according to the New Testament, to witness to God's will for the world as his will has been disclosed to the church. The church is not an end in itself; neither is it the Kingdom of God. Its primary purpose is to point men beyond itself to God the Creator, the Sovereign, and the Redeemer of the world as well as of itself. It is called to walk by the Spirit, which is the Spirit of love. It is called to be obedient to its Lord, who is Lord over all things and summons his followers to discipleship in the world into which he was incarnated and for which he laid down his life. It is commanded to love God – the one God of Israel – with heart, soul, mind, and strength. Its members are commanded to love their neighbors for whom Christ died – including the publican, the Samaritan, and even their enemies – as themselves and to minister to their mundane needs (Matt. 22:37-39; 25:31-46; Luke 10:29-37). In all these ways the church points men beyond itself to God and calls them into that koinonia which Christians share with one another, which is built upon that koinonia which believers have " with the Father and with his Son Jesus Christ " (I John 1:3).

VI

THE CHURCH AND THE WORLD
IN THE NEW TESTAMENT

A. THE CHURCH VIS-À-VIS THE WORLD

From its earliest beginnings, whenever the church has sought to understand its own identity and purpose, it has always done so " vis-à-vis the world." [1] Whether it has wished to do so or not, the church has always found it necessary to relate itself in some way to the religious, political, economic, intellectual, social, and artistic life of the culture in which it has been placed. This was true of the New Testament writers who were faced with a variety of cultures in Palestine, in Asia Minor, in Greece, and in Rome. That it continues to be true is clearly evidenced in the present day by the inevitable involvement of local churches and denominational groups in the struggle for social justice and in their efforts to be relevant in some way to the life of contemporary men. But the need for the church to relate itself to man's life in culture has been dramatized most of all in recent years in the ecumenical movement. The first three Assemblies of the World Council of Churches focused attention upon various aspects of this overarching problem. Thus the theme of the Amsterdam Assembly (1948) was " Man's Disorder and God's Design "; that of the Evanston Assembly (1954) was " Christ — the Hope of the World "; and that of the Third Assembly held at New Delhi (1961) was " Jesus Christ the Light of the World." Similarly, one of the primary aims of Pope John XXIII in convening the Second Vatican Council was that of bringing the Roman Catholic Church into "closer accord with the needs and conditions of our times."[2] Significantly, the concluding session (1965) of Vatican II was devoted to a consideration of the theme "The Church and the Modern World."

In the present chapter we turn, therefore, to an analysis of the relationship of the church to the world from the standpoint of Biblical faith. H. Richard Niebuhr made clear in his classic study *Christ and Culture*[3] that a number of radically different answers have been given to this problem both in the New Testament and also throughout the history of the church. In part, the variety of such answers has been the result of different understandings of the meaning of the gospel; and, in part, it has been due to the different cultural situations in which individual Christians have found themselves. Due to the dynamic character of both the church and the world as well as the complex and changing relationships between the two, no single answer to this problem can be given that is applicable in the same way at all times and under all cultural conditions. As long as the church endures, Christians will need to continue to search for that answer which is most responsible, that is, most obedient and most loving in each particular day and each cultural situation. The problem will never be finally resolved until both the church and the world find their fulfillment in the Kingdom of God.

But this recognition of the continuing and inescapable need of the church to relate itself to the world rests upon a Biblical understanding of both the church and the world. In the preceding chapter we examined the New Testament conception of the church. In addition, some consideration was given to the Hebraic conception of the world as God's creation in our discussion of the faith of Israel. We now need to make this latter aspect of Hebraic faith more explicit and, in particular, to see how the concept of "the world" is used in the New Testament itself. In the remainder of the present chapter we shall focus our attention upon the world as the sphere of the church's work and upon the purpose of the church understood in relation to the world.

In order to understand the relationship between the church and the world from the standpoint of Christian faith, it is essential that we give more detailed attention to the Biblical understanding of the world. In the first place, it is important to note that the concept has a variety of different meanings in the Bible. Moreover, many of these meanings are quite foreign to our contemporary thought patterns.

The variety of usages of "world" is especially pronounced in our English translations of the Scriptures as compared with the original Hebrew and Greek texts. For example, in the Revised Standard Version four Hebrew words and two Greek words having a spatial reference are translated "world." [4] Moreover, other words with a primarily temporal rather than spatial meaning are sometimes rendered into English as "world." One of the most important of these is the Greek noun *aeon*. In the King James Version *aeon* is translated as "world" more than thirty times, but in the Revised Standard Version it usually appears as "age."

Not only are a number of Hebrew and Greek words translated into English as "world," but some of the former have a variety of meanings in themselves. For example, the Greek noun *kosmos*, as it is used in the New Testament, may signify the earth as the stage for man's life (Rom. 4:13; I Cor. 14:10), or it may refer to the universe as a whole (Gal. 4:3; Phil. 2:15). Again, it may refer to mankind rather than to the stage upon which men live (Rom. 3:6, 19; 5:12 f.; II Cor. 5:19). When it is used in the former sense, it sometimes has essentially a historical meaning and refers to the sphere of human relationships or the world of men, as when Paul writes, "Your faith is proclaimed in all the world" (Rom. 1:8). More characteristically, however, when *kosmos* is used to refer to mankind, it implies a theological judgment upon the attitudes, the anxieties, the wisdom, and the enmity of the world – including both men and spiritual powers of evil which are regnant in this earthly sphere of life — against God.[5] This last usage of *kosmos* is especially typical of Paul's letters and the Johannine writings. Understood in this last sense as a realm of life which is in rebellion against the divine will and rule, *kosmos* is primarily a historical concept rather than a space concept; as such it is sometimes used interchangeably with *aeon*, to refer to the present age in contrast to the eschatological "age to come."

From what has been said above, it is clear that the Bible does not confront us with a single view of the world. Many ideas are associated with this term, especially as it is used in our English translations; and the particular connotation that the term " world " bears varies a great deal from one context to another. Although these meanings cannot be fit together into a systematic world view, it is possible to speak meaningfully of certain conceptions of the world that are recurrent in Biblical thought. The meaning of each of these themes is derived from Biblical faith in God, and the different conceptions are seen to have a fundamental unity within the framework of the Biblical perspective.

Viewed in this light, the Bible makes three basic affirmations about the world. These do not exhaust the meanings that this concept has in the Scriptures, but they are particularly relevant for a proper understanding of the relationship of the church to the world both in the New Testament itself and in our own day. In the first place, according to the Bible, the world as God's creation and as the sphere of human existence and activity is good. Secondly, the world as the sphere of man's disobedience, alienation, and estrangement is sinful and fallen. And, thirdly, the world as fallen — lost, alienated, and in bondage — is the object of God's redemptive love.

1. The World as God's Creation: The Sphere of Human Activity

Since we have previously discussed the Biblical understanding of God as Creator, there is need at this point only to recall the major ideas that have already been dealt with in a differ-

ent context and to relate them to the over-all concept of the
world. It is especially important to see the relationship of the
concept of Creation to that of the world in the New Testament,
since relatively little attention is given to the former in this
portion of the Bible. The central theme of the New Testament
is redemption or salvation rather than the creation of the world.
Although reference is sometimes made to the fact that God —
or Christ — created the world in the sense of the earth or the
universe, Jesus and the writers of the New Testament seldom
spoke explicitly of Creation as such. Yet they everywhere assumed — as the Old Testament had clearly declared — that God
had created "the heavens and the earth" (Gen. 1:1). God is
not a part of the world or the cosmos; rather, he is transcendent
over it. Moreover, everything that he has created — that is, everything that is outside of himself or over against him as creature — is good, for God is good and he created it.

Such an attitude toward God's creation is clearly reflected in
numerous parables and sayings of Jesus recorded in the Gospels. It is shown, for example, in the natural and spontaneous
way in which he speaks of God's care for the birds of the air
and the lilies of the field and of the divine ordering of seed-
time and harvest. It is evidenced, most of all, in the joyfulness
that was so characteristic of his attitude toward life and the
world — a joyfulness that cannot be understood apart from his
trust in God as the Heavenly Father who has called creation
into being, who cares for all that he has made, and who rules
over all as Lord of "heaven and earth."

The Biblical affirmation of the goodness of creation — including plant and animal life, mineral resources, man's physical nature, food, clothing, shelter, the beauty and grandeur of
the natural world, and the splendor of the heavens — represents
a repudiation of every form of asceticism based upon the belief that the physical world is evil. Moreover, the doctrine of
Creation — with its radical distinction between the infinite Creator and the finite world that he has made — also represents a
radical rejection of every form of materialism based upon the

view that man's true good is to be found in the acquisition of material things, no matter how necessary these may be for human life. The physical world as God's creation and as the sphere of human existence is good, but it is not the chief good for man. The material world is temporal, but man is destined for eternal life. The distinctive quality of man's nature consists of the special personal relationship in which he stands to God and to his fellow humanity. Man was made to live in fellowship with his Creator, upon whom he is ultimately and absolutely dependent, and in community with his neighbors. Hence, to be preoccupied with the creation and seek it rather than the Creator is idolatry (cf. Rom. 1:25). To place one's trust in material things and to seek one's true being in the accumulation of physical possessions is to miss living an authentic *human* existence. Jesus put the matter quite succinctly when he asked, "For what does it profit a man, to gain the whole world and forfeit his life?" (Mark 8:36).

2. The World as Fallen: The Sphere of Sin, Alienation, and Anxiety

On the one hand, considered in relationship to the Creator, the world as God's creation is good. God has placed the earth at man's disposal to meet his needs; nothing that he has created is unclean or untouchable. (Gen. 1:31; Rom. 14:14, 20; I Cor. 10:25-26.) All that he has made is to be accepted and used with gratitude, joy, and thanksgiving. But, on the other hand, the world as the sphere of human existence has become the scene of evil, of disobedience to the Creator, and of estrangement from the Source of man's true life. It was intended to be the setting for life lived in community with God and in obedience to his will; but it has become the stage for man's disobedience and fall. Hence, in the New Testament — particularly outside of the Synoptic Gospels and The Acts — the term "world" is frequently used to symbolize the sphere of life that is in opposition to God's will and rule.

The Old Testament does not have an equivalent term for the

abstract Greek noun *kosmos* (cosmos, universe). The early Hebrews spoke instead in more concrete terms of "heaven and
earth," the present age, and the earth as the sphere of human
existence. In like manner, they spoke of kings, peoples, and nations rather than of the "world" as mankind. Similarly, they
described sin and evil concretely in terms of man's rebellion
against God, in terms of his transgression of the revealed Law,
and in terms of specific acts of injustice.

However, in the intertestamental period and in the early
Christian era, Hellenistic Jews and Greek-speaking Christians
appropriated the Greek word *kosmos* and used it to refer not
only to the earth and its inhabitants, but also to the whole
range of earthly conditions — the joys and sorrows, the cares
and anxieties — under which human life is lived. In this latter
sense *kosmos* referred primarily to a sphere of life centered in
the "affairs of the world" in contrast to the "affairs of the
Lord" (I Cor. 7:32). In addition to this term, the early Christians continued to use a number of other words to describe
various aspects of man's mundane existence.

In the Synoptic Gospels and in The Acts the term "world" is
frequently used in a morally neutral sense and without any
idea of theological disparagement to refer either to the earth as
the geographical-historical setting of human life and activity or
to the peoples of the earth (Matt. 13:38; 24:14; Mark 16:15;
Luke 2:1; Acts 11:28; 17:6, 24; 24:5). When the conditions of
earthly life are contrasted with life in the eschatological Kingdom of God, the contrast is usually drawn in terms of time
concepts, such as "the present age" or "this age" or "the
close of the age," versus "the age to come" (Matt. 12:32;
13:39; 24:3; 28:20; Mark 10:30; Luke 16:8 [margin]; 20:34,
35). Moreover, although Jesus and the Synoptic writers assume
that men and the life of the present age are faced with an im-
minent eschatological judgment, the attitude that they reflect
toward this age — that is, toward the world — is less negative
than that of Paul and the Fourth Evangelist. In the Synoptic
Gospels the great danger posed by life in this age is the threat

of anxiety: the danger, namely, that the cares associated with earthly existence will distract man from his true good and cause him to lose his soul.

In other parts of the New Testament, however, there is a much stronger tendency toward moral dualism between life in this world and the Kingdom of God. This tendency is particularly pronounced in the Pauline and Johannine literature, but it is also present in a number of other epistles (Heb. 11:7, 38; James 1:27; 4:4; II Peter 1:4; 2:20). In these writings, but especially in the Johannine literature, there is also a much stronger condemnation of the world than is found in the Synoptic Gospels and in The Acts (John 9:39; 12:31; I John 2:15-17). In the Fourth Gospel, for example, Jesus is pictured as coming into this world in order to judge the world (John 9:39). In The First Letter of John the world is identified with lust and pride (I John 2:16); as such, it stands in opposition to God and is doomed to pass away. As we shall see, Paul characteristically speaks of the world as life "according to the flesh" as opposed to life according to the Spirit (Rom. 8:12-13; Gal. 6:8). Similarly for James pure religion includes keeping oneself "unstained from the world" (James 1:27), and "friendship with the world" is equated with "enmity with God" (James 4:4).

Speaking generally of those places in the New Testament where the world is most strongly condemned, the primary meaning of the concept is a realm of "moral uncleanness and sin." [6] It is a sphere of life that stands in opposition to the will and rule of God. Hence it stands under the divine judgment and is condemned on account of its sin. Because of its sin it is alienated from its true Source of life; hence, it has become a realm of corruption and decay which is even now passing away. Understood in this sense, the world is morally unclean and impure, but its deepest tragedy is that it is now in *bondage* to evil. Moreover, insofar as human life is determined by this fallen world, it is a life of captivity to the forces and powers of evil which are regnant in the world — its anxieties, its lust, its avarice, its moral blindness, its narrow loyalties, its materialism, its depersonalized existence, and its ultimate meaninglessness. These forces have gained sway over man's will, and he is unable to free himself from their power. Yet the responsibility for this bondage lies in man's own sin.

In the period between the Old and New Testaments the concepts of Satan and of fallen angels gained wide acceptance in Jewish and Christian circles. These powers appear frequently in the New Testament as the explanation for the power and presence of evil both in individuals and in society. Thus, it is Satan who tempts Jesus during the forty days in the wilderness following his baptism (Mark 1:13). On one occasion Jesus tells the seventy disciples, "I saw Satan fall like lightning from heaven," thus signifying the routing of the forces of evil (Luke 10:17-18). Again and again Jesus is pictured in the Gospels as performing works of healing by casting out demons.

Whereas belief in demons was thus found in Palestine, in both Jewish and Christian circles, in the New Testament period, this belief was on the whole subordinated to the monotheistic conception of God as the Creator and final sovereign over all. This is clearly the case in the Gospels, where the evil spirits are overthrown by the power of God's Kingdom which is even now breaking into the present world order.

In Hellenistic and Roman circles, however, these powers were conceived of in terms of a thoroughgoing cosmic dualism. Paul refers to these mythological figures as "angels," "principalities," and "powers" (Rom. 8:38). They controlled not only human lives but also the course of the universe itself. Evil was considered to be beyond the control of God; hence, its origin and its power were ascribed to evil, cosmic spirits which were arrayed against the forces of good (truth, light) in a great universal struggle and which held men in their grip.

Belief in such forces was part of the religious background of the converts from paganism to whom Paul was writing. Even though he was not interested in defending one cosmological explanation of evil over against another, Paul nevertheless

found it necessary to interpret the meaning of Christian faith
— especially salvation — in terms of the world view that was
common among the Gentiles. Although admitting the existence
of such demonic powers, Paul completely rejected every form
of ultimate cosmic dualism. Instead of being eternal powers of
evil and darkness existing alongside equally eternal powers of
good and light, these cosmic forces, Paul declared, all belong to
God's creation (Rom. 8:39; cf. Col. 1:15-16). Moreover, God
can still make use of them, for he is still sovereign over them.
Before the Creator they are weak and impotent. Yet, they gain
dominion over man by deceiving him and beguiling him into
choosing evil as his true good. Once man has chosen to serve
them rather than God, he is unable to break their grip upon
him.

Paul's central concern in relation to the "principalities and
powers" had to do with their role in the lives of believers. In
his triumph over the forces of evil that had been responsible
for the crucifixion, Christ had already broken their power, Paul
proclaimed. They are, therefore, now "doomed to pass away"
(I Cor. 2:6). They have been "disarmed" and defeated; hence,
they are no longer able to harm man. Since God in Christ has
triumphed over every power that is hostile to himself, nothing
is henceforth able to separate the believer from God. "For I
am sure," Paul wrote to the Roman converts, "that neither
death, nor life, nor angels, nor principalities, nor things present, nor things to come, nor powers, nor height, nor depth, nor
anything else in all creation, will be able to separate us from
the love of God in Christ Jesus our Lord" (Rom. 8:38-39).

The bondage of the world is described in many ways in the
New Testament. As noted above, Paul speaks of it as life "according to the flesh." But this phrase means far more than sins
associated with man's physical passions and appetites; it also
includes those sins of the spirit which are the fruits of life lived
with the self rather than God as its center. Thus Paul includes
strife, jealousy, dissension, party spirit, envy, idolatry, and
selfishness in a list of "the works of the flesh" (Gal. 5:19-21).

Elsewhere he speaks of man's bondage to the world in terms of his moral life lived under the tyranny of law rather than in the freedom of sonship. Or, again, it is bondage to sin and death as well as subjection to the law (Rom. 3:9; 5:12).

The Johannine writings typically describe the world in terms of a number of absolute contrasts between the nature of the world and the divine reality symbolized by the Word (Logos). The world is the realm of darkness which stands in opposition to the light (John 1:4-11). It is also a realm of falsehood that is at enmity with truth. Darkness and falsehood hold the world in captivity, and only the true light and truth which are manifest in Christ can free men from their dominion. Like the letters of Paul, the Johannine writings also describe this bondage of the world both in terms of the rule of the devil over the world (John 12:31; 16:11) and in terms of its bondage to sin (ch. 8:34) and death (ch. 8:21, 24). Not only will those who do not believe that Jesus is the Messiah die in their sins, but the world is already dead. In contrast to those who reject Jesus, however, those who believe in him have " passed from death to life " (ch. 5:24), as have also those who love the brethren in obedience to Jesus' commandment (I John 3:14). The world is thus a realm where death holds sway over men; but even more ghastly is the fact that because of its bondage to death the world is now the enemy of life.

In summary, the concept of world has a variety of meanings in the New Testament. Particularly in those translations in which the Greek word *aeon* is rendered into English as " world," the term has a predominantly temporal reference and refers to the present age in contrast to the eschatological Kingdom of God. This usage, we have seen, is especially common in the Synoptic Gospels, and it is also found in Paul's letters. In contrast to this historical-temporal meaning, the concept is typically used in the Fourth Gospel and in the epistles to refer to a sphere of life that is under the dominion of evil. Used in this latter sense, the term " world " frequently — particularly in the Johannine literature and also in the Pauline epistles — has an existential meaning and refers to a quality of existence that is characterized by darkness, falsehood, bondage, and death as opposed to man's true, authentic existence, which is characterized by light, truth, freedom, and life.

3. The World as the Object of God's Reconciling Love

The central affirmation that the New Testament makes about the world, however, is that it is the object of God's reconciling love. Moreover, the New Testament leaves no doubt that the world that God thus seeks to reconcile to himself is the fallen world — human life in its disobedience, its emptiness, its lostness, and its bondage to sin and death.

It is true that the Synoptic Gospels characteristically describe the purpose of Christ's coming in concrete, Hebraic terms, whereas the Fourth Gospel typically uses more abstract, symbolic language; but throughout the Gospels the fundamental message is the same. Jesus did not come to call the righteous, but sinners to repentance. (Luke 5:32.) He came to seek and to save those who were lost, and he spent his life ministering to them. He told of his Father's love for them and spoke of their value to God. Finally, he laid down his life for them and prayed for his tormentors even in his death, thereby revealing the depth of the divine love for the world. Or, again, in the language of the Fourth Gospel, God did not send the Son into the world to condemn it, but rather that it " might be saved through him " (John 3:17).

Paul captured the heart of the gospel message when he wrote, " God was in Christ reconciling the world to himself " (II Cor. 5:19). In Christ God had shown that the world is ultimately loved, accepted, and affirmed despite its disobedience, its estrangement, and its guilt. For the depth of God's love for sinful mankind was revealed precisely in the incredible and totally unexpected event that " while we were yet sinners Christ died for us " (Rom. 5:8). Moreover, in Christ, God had reconciled " all things, whether on earth or in heaven," to himself (Col. 1:20). In the Son he had revealed his will and his purpose to bring all things to the fulfillment of their true nature for which they had been created.

For fallen humanity such fulfillment involved a radical transformation of human existence — a transformation so radical, indeed, that Paul called it a " new creation." This " new creation," however, was not the negation of the old creation and the substitution of an entirely different person for the old self. On the contrary, the gospel proclaimed the never-ending divine love for fallen, sinful humanity and the reconciliation of this disobedient, estranged mankind to community and fellowship with him who had called it into being. The reconciliation of fallen humanity to God meant the establishment of fallen man in his true humanity. And the good news of the gospel was that such a radical transformation of human life had now become a present possibility. This new creation was even now coming into being, as evidenced by the radically new quality of life — the new meaning, the new power, the new freedom — that was mediated to men through Christ. In him the Creator had most clearly revealed himself to be love, for in him God had disclosed his will to reconcile the world unto himself and in so doing to make all things new. In Christ power and love were thus seen to be ultimately united in God, the universal sovereign over all that he has made.

C. THE WORLD AS THE SPHERE OF THE CHURCH'S WORK

As we have seen, the essence of the gospel is that Christ came into the world — a world that was fallen and alienated from God — in order that it might have life. This is the meaning of the incarnation — that God manifested himself in human life and history, that is, in the world. Jesus was crucified by the world. Nevertheless, it is this same world that Christ has claimed for himself through the disclosure of the depth of the divine love even for those who rejected him. The Lord of the world took the form of a servant in order to save the world, and in taking the form of a servant he revealed himself to be its true Lord.

Moreover, just as Christ was in the world so his followers are to be in the world. Jesus assumed that the arena of human need was the place where his followers would be found doing the divine will. On the day following the transfiguration, he was himself found in the valley at the foot of the mountain healing a child (Luke 9:37-42). And, even as he had healed the diseased and cast out evil spirits, so he sent his disciples forth "as lambs in the midst of wolves" to heal the sick and proclaim the nearness of the Kingdom (Luke 10:1-9). He summarized the entire claim that God makes upon man in two commandments, love for God and love for the neighbor; and he illustrated what it meant to love the neighbor in a concrete way by telling a parable about a despised Samaritan. Likewise, he pictured the Last Judgment in terms of the readiness that each person had shown to minister to the needs of even the least of God's children.

Even in those parts of the New Testament where the note of moral dualism between the world and God is strongest, asceticism and every form of ultimate metaphysical dualism are both rejected. The Fourth Gospel, for example, represents Jesus as sending his disciples into the world even as he had been sent into it (John 17:18). Though they were in it, they were "not of the world" even as he was not of the world (ch. 17:14). Jesus prayed not that the Father would take the disciples out of the world, but that he would "keep them from the evil one" (ch. 17:15). Similarly, although Paul recognized the tension between the Christian faith and the world, he recognized that the place where the Christian is called to live is in the world "in the flesh." For himself, he would have preferred "to depart and be with Christ"; but it was necessary for him to remain in the flesh on account of his brethren (Phil. 1:21-26). Or, again, while insisting upon the need for moral discipline in the church at Corinth, Paul made it clear that he had not meant to imply that Christians should not associate with immoral people in society generally, since Christians would then need to go out of the world (I Cor. 5:9-11). His whole

life as a missionary to the Gentiles bore witness to his belief
that the church had been given a "ministry of reconciliation"
(II Cor. 5:18) and that its place was in the world which Christ
had come to reconcile to himself. The Christian life, he declared, is a life of "faith working through love" (Gal. 5:6). It
rests upon the acceptance of the forgiveness of one's sins, but
the acceptance of God's love (justification through faith) serves
as a springboard for life lived in obedience to Christ out of
gratitude for God's love. Because Christ has overcome the
powers of this world, he has shown that he is Lord of the
whole creation; and since his followers are, through faith, no
longer under the dominion of the rulers of the present age,
they are free to obey the rightful Lord of the world in all
things.

   In a word, then, the world is understood in the New Testament as that community which Christ came to save by revealing God's love for fallen humanity and also as that community
into which Christ sends his disciples to be his witnesses and
his agents of reconciliation. But the basic question that the
church faces today as it seeks to understand its mission in contemporary culture is this: *What does it mean for the church
to be in the world?* What, in the first place, is its purpose in
going into the world? Is it to gain new members in order to en-
large the rolls of the churches? Is it in order to dominate and
control the secular life of man in keeping with its own vested
interests, and according to its own distinctive moral standards?
Or is it perhaps to minister to the needs of human beings by
taking upon itself the form of a servant? We need to ask, in
the second place, how it is possible for the church to be in the
world and yet maintain its identity apart from the world. How
can it be socially relevant without itself becoming secular?
How can it proclaim a social gospel without becoming primarily an agency of social reform? Finally, in the third place,
who is the church and where is it found? What new forms are
needed to enable it to enter into the life of the contemporary
world? More particularly, what must be the role of the laity if

the church is to succeed in articulating the Christian faith and making it relevant to the issues and decisions that men face in their daily occupations, in the use of leisure, in politics, and in the quest for peace and world community? These are some of the major issues that will concern us in the remainder of our study.

But in order to speak meaningfully about the relationship of the church to the contemporary world, it is necessary to define each of these terms as precisely as possible for purposes of the present discussion since each may be used in a variety of ways. Moreover, we need to define both these concepts in such a way as to restate their basic Biblical meaning in contemporary language. For purposes of the present analysis, *the church* may be defined as *that community in which the Lordship of God-in-Christ is acknowledged.* The church is that body of believers — the new covenant community, the body of Christ, the koinonia — which witnesses to the reconciliation of man with God which has been effected through Jesus Christ, and to the Lordship of God revealed in Christ over both the church and the world.

The church exists as an empirical, human community among other human communities such as the family and the state. The church is that body of believers — the new covenant community, the body of Christ, the koinonia — in which " the word of divine forgiveness is spoken in commission and heard in faith." [7] It is at the same time that community in which the Redeemer is known to be the Creator and Judge, where the sovereignty of God-in-Christ over all his works is recognized, and where the divine command that man shall love God and the neighbor is also " spoken in commission and heard in faith."

Whereas the church is a human community, it differs from all other human communities in that its center is Christ. He is not present merely as a third or fourth person where two or three are gathered in his name; rather, he is the One who is at work in the gathering of the two or three in his name. The church is a community of those who take their stand before God with Christ. The knowledge that its members have of God, their hope for the future, their assurance of the forgiveness of their sins, and their fellowship (koinonia) with each other and with God are mediated to them through Christ. He is its center, but he points beyond himself to his Heavenly Father.

When the world is defined similarly in theological terms vis-à-vis the church, *the world is that community, or realm of human existence and activity, to which the church is sent to proclaim the gospel.* It is that sphere of human life, wherever it exists, in which the Lordship of God-in-Christ is not acknowledged, in which the word of divine forgiveness is not heard in faith, and in which God is not worshiped. As such it is that community which the church confronts with its message of reconciliation and judgment. Yet the church is not itself the source of that judgment and reconciliation, but rather that community which points to the divine judgment that is being passed upon both the world and the church and to the divine grace by which both the world and the church may be renewed and made whole.

Understood in other terms, the world is that realm of life which is preoccupied with the temporal as its "ultimate concern" (Paul Tillich), whereas the church is ultimately concerned with the nontemporal Source of the existence and meaning of the temporal. The world as such, apart from the gospel (or some other culture-transcendent faith), is always finally concerned with the temporal; and it cannot be otherwise, for apart from such faith it has no knowledge of the nontemporal. The church, on the other hand, understands that the temporal world was created by God and that it is therefore dependent upon him, even as the church has been brought into being by God's action in Christ and is constantly dependent upon him. Unlike the world, the church knows that both it and the world exist by the grace of God and for the purposes of God. It is for this reason that the church always confronts the world as the neighbor who is to be loved in his need and to whom the gospel is to be proclaimed. From the standpoint of the faith of the church, there is one Lord — one Creator, one Judge, one Reconciler — one Sovereign over both the church and the world.

On the basis of what has been said thus far, it is clear that the church and the world cannot be defined theologically in terms of mutually exclusive institutional forms or even of mutually exclusive concerns. Both the church and the world have institutional embodiments, and both may exist outside the empirical churches as well as within them. Wherever the Lordship of God-in-Christ is acknowledged in the life and work of culture as well as in the sanctuary, there the church exists; and wherever the Lordship of God is denied in the sanctuary as in man's social, political, and economic affairs, there the world exists as the community to which the church is summoned to bear witness. It is also clear that the church and the world cannot be defined in terms of a simple distinction between the temporal and the nontemporal, between the secular and the sacred, or between the cultural and the spiritual. Like the world, the church lives in the midst of man's temporal, secular, and cultural life and is inextricably related to all of these; but, unlike the world, the church is neither exclusively nor ultimately — that is, finally — concerned about these affairs, for it sees them in relationship to him who is the Ground or Source of the temporal as well as the nontemporal, of the secular as well as the sacred, and of the cultural as well as the spiritual.

D. BONHOEFFER: THE CHURCH EXISTS FOR THE WORLD (HUMANITY)

The person who perhaps more effectively than any other single individual in the middle of the twentieth century has called the church into the world is Dietrich Bonhoeffer, who was put to death by the Nazis in 1945 for his part in a plot to overthrow Hitler. Bonhoeffer was keenly aware of the alienation of the church from contemporary man and society, and he believed that the responsibility for this alienation lay primarily with the church.

Bonhoeffer saw two main reasons why the church had alienated itself from the contemporary world. In the first place, it had relegated the Christian faith to a place on the periphery of life — a " corner " of the world — where it had become only a matter of incidental and relatively trivial interest. Christianity had become preoccupied with the salvation of individual souls for a life beyond the grave; as such, it had become an escape from the God of the Bible, who is the Creator and Sustainer of this world and calls men to a life of obedience here and now. Christian faith does not mean the salvation of man by taking him out of this world — for example, to some Beulah land far from the cares, needs, fears, and struggles of human life; rather, it means the transformation and renewal of man for life in the midst of this present humanity with all its struggles as well as its joys. This is the meaning of the Biblical faith that God is the Creator. It is also the meaning of the incarnation and the resurrection as the experience of becoming a " new being." But the this-worldly dimension of Christian faith becomes particularly clear when the New Testament is viewed in the light of the Old Testament. Thus Bonhoeffer wrote:

> I should like to speak of God not on the borders of life but as its centre, not in weakness but in strength, not, therefore, in man's suffering and death but in his life and prosperity. . . . God is the "beyond" in the midst of our life. The Church stands not where human powers give out, on the borders, but in the centre of the village. That is the way it is in the Old Testament, and in this sense we still read the New Testament far too little on the basis of the Old.[8]

The second main reason that Bonhoeffer gave for the alienation of the church from the world was its desire to dominate the latter by imposing its own theological beliefs upon the secular world in such matters as science, philosophy, politics, and morality. The church, he declared, had arbitrarily insisted upon the secular world's acceptance of its own theological hypotheses and its traditional ethical standards as the only possible valid answers to the issues and problems with which specialists in these fields are concerned. " In the name of intellectual honesty," he wrote, "these working hypotheses should be dropped or dispensed with as far as possible." [9] This is what he meant when he asserted that the world had "come of age." Through reason and science it had achieved a certain self-understanding which, though limited and in some ways distorted, answers many questions about the world — questions of physics, politics, economics, medicine, and the like — far more satisfactorily than the church can answer them by appealing to Scripture or special revelation. For the church to continue to attack the "adulthood" of the secular world and to continue to attempt to dominate and control it, he insisted, is pointless, ignoble, and unchristian.

But for Bonhoeffer the adulthood of the world did not mean — as some "death of God" theologians interpret him to mean — that there is no place or need for God in the contemporary world and that the God of Christian faith is therefore dead. Such "death of God" theologies rest upon the false assumption that God and some particular traditional, anthropomorphic conceptions of God are one and the same thing. Such conceptions of God do indeed die, but the One who judges them and condemns them to death as idolatries is the Living One whom atheists and humanists also seek even in their denials of every effort to identify God with some particular culture-conditioned conception of him.

The God of Christian faith does not exist merely as the answer to men's unanswered questions about the world, about life, or even about death, Bonhoeffer declared. God is not simply a "stopgap" for the incompleteness of human knowledge. If he were, he might someday prove to be expendable. Such a deity might someday be judged to be dead because in point of fact he would never have really existed except as a projection of men's minds. Recognition of the adulthood of the world meant, therefore, that the way has been cleared by contemporary scientific and secular knowledge for modern man to be confronted by the God of Biblical faith in a way that was not open to him in a prescientific, preindustrial stage of culture. Hence, Bonhoeffer hailed the advent of this modern, adult world and summoned the church to proclaim its faith in terms that recognized the acceptance of man's cultural advances and acknowledged the justice of the demand for intellectual and moral integrity which has led contemporary man to reject the message of the church as it has been proclaimed in traditional pietistic, anti-intellectual, and otherworldly terms. The "Lord of heaven and earth" who became manifest in history in the Person of Jesus Christ, Bonhoeffer was saying, is the Lord of man's knowledge (reason) as well as his ignorance, of his strength as well as his weakness, and the God who is threatened by the truth that is discovered in culture is not the God of Christian faith.

In a sense, the fundamental charge that Bonhoeffer leveled against the church was that it was more concerned about religion than it was about faith. It was more concerned about its own self-preservation than it was about the world. It had substituted an authoritarian creed, metaphysical dogmas about the world, and a highly individualistic and otherworldly conception of salvation for faith understood as a living, existential awareness of the Lordship of Christ over the totality of human life and the world. In a word, it had staked out a corner of the world, withdrawn into it as a fortress, and forsaken the rest of the world to its own lostness and alienation from God.

Hence Bonhoeffer, particularly in his later writings, summoned the church to be faithful to its mission of going into the world. "The church is her true self," he wrote in an outline for a book that he was never able to complete, "only when she exists for humanity." [10] The church is true to its own nature only when it is busy taking risks and spending itself in the services of humanity. The church cannot escape its responsibility for the historical future of mankind because of its vision of an eschatological fulfillment of human life and history. On the contrary, it is summoned to accept its responsibility for the cultural life of the world and to take its place with secular man in bearing this responsibility. But the church must give up its authoritarian claims; it must submit itself to the realities and concrete requirements of life in culture, "not lording it over men, but helping and serving them." Its mission is to tell men, in terms that are concrete and relevant to their vocational life, whatever their daily occupations may be, what it means to live in Christ and to exist for others.

The church must prepare the way for the hearing of the gospel by entering into the life of the world and taking upon itself the consequences of the world's alienation, its guilt, and its dehumanization; for only thus can the church convince the world of its lostness, its guilt, its idolatry, and its inhumanity.[11] Moreover, the church will be able to speak with authority to the world concerning the Lordship of God-in-Christ only if it goes into the world, takes its place along with the world, and exists for the world. Only then will it be able to speak, by deed as by word, about the meaning of faith in the living God who "takes hold of man in the center of his life," rather than merely about religion.

PART THREE: TOWARD A PROPHETIC COMMUNITY

VII

THE TENSION BETWEEN THE CHURCH AND CULTURE

In this concluding section of the present study, attention will be focused upon some of the implications of the Biblical conception of the nature and purpose of the church for the renewal of the churches in the present day. As we saw in Part One, the churches in America generally reflect the divisions of secular society along class and racial lines; moreover, they tend to sanctify the values that are dominant in our American way of life. Thus they tend to transform religion into an ideology and use it as a propaganda device to defend and promote the special interests and values of their members.

In Part Two, we examined the Biblical conception of God as that universal, sovereign, and righteous Will which transcends all man's cultural attainments, including his religious institutions and creeds, and stands in final judgment upon them. We examined Israel's understanding of herself as a covenant community and the relationship of the Old Testament to Christian faith. Against this background we considered the church's understanding of itself as a community of faith in which the universal Lordship of God-in-Christ is acknowledged and as a body of believers who are sent by Christ into the world to be his witnesses and his agents of reconciliation in the present age.

Seen in the light of the radical monotheism of Biblical faith and the New Testament conception of koinonia, the church is in its very nature a prophetic community. It exists in the world, but its purpose is to point men to God, the true center of their existence and the ultimate ground of meaning and value. Viewed from the perspective of a Biblical understanding of the church, it is evident that the church today as it actually exists in the form of local congregations and denominations is in need of radical transformation and renewal. Instead of reshaping the communities in which they are set, the churches tend to reflect and deepen the divisions of secular society and to sanctify the prevailing values and patterns of culture. They have lost their capacity to leaven society and to give light in the midst of the world's darkness. Because they have become captive to the particular cultures and subcultures in which they are set, they appear to be irrelevant and even hostile to the deepest interests and needs of people with different cultural backgrounds. Thus, they have often become agents of conflict between classes, races, nations, and warring ideologies, rather than agents of reconciliation.

Moreover, even for their own members the churches have frequently become places of escape from life and God. They have often been indifferent not only to the claims of justice but even to the barest necessities of men. They have been agents of oppression, bondage, and inhumanity. More frequently still, they have become fellowships of people who share certain religious interests and emotions but are prevented by their very religiosity from encountering the judging and renewing grace of God.

If the church today is to experience the renewal for which it prays despite its unfaithfulness and its idolatry, what is required of it? How can it proclaim its universal message with authority, with power and relevance, to men in the modern secular world? In a word, how can it again become a prophetic community? To raise the question about the renewal of the church in these terms does not imply that the church can re-

new itself by its own power and works. Just as faith is ultimately a gift rather than a human achievement, so the transformation of the church will be finally the work of God rather
than a work of men. But, to continue the analogy, faith is not
simply a gift that is passively received; rather, it is also a human act of commitment of oneself in trust and obedience to
God. Similarly, the renewal of the church involves the latter's
response in repentance, in trust, and in obedience to God's
continuing gift of himself and revelation of his will for the
church.

In this final section of our study we shall therefore attempt
to describe in contemporary language some of the characteristics of a prophetic church insofar as its relationships to culture are concerned. In the present chapter we shall deal primarily with the need to safeguard both the external and the
internal freedom of the churches. In the final chapter we shall
be concerned more explicitly with the renewal of the church
through its involvement in the life of secular society. A major
purpose of both these chapters is to make clear the need for
a recovery of the universal dimensions of Christian faith, particularly the sovereignty of God and the solidarity of mankind in a universal community.

A. TYPICAL RELATIONSHIPS OF THE CHURCH TO CULTURE

It has already been pointed out that the church exists for the
sake of humanity and that the world is, therefore, the sphere
in which the church must do its work. But if the church is
called to go into the world, it is also commanded to maintain
its own identity over against the world. It is summoned to live
" in the world," but it is forbidden to be " of the world." This
twofold relationship of the church, and of the Christian, to secular culture is expressed in a variety of ways in the New Testament. It is implicit in Jesus' words to the disciples: "You are
the salt of the earth," and "You are the light of the world"
(Matt. 5:13, 14). It is also implied in Paul's exhortation, "Do
not be conformed to this world but be transformed" (Rom.

12:2). But this paradoxical relationship between the church and the world is described most explicitly in the Fourth Gospel, where Jesus speaks of sending the disciples "into the world" but at the same time declares that they "are not of the world," just as he has not been of the world even while he has been in it (John 17:11-18).

A church that is not *in* the world has forgotten what the incarnation is all about; but a church that is *of* the world has forgotten both the divine judgment that is being passed upon the world and also the promise that human life can be made new. It is not surprising, however, in view of the double requirement to be *in* the world yet *not of* the world, that throughout the history of the church large numbers of Christians have emphasized one aspect of this relationship to the exclusion of the other. On the one hand, many churches, seeking to remain uncorrupted by secular society, have chosen the path of *withdrawal* from culture. Others, remembering only the requirement that they be in the world, have become *folk churches;* as such they have viewed themselves as the guardians of the particular cultures in which they have been set. But from the beginning there has been a third group of churches which have endeavored to enter into the life of the world and bear witness to the relevance of Christian faith for the totality of human existence without themselves becoming captive to the values and idolatry of the world. Such churches have understood the normative relationship between the church and the world in terms of creative *tension* or polarity.

In order to gain a broader perspective for understanding the responsibility of the church in relationship to present-day society, it will be helpful to examine each of these three typical attitudes that the churches have taken toward the world. In the present discussion, attention will be focused primarily upon the expression of these attitudes in contemporary Protestantism, although each of these views is also found in contemporary Roman Catholicism and although each represents an answer to the church-world problem that runs back through the history of Christianity to its beginnings in the New Testament period.

1. Withdrawal from Culture

Sometimes the churches that have sought to withdraw from culture have appeared among sectarian groups which have understood the relationship of the church to the world as one of radical opposition. According to this view, the church is composed of a group of believers who are summoned to come apart from the profane world of business, politics, liberal education, public entertainment, and war in order to establish a separate community of the elect. Consequently, the church is looked upon primarily as the defender of orthodox beliefs and traditional morality. It becomes essentially a fortress into which Christians retreat and in which they seek to find their security against the onslaught of a corrupt society. Instead of being *for* the world, the church is basically *against* the latter, and its message to the world consists of the announcement of God's judgment upon society. Contemporary examples of this sectarian attitude are found in the frequent and bitter attacks by many theologically conservative groups upon the National Council of Churches, the World Council of Churches, and the social action agencies of the major denominations which try to make clear the relevance of Christian faith to contemporary life.

In present-day Protestantism, however, the effort to withdraw from culture generally takes a much less militant form than that represented by sectarianism. Instead of emphasizing the opposition between the church and culture, Protestant churches that remain aloof from the conflicts and dilemmas of culture today usually divide human existence into two mutually separate realms. Sometimes these realms are described in terms of the spiritual and the temporal; again, they are spoken of as the spheres of the religious and the secular or the sacred and the profane. The two realms are mutually exclusive: the spiritual-religious-sacred domain is the sphere of the church;

the temporal-secular-profane, that of culture. Each realm — or kingdom — has its own authority, its own values, and its own distinctive morality.

In contrast to the sectarian rejection of culture, this form of withdrawal might be described as a parallelist conception of the relationship of the church to society. Typically, this view has been associated with pietistic forms of Protestantism, both in Europe and in America, going back to the Reformation. Theologically, it stems more out of the Lutheran wing of the Reformation than out of Calvinism. In pietism, the life of faith is looked upon as a life that is hidden with God. Faith is essentially an attitude of inner, spiritual trust in God and the acceptance of the forgiveness of sins. Religion provides a retreat from the frustrations and tensions of secular life; it enables the believer to live in the midst of the world by holding out the promise of justification by grace instead of by works. If the pietist does not go so far as to sin in order " that grace may abound " (Rom. 6:1), he is nevertheless in danger of forgetting that " faith by itself, if it has no works, is dead " (James 2:17).

But this form of withdrawal from culture is not limited to such theologically conservative forms of pietism as still linger on in Protestantism, especially in the South; it is represented by more sophisticated forms of contemporary theology. It is found, for example, in some neo-orthodox forms of Protestantism insofar as the revival of Reformation theology becomes primarily an attempt to recover the teachings and doctrines of the Reformers without relating them to the intellectual and cultural demands of the twentieth century. It is also evident in certain contemporary existentialist forms of theology which seek to understand man primarily in individualistic terms, thus abstracting him from the community of which he is inextricably a part. More commonly still, the withdrawal conception of the relationship of the church to society finds expression in the implicit dualism and the practical polytheism which are to a large extent characteristic of popular religion in every age.

When the withdrawal conception of the church vis-à-vis the world is analyzed from the perspective of Biblical faith, it becomes clear that it constitutes a denial both of the Biblical understanding of man and of Biblical monotheism. Insofar as the withdrawal churches limit religion to concern with personal salvation and an individualistic morality, they fail to take seriously the goodness, or value, of culture for the fulfillment of human life. According to the Biblical view of man, he was created for life in community, and both the need for culture and the ability to produce culture are grounded in the nature of man as he was created. Life in society thus has positive value, and its true meaning (goal) is grounded in the will of the Creator who has ordained that man should live in community and has made him social by nature.

Not only does the withdrawal view of the church represent a denial of the Biblical conception of man; it also fails to take seriously the sovereignty of God in and through history. By restricting the will and power of God to the inner, spiritual life of man, it constitutes a return to tribalistic, polytheistic religion. The outward, external sphere of secular culture remains under the rule of alien forces and powers. God no longer executes judgment within history, and he no longer summons men and nations to do his will in the great political and social struggles of the day. The Lordship of Christ is limited to the private, personal life of the withdrawn community. The vision of the Christ who makes all things new is either restricted to the inner realm of the spirit or postponed to an otherworldly eschatological future. Understood in these terms, both the church and Christian faith become irrelevant to culture, and they are doomed to remain on the periphery of life.

2. The Folk Church

The second conception of the relationship between the church and the world that we noted above was that of the folk church. According to this view, the task of the church is to support and sanctify the highest ideals and noblest institutions

of a particular cultural or subcultural group. In Germany prior
to World War II the Lutheran Church became such a *Volks-
kirche*. Having the status of an established church, it was the
official denomination; and as such it was used by the state to
promote and sanction the nationalistic, militaristic, and anti-
Semitic policies of the German *Reich*. But the idea of a folk
church is not limited to an officially established denomination
which is supported and controlled by the state or to a society
in which there is a strong sense of ethnic identity as the basis
of a folk culture. Rather, it is present wherever the church
gives its primary loyalty to the culture of which it is a part
and sanctifies the pattern of life that the latter represents — be
it German or southern or American — as "the Christian way."

In our examination of the class, racial, and ideological character of the churches in this country, we found abundant evidence of their tendency to become folk churches. We found
that the churches tend not only to reflect the class and racial
divisions of secular society but also to rationalize and deepen
these divisions. Moreover, they tend to equate the Christian
faith with those values, ideals, and institutions which their
constituents cherish most: conformity, success, the *status quo*,
peace, harmony, and free enterprise; or, on the other hand,
with nonconformity, reform, protest movements, social welfare, and greater public control of the economy. In general,
the main-line churches in the United States have largely identified some form of free enterprise and democracy with Christianity. They have assumed that the latter represent the will of
God for all peoples everywhere, quite forgetting that throughout the history of the church — and also in large portions of the
world today — most Christians have lived under other forms of
economic and political institutions.

In its effort to be in the world and at the same time relevant
to the world, the folk church becomes a form of "culture-
Christianity."[1] Instead of transforming culture, it becomes conformed to society. In this process it not only loses its identity as
the church of Christ vis-à-vis the world, but it also thereby

loses its universal appeal. It gives primary importance to the preservation of cultural forms rather than to human beings and their personal needs. Because it is ethnocentric, it ceases to be relevant to the needs of men in other cultural circumstances. Stated in theological terms, the folk church ceases to be the universal church because it places its faith in an idol rather than in the one universal God who transcends all man's cultural achievements and judges every culture, as well as every group within culture.

In many respects the practical effects of the folk church upon culture are similar to those of the churches that seek to withdraw from society, for in both cases culture remains essentially autonomous. There is, however, one major difference between the two approaches: the folk church does explicitly and intentionally what the withdrawal churches do implicitly and often by default. Whereas the separationist church leaves culture unaffected by religion, the folk church gives religious sanctions to the goals and values of culture. On the one hand, it deifies the *status quo* — whether it be slavery or segregation or a particular economic or political system; and, on the other hand, it sanctions holy wars and crusades to defend and spread those institutions — for example, capitalism, democracy, or religion — which a particular society holds most dear.

When the folk church is examined in the light of the New Testament, it is evident that, while it succeeds in being in the world, it fails to heed the injunction not to be of the world. In the first place, being immersed in the world and having accommodated itself to the latter, the folk church is no longer able to discern how it has violated the First Commandment by placing a tribal deity before Yahweh and bowing down and worshiping it. Instead of seeking God for his own sake, the folk church turns to him for utilitarian and pragmatic reasons. Religion is a good thing because it produces prosperity and national strength.

In the second place, the folk church tends to equate the existing social order — or its blueprint for a future society — with the Kingdom of God. In so doing, it forgets that, while the Kingdom is manifest within the present historical order, its final consummation is eschatological. It forgets, also, that insofar as the Kingdom is manifest within history — within the heart of the believer, in the koinonia of the church, and in the social order — it is not something that men build by their own efforts, ingenuity, and goodwill; rather, it is a gift that God bestows upon those who will receive it and subject themselves to his Lordship.

Thirdly, since it is immersed in culture to the point of conformity with the values and norms of the latter, the folk church is no longer free to be prophetic. It is no longer able to perceive the radical difference between the sinfulness of man and the holiness of God. It is no longer able to discern the extent to which even the most idealistic and altruistic forms of human achievement are perverted by egoism and pride and therefore fall under the divine judgment. By sanctifying the existing forms of culture, it hides men from God and from an awareness of their need for his judgment and grace; and in so doing it tempts both individuals and social groups, including the churches, to make messianic claims for themselves as the special bearers of the divine will in history.

3. A Pattern of Creative Tension

The third major Protestant conception of the relationship of the church to secular culture is one of tension. H. Richard Niebuhr describes it as a relationship of " polarity." [2] It might also be called a relationship of interaction between the church and the world. Like the folk church, the church that exists in tension with culture sees the necessity of being in the world and being relevant to the needs, values, and goals of men in culture; but, unlike the folk church, it recognizes that it is forbidden to become conformed to its secular environment, thus losing its power to summon men to repentance and renewal. Like the sect, it sees that the church is called to maintain its separate identity from the world; but, unlike the sect, it recognizes that it is called to do so in the midst of the world.

The concept of the church and secular culture as existing in permanent tension attempts to take into account both the yes and the no that always need to be spoken by the church to culture. The sect — "the church against the world" — addresses only an unequivocal " No! " to the world. The parallelist church fails to enter into any real communication with culture. The folk church, on the other hand, speaks only an unqualified " Yes! " to secular society. In contrast to all of these, the church that interacts with culture seeks to maintain a relationship of polar and dynamic tension between the church and society. Sometimes this relationship involves cooperation of the church with the secular community; sometimes it involves the former setting itself in opposition to the latter; but always it involves the church's recognition that it and the world exist together before God and that both are instruments of the divine will. Neither the church nor secular culture is the Kingdom of God, but both are instruments of that Kingdom. God's judgment falls upon both, but God uses both for the accomplishment of his will.

Both the church and the world exist before God and live under his sovereignty, although the world is not aware that this is so; hence, the two communities remain two, having different centers and different objects of final loyalty. The church can be the church only if it maintains its identity over against the world; it can fulfill its mission to the world only if it remains distinct from the world. No matter how much the church may cooperate with the world and champion the truth and justice that are in secular culture, and no matter how much the former may oppose the untruth and injustice of the latter, the mission of the church to the world remains essentially the same, namely, to point the world to its true Lord. For it is only the church — that is, only the community of faith — that knows that the God who was made manifest in Christ as the Savior of men is in actuality the Creator, Judge, and Reconciler of the whole world. Because the church knows this but the world

does not know it — and cannot know it by itself — the church is
sent into the world to be a witness to the Lordship of God
over the world and to be an agent of reconciliation of the
world to its Lord.

But the church is able to remain in the world and maintain
its identity over against the world only if it constantly points to
a more ultimate relationship in which both the church and the
world stand before God. The task of the church, therefore, is
to witness not to itself but to Christ and to the One to whom
Christ bore witness. Yet, the great temptation of the church as
a human insitution is to seek its own glory. Like the world, the
churches as human institutions are always tempted to make
arrogant claims for themselves — for their goodness, their
achievements (size, possessions, influence), their authority —
rather than summoning men to glorify and obey God.

As a human community the church is composed of people
who are sinful and whose faith is often small and faltering. It
is always threatened by the spirit of the world — that is, by
worldliness, self-seeking, pride, and idolatry. But, unlike the
world, the church — when it is faithful to the gospel — submits
its own life to the judging and transforming love of God
through confession, through prayer, and through listening to
the Word of God which is spoken to it through Scripture,
through the secular world, and through the Spirit in the church.
It recognizes its need for continuing repentance, continuing
forgiveness, and continuing transformation.

The church, therefore, does not point to itself as the source
either of the world's judgment or of its renewal. Rather, as a
community that lives by faith, it points the world to One by
whom the world is judged even as the church is being judged;
and it witnesses to the liberty, the power, and the fullness of
life that are the fruits of trust in God and obedience to his will.
It witnesses to the world concerning what it means to live by
the faith that the ultimate Power in the universe is love. It
testifies to the world that man can live a truly human existence
only when he lives in fellowship with God in whose image he

is made, and that man's deepest and most abiding joy is to be found in this fellowship (koinonia) with his Creator. This is the " good news " that the church is sent to proclaim to the world both by word and by deed.

It is all too evident that the churches, since they are human institutions and as such are frequently conformed to their secular environments, often proclaim the gospel without power and are often indistinguishable from the world in their deeds. Yet the church has endured, the gospel has been proclaimed with power, and the church has shown signs of its faith in works of love. According to the measure of its faith and love, it has been an agent for the mediation of forgiveness, reconciliation, healing, and greater social justice. Its faith has been active in love for the neighbor, both near and far, both believer and nonbeliever. Here and there, now and then, it has been like leaven in society or like a light amid the world's darkness. Yet amid all such works it testifies that these are also ultimately gifts which spring from grace. Therefore, it points the world not to itself but to its Lord, and summons the world also to live by faith in God who alone has power to save it from its own self-destruction and restore it to its true life.

Thus the church and the world exist together before their common Lord. Both live by the divine love that they receive, and both are chastened by the divine judgment. Both will continue to exist side by side until the end of history, and the task of the church vis-à-vis the world is to interpret to the world what it has seen and heard about God and the relationship in which both the church and the world stand before God, that the world might believe and that, believing, it might have life (cf. John 20:31).

B. THE GOAL OF THE CHURCH: THE TRANSFORMATION OF INDIVIDUALS AND COMMUNITIES

In the preceding section we emphasized the need to preserve a relationship of dynamic tension between the church and culture. But clearly the goal of the church vis-à-vis the world cannot be adequately described in such negative terms. The purpose of the church is not to live in tension with the world, although the former can fulfill its mission only if it preserves its identity over against the latter. Rather, the purpose of the church is to effect the transformation both of individuals and communities by summoning both to repentance and to a reorientation of their lives about their true Center.

The church does not aim simply at the transformation of individuals alone; for the latter have their being in the communities of which they are a part, and their lives are in large measure shaped by these communities. The concept of an individual in total isolation from community is an abstraction. But neither is the church merely — or even primarily — an agency of social reform. Rather, it witnesses to the God of individuals and nations, a God who demands righteousness and justice in man's collective life as well as love for the individual neighbor and humility before himself (cf. Micah 6:8).

In *The Purpose of the Church and Its Ministry*, Prof. H. Richard Niebuhr described the goal of the church in terms that have become classic: " the increase among men of the love of God and neighbor." [3] Although the purpose of the church may be defined in many different terms and although doubtless no single formulation of its goal is entirely adequate, this description of its task is patterned after Jesus' summary of the divine will for man. It reminds the church in its search for renewal that a living relationship to God is more important than creeds and forms of worship, although both the latter are necessary for the nurture of this relationship; and it reminds the church, also, that the requirement of the second great commandment is inseparable from that of the first. This definition of its purpose likewise makes it clear why the church cannot fulfill its mission in the world without entering into the life of the world and sharing in its burdens; for love is a possibility and a need wherever persons exist in relationship to one another, whether as individuals or in groups.

It is, of course, possible to turn Niebuhr's definition of the purpose of the church into a sentimental and moralistic formula just as Jesus' summary of the whole duty of man in the twofold commandment to love God and neighbor has been sentimentalized and moralized. Seen, however, in its proper context of the Christian understanding of God, of the meaning of love (agape), and of the way in which love becomes a possibility in human life, Niebuhr's definition of the goal of the church is also an apt definition of the purpose of Christianity itself — of the incarnation, the crucifixion, and the resurrection.[4] In the context of the New Testament meaning of love for God and love for the neighbor, it is evident, moreover, that the increase of love for God and the neighbor depends upon the increase of faith, or trust in God, which in turn depends upon the disclosure of the divine love. For it is the disclosure of God's unmerited love that creates the possibility of trusting him and prompts the desire, born out of gratitude, to love God with heart, soul, mind, and strength and to love the neighbor as one for whom Christ died.

It is not possible within the limits of the present discussion to do more than suggest the depth of the transformation of human life that is implied in the phrase "the increase among men of the love of God and neighbor." In an earlier section (Chapter IV), an attempt was made to spell out the meaning of love for God in terms of radical monotheism and trust in God alone as the Center and final Ground of all meaning and value. An effort was also made to interpret the meaning of love for the neighbor in terms of man's response to the creating, judging, and reconciling will and action of God in a universal community under one Heavenly Father. Subsequently (Chapter V) a similar attempt was made to define the concrete meaning which love for God and love for the neighbor had in the daily life of the New Testament church, understood as the new covenant community, the body of Christ, and the koinonia.

Using Niebuhr's definition of its purpose, the church might be defined, then, in terms of love as that community which is

aware of the love of God in Christ and which seeks to respond
to the divine love by loving both God and the neighbor. It is a
community that has been reconciled to God and that seeks to
be an agent of reconciliation of others to him. Yet the reconciliation to which it witnesses is a reconciliation that is more of
a process that has begun than an act that has been completed.
The church lives in the memory of God's reconciling acts in
history, in Christ, and in the church itself; it lives in the present
experience of being reconciled to God and through him to the
neighbor; but it also lives in hope – in hope that is born of
memory and present experience – that the process that has begun will be fulfilled by him who makes all things new. As a
community of those who are reconciled to God and to each
other, the church is summoned to go into the world as an agent
of reconciliation. In the fulfillment of this task, proclamation
of the gospel and works of love are both necessary. Love and
reconciliation cannot finally be witnessed to by word alone, nor
can they be brought into being by commanding men to love.
What they mean can be made manifest only as they become incarnate in the midst of human need, thus preparing the way for
the hearing of the gospel.

C. FREEDOM AND THE PROPHETIC COMMUNITY

In order to accomplish its purpose in the world – namely the
transformation of individuals and communities – the church
must be free to witness to the sovereignty of God over all men
and over all human communities, and to the solidarity of mankind in a universal community. Basically, the tension between
the church and culture arises out of the conflict between this
radically monotheistic faith of the church and the rival forms
of social faith to which various political, economic, and racial
groups look for meaning and value. This is true not only of the
conflict between the church and nationalistic and economic
forms of totalitarianism such as Nazism and Communism; it is
also true of the struggle between Christian faith and every
other social, economic, political, and even religious form of

idolatry and polytheism. This conflict of faiths underlies the continuing tension between the church and culture – a conflict that, as we have seen, runs through the churches themselves. Moreover, Christian faith teaches that this conflict will continue to the end of the present historical order, for neither the church nor culture can be equated with the Kingdom of God in its fullness. Hence, as long as the church remains true to its mission, tension between the two will remain. Such tension, however, is neither evil nor undesirable. It is, in fact, the necessary prerequisite to a creative relationship of the church to culture.

But in order for this tension between the church and culture to be creative, both the church and secular society must be free from the domination of each other. Man's life in culture – in science, in business, in the struggle for human rights, in the quest for world community – needs the resources of religious faith and the church; but, because of its tendencies toward self-deification, the church needs the restraint of culture with its demands for intellectual integrity and relevance to the totality of human existence. In theocratic societies, state churches tend inevitably to become oppressive and tyrannical. In the name of religion they deny human freedom, and thus they inevitably undermine the integrity of religion itself by seeking to force it upon society as a whole. Not only does such coercion produce hypocrisy in religion, but it also leads to the repression of man's life in culture. On the other hand, atheistic and officially antireligious societies, which either suppress or control organized religion, also deny human freedom and produce other forms of tyranny. They develop their own ideologies which they seek to impose upon their own members. They generate their own pressures toward nonreligious conformity and toward some form of totalitarianism. Thus, they too ultimately dehumanize man by robbing him of his individuality and freedom.

In our earlier discussion of the emergence of religious pluralism and the meaning of a secular society (Chapter III), we emphasized the need for the latter to be free from domination by any form of established or state church. In the present context we are primarily concerned with the broader freedom of the church which is necessary in order that the latter may fulfill its mission as a prophetic community in the midst of the world. This freedom is both external and internal. In the first instance, the church must be free to proclaim its faith in a relevant way to society and free also to work for its implementation in the life of the community. But secondly, the church must have internal freedom since it is a human institution and therefore stands in constant need of self-criticism and internal reform.

1. The Church and External Society

In this country we have had a strong tradition of religious liberty from the beginning of our national existence. As we have seen (Chapter III), the guarantees of religious liberty in the federal Constitution provided for the institutional separation of church and state. The motivation for these provisions was essentially twofold. On the one hand, they were designed to protect the country from religious persecution; and, in the second place, they represented an effort to safeguard the freedom of the churches from control by the state. Eventually these principles were also adopted at the state level. Moreover, the application of them has subsequently been extended to the areas of public education, selective service, the requirement of oaths for office, and Sabbath laws, so that we have become increasingly a pluralistic society in which no particular religious group is given preferential treatment in the political life of the nation. Thus — insofar as the law of the land is concerned — all religious groups have the same freedom and the same protection of their rights to engage in public worship and to seek to influence the formation of public policy.

But freedom has many dimensions. It has many prerequisites. It is never fully achieved in human society, and a constant effort must be made to preserve it and to provide new forms in which it can find ever new, dynamic expression. Despite our zealous guarding of the freedom of the churches from state control, it is perfectly clear that in most communities in this country the churches are not free to be prophetic. Neither the minister nor individual laymen nor the congregation as a whole are free to challenge the conventional morality and patterns of behavior in the community at large without fear of reprisal. In itself there is nothing unusual about the fact that society demands conformity to its values and its conventional behavior; but the irony of this situation in America arises out of the fact that approximately 65 percent of the total population are members of organized religious groups rooted in traditions that teach that men ought finally to obey God rather than men, that all men are fundamentally equal, and that God demands social justice as the expression of faith. Not only so, but most of these church members pay lip service to the principle that the church must be free, and they strongly condemn those totalitarian countries in which organized religion is either suppressed or openly controlled by the state.

There are many ways of suppressing the freedom of the church besides the political means that are employed by states that are officially atheistic, tribalistic, or theocratic. As minority groups within the churches and especially the victims of social injustice outside the churches have made clear, the church is not free when it becomes a part of the establishment in a society, an instrument to protect the vested interests of the privileged groups and control the masses.

Perhaps the greatest single hindrance to the recovery of the church as a prophetic community in this country today is the illusion that the United States is a Christian country and that it has been so from the beginning. This illusion is widely shared by the membership of the churches. As a result, the prevailing patterns of American life are defended in the name of Christianity against attack and criticism by the more prophetic voices within the churches, including individual ministers, social action agencies of local churches and denominations, and the National Council of Churches. In some respects such culture-Protestantism is particularly strong in the South, where the population is more religiously homogeneous (Protestant) than it is in other sections of the country. Thus, in the South, Protestantism tends to be identified with a combination of pietism, agrarianism, exaggerated individualism, antiunionism, and anti-intellectualism. In other sections of the country, however, culture-religion takes different forms, both Protestant and Roman Catholic.

Under such circumstances the alleged freedom of the churches is a myth. In this situation the churches are, in many respects, just as effectively captive to culture as those in Communist lands. Churchmen in this country were generally shocked by this charge when it was made a few years ago by the famous Swiss theologian Karl Barth, in a letter to a pastor in East Germany. This minister had written Barth for advice concerning what a Christian pastor might do in a Communist land that was militantly opposed to the church. Barth recognized the difficulties faced by a pastor under such circumstances. Nevertheless, he warned, the East German minister should not pray for a victory of the West over Communism, for then the plight of Christians might be even worse! Barth's essential point was quite clear. Western churchmen, he said in effect, are offended when they hear clergy from Communist countries echo the propaganda of their governments. But, he noted, Western churchmen also do precisely the same thing when they too echo, and sanction, the propaganda of their governments and their economic institutions. If it is hard to be a Christian pastor in a Communist country, Barth was saying, it is also hard to be a Christian in any other society, and particularly in one that makes religious pretensions of its own.

The bondage of the Christian and the churches in a "Christian" society has never been more forcefully depicted than it was by the Danish theologian Søren Kierkegaard when he lashed out against the hypocrisy of conventional, official religion in his *Attack Upon Christendom*, about a hundred years ago. The fundamental question that Kierkegaard asked in this book furnishes a striking counterpart to that raised by the East German pastor. For what this Danish prophet wanted to know was this: How can a person be a Christian in Christendom?

It is the major function of a prophetic church to expose such hypocrisy and to point both individuals and communities to the divine judgment under which all human achievements stand to the end that men, in both their individual and collective life, may be transformed and fulfilled. In actuality, however, the churches generally follow rather than lead secular groups in the awakening of a social conscience. Indeed, one leading contemporary sociologist of religion goes so far as to say, "The church cannot change basic secular institutions; it will sponsor modification of them only when important groups have moved in that direction." [5] If any evidence in support of Professor Yinger's judgment is needed, it is sufficient to cite the role of the churches in the contemporary struggle for civil rights.

2. Freedom Within the Koinonia

In addition to freedom from external control by society, the church also needs internal freedom if it is to remain a prophetic community. This is true, first of all, because freedom is a prerequisite for genuine community of any kind; and it is true, in the second place, because the church as a human community stands in need of continuing reformation and self-criticism in order to protect it against complacency, pride, and self-idolatry.

The present century is an age in which freedom and human dignity are on the march all over the globe. Rapid advances in education, in technology, and in communication have opened up tremendous new possibilities for freedom to men everywhere. There has been a worldwide revolt against old political and economic forms of imperialism and against authoritarianism and dogmatism in religion and morality. In the light of the new possibilities for freedom from old forms of political and economic exploitation and indeed from poverty, ignorance, and disease, we have gained new insight into the meaning of freedom in our day. Moreover, such is the nature of freedom that the very possibilities of greater liberty also provide the possibilities for new, more totalitarian forms of tyranny and oppression than existed in earlier societies.

Not only are men seeking new forms of freedom in our day, but they are also seeking it in a new context — namely, that of man's increasing interdependence. In this new context of mass society, any individualistic conception of freedom has become anachronistic. Modern man is now faced with only two possibilities: freedom in community or some form of collectivism in which freedom is denied.

In the midst of the quest for greater freedom in increasingly larger social groups, the church exists as a community that witnesses both to the dignity and worth of each individual and also to the brotherhood of all men under one common father. Moreover, it is called to manifest this community in its own life as the koinonia, the very existence of which serves as an agent of reconciliation in the midst of all of man's broken communities and alienation from his fellowman. The church is summoned to be a fellowship of peoples of all races, walks of life, and ethnic origins, drawn together by a common faith and sharing their great variety of gifts — their traditions, their special skills, all that makes each group distinctive — for the mutual benefit of all. Every individual and every group has its place in God's creative and redemptive purpose; he wills a universal community in which each is free to contribute, according to his special gifts and abilities, to the growth and fulfillment of the whole.

When one looks at the history of the churches, however, it is clear that they have been torn by the same struggle for internal liberty as other institutions. Like the state and other secular groups, the churches have also denied freedom to their own members. They have rejected the prophets and critics who have arisen in their midst, because they have been more concerned with their own power and prestige as institutions than they have with justice, more concerned with the appearance of religion than with integrity, and more concerned with conformity than with freedom. Yet, despite the long history of tyranny in the name of religion, both within Roman Catholicism and in Protestantism, the churches have also sown the seeds of freedom insofar as they have proclaimed the fundamental equality of all men and insofar as they have taught that man's final duty is to obey God rather than men.

The worldwide march of suppressed peoples toward greater freedom — from racism, from economic exploitation, from colonialism — has confronted the churches with the demand for full and equal participation of all racial, ethnic, and class groups both in the churches themselves and also in the total life of society. For example, until well into the twentieth century foreign missions were almost entirely dominated by the white leadership from the West. In recent years, however, there has been a growing demand for indigenous leadership in the younger churches of Asia and Africa, and such leadership is rapidly replacing that of the white missionaries in these lands. To a large extent this development has been necessitated by the mounting distrust of the white man and a growing revolt against domination by the West. But, on the whole, this change has been welcomed by the sponsoring churches of the West; for they recognize that if it had not taken place, the church would have been rejected in Asia and Africa as the handmaid of economic and political imperialism. It is only within the last few years, however, that native-born leaders have been given the highest positions of ecclesiastical leadership in many of the denominations in these countries.

Yet in this country Negroes continue to be excluded from many predominantly white denominations and local churches; and if they are permitted to join such groups, they are generally excluded from full and equal participation in the life of these churches. Since World War II, however, the civil rights movement has given the churches a new understanding of freedom and of their own guilt in denying in practice what they profess in creed. It has exposed the hypocrisy of racial divisions in the body of Christ and the sentimentalism of love without a concern for social justice. It has forced the white churches to recognize their own involvement in paternalism and their denial of dignity, equality, and freedom to their fellow Christians.

Not only has the Negro revolution brought the churches under judgment for their exclusion of the Negro from Christian fellowship, but it has revealed an even deeper sickness within the churches. For it has created a crisis in the institutional churches in which freedom of conscience, freedom of speech, and freedom of the pulpit are denied by the churches themselves. When these freedoms are forfeited, the church loses its integrity, and it is cut off from any possibility of reform and renewal. These same freedoms are, of course, also threatened in the effort of the churches to deal with other controversial movements such as Communism, the radical right, or organized labor; but in many respects the Negro revolution has pointed up the crisis in the churches most clearly at this point because racial segregation represents the most obvious denial of Christian brotherhood and the unity of the church.

What, then, has the contemporary worldwide struggle for freedom taught the churches about the meaning and urgency of freedom in the church as well as in secular society today? What new dimensions of freedom has it revealed? In the first place, it has become increasingly clear that freedom is prerequisite for human dignity. This is true in democratic America just as much as in Communist Russia or China. It is true both for the clergy and for the laity. Freedom is indivisible. It includes the freedom of the minister to proclaim the gospel according to his conscience, and it also includes the freedom of laymen — including the church school teachers and the membership of the churches generally — to witness to the meaning of Christian faith in word and deed within the church itself without fear of intimidation and reprisal. Moreover, it includes the freedom of minister and layman alike to act according to their consciences in the secular community as well as in the church.

Not only has the freedom movement made it clear that freedom is prerequisite for human dignity; it has also, in the second place, given the churches a deeper understanding of the meaning of freedom. It has unmasked the hypocrisy of traditional ecclesiastical and secular pretensions to liberty, equality, and brotherhood. In order to be genuine, freedom cannot be limited to toleration or paternalism or even to the right to meet together and "have one's say." On the contrary, freedom as an expression of human dignity implies the right to be heard. The difference between "being heard" and "having one's say" is fundamental. It was strikingly illustrated at the Republican National Convention in 1964 during a debate concerning the relationship of the Republican Party to certain right-wing political groups, including the John Birch Society. In the course of the debate Governor Nelson Rockefeller, of New York, urged the convention to renounce the support of such groups, but he was not given even the outward appearance of being heard. The chairman of the convention found it necessary to rebuke the delegates and the audience for the denial of this fundamental right in a democracy. This episode was particularly shocking because the denial of freedom was so open and undisguised. Yet it was by no means unique. Genuine freedom — whether in secular political life, in economic organizations, or in ecclesiastical institutions — implies the *freedom to participate creatively in policy formation and in the making of significant decisions* about important, and therefore controversial, issues that affect oneself and one's relationships to one's fellowmen. This is also true of the various racial groups and economic classes that are included in local churches and in the regional and national governing bodies of the different denominations. Insofar as such participation at the level where decisions are being made continues to be denied, the claim to freedom and equality remains empty and hypocritical.

Such freedom to participate in policy formation — whether in the churches or in industry and politics — implies, moreover, a fundamental equality among men. Freedom is inconsistent with every form of minority status. The rapid surge toward nationhood on the part of colonial peoples in Asia and Africa since World War II and the current demand for reapportionment of state legislatures and realignment of Congressional districts in this country, as well as the Negro revolt and the growth of religious pluralism, have given us a new understanding of the prerequisites for freedom in the twentieth century. These movements have made it clear that paternalism and charity are incompatible with freedom because they constitute a denial of equality.

The significance of equality for freedom is well illustrated in the area of communication between the races. In the South, for example, genuine communication between the races has been virtually impossible down to quite recent times even though whites have had daily contact with Negro employees and service personnel. This has been true even in those communities and organizations in which there have been interracial meetings and collaboration in political and civic affairs. In such situations the Negro has been expected to accept the overall pattern of segregation and accommodate himself to it. Under such circumstances genuine communication was impossible because the relationships between the races were unequal. Since the Negro was almost completely dependent upon the white man, the former was not free to express his true grievances, his deep sense of injustice, and his resentments against white society without fear of reprisal.

Indeed, this situation continues to be dominant in large sections of the country even today. Nevertheless, here and there, in the churches as well as in the community at large, a more mature freedom based upon the recognition of mutual equality is being achieved. Where this has happened, the result has been a gain for the community as a whole, including whites as well as Negroes. The achievement of such freedom has been the real aim of the Negro-led freedom movement beginning in

Birmingham in 1963 and reaching a series of peaks in the March on Washington in that year, the Civil Rights Act of 1964, and the Voting Rights Act of 1965.

The achievement of *de facto* equality and freedom between groups that have previously been unequal is often a painful and threatening process to members of the dominant group. It involves crisis and conflict.[6] It implies the possibility that the previously dominant group may be outvoted; hence, it creates a basic insecurity on the part of the latter. But the acceptance of such a process implies a basic respect for the worth and the individuality of each person. Hence, it is a sign of growing maturity in the churches and in our national life that both the churches and secular institutions are coming to recognize that equality is prerequisite not only to human dignity but also to liberty itself. Moreover, such is the nature of freedom and human dignity that they cannot be denied to any man or any group without thereby placing in jeopardy the value and the liberty of all.

Not only is freedom essential both as a safeguard and as an expression of man's basic worth as an individual; it is also essential for the creation or attainment of genuine community, whether in marriage, in the family, in the church, or in the community at large. As we have seen, one of the most meaningful descriptions of the church in the New Testament is that of koinonia. Understood in this light, the church was a fellowship of faith — a community of many people with diverse gifts drawn together by a common faith from across all kinds of human divisions. Each member was encouraged and challenged to use his special gifts — as apostle, as prophet, as evangelist, as pastor, or as teacher — for the mutual upbuilding and enrichment of the koinonia that it might grow in knowledge, in unity, and in fullness of faith. Each member was admonished to speak the truth in love to all the rest so that each might attain to mature manhood and contribute to the growth and strengthening of the koinonia.

Freedom, as the writer of Ephesians saw, is prerequisite both for the creation and for the preservation of genuine community. By itself, freedom is largely a negative principle; hence, it cannot constitute the unifying bond that binds a group together into a true community. Nevertheless, freedom is essential as a prerequisite for community. The unifying bond itself, however, is a shared faith, or — as Augustine put it in *The City of God* — a common love, a mutually shared devotion to a common object of loyalty or value. This common loyalty is what creates a community, even a fleeting one, out of a group of spectators at a football game or out of an audience that becomes one in its response to an artist's performance of a great musical composition. Community is not determined by geographical proximity; neither can it be created by force. Without a commonly shared love, a group of people may constitute a crowd of spectators, they may form an organization, they may be incorporated into the external form of a city; but unless there is a unifying center of value, an object of common loyalty, there is no real community.

Freedom, then, is not the unifying principle of community, but it is the soil in which this principle must grow. When the liberty and individuality of either partner is denied, marriage becomes an empty shell instead of a community of mutual love and trust. Without liberty of conscience and freedom in fellowship, the church becomes primarily an organization or an institution instead of a community built upon a common love for God and a mutual recognition of each member's worth, his gifts, and his individuality.

From the standpoint of Christian faith, the koinonia which the church is called to manifest in its own life provides an analogy of the nature of genuinely human community in all man's relationships, wherever they are found, because they are grounded in the nature of man as God created him.

God created man with the capacity for individuality, and he wills him to be free. God also created man to find his fulfillment — his true humanity — in community, and the very possibility of community depends upon the mutual recognition of each person's freedom, his uniqueness, and his equality.

VIII

RENEWAL THROUGH ENGAGEMENT
WITH CULTURE

In the previous chapter we examined some of the reasons why freedom — both for the individual believer and also for the institutional churches — is a necessity if the church is to be a prophetic community. Freedom provides the climate in which the will of God can be proclaimed and heard according to conscience both within the churches and also within the secular community. Freedom provides the external possibility for the church to be relevant to culture and to witness, by word and action, to the meaning of faith in relation to society. It provides the context in which the church can become involved in the fundamental issues facing the secular community. But freedom, we have also noted, does not itself constitute the positive content of the church's witness.

In this concluding chapter we turn, therefore, to a consideration of the church's social responsibility in more positive terms. As a community of faith the church exists in the midst of the secular community, but it also lives in tension with the surrounding culture — with its values, its norms, its idolatry, and its polytheism. As a prophetic community the church must make clear the meaning of its faith for the crucial issues and choices that contemporary man faces in the secular world; for these are the issues with which he is most existentially concerned, and these are the decisions in which his freedom and his responsibility for the neighbor come to most concrete focus.

For this reason the engagement of the church with culture is indispensable for the renewal of the church. Not only is it prerequisite for the recovery of the church's relevance to contemporary life, but it is necessary, most of all, for a renewed understanding of the meaning of faith itself.

A. THE CONTEMPORARY SECULAR WORLD

It has been noted, in a previous chapter, that the development of religious pluralism in this country has been accompanied by an increasing secularization of the public life of the nation. As a people we have moved increasingly toward a pluralistic, secular state, insofar as separation of church and state is concerned. This fact has been widely acknowledged and accepted by the churches, for the latter have recognized that it is the natural outgrowth of religious freedom.

But the transition to a pluralistic, secular state is only one, relatively minor manifestation of a far deeper and more pervasive secularization of modern life as a whole. A veritable revolution has taken place in man's world view and in his control over nature since the rise of modern science. As the result of his increasing mastery over nature, modern man has more and more rejected the appeal to God as a hypothesis to answer unresolved questions about the physical world, including the origin of the universe and even of life itself. Modern man has acquired a new independence and autonomy in the realm of science and technology, and often these advances have been made against the opposition of institutionalized, traditional religion. The church and religion have, to a large degree, become irrelevant to the most meaningful areas of contemporary man's experience, to the decisions that he inevitably faces in culture, and to the determinative centers of power in modern society. Such an experience is not limited to people outside the churches; it is also characteristic of great masses of the membership of the churches, and for this latter group the sense of irrelevance is frequently the source of deep-rooted anxiety and guilt.

Thus in the contemporary world the church faces a new cultural situation: the reality of a largely secular society. The age of Christendom — that is, of a religiously homogeneous society based upon a common faith and morality — has passed. The breakup of this religious and moral unity has been a gradual process whose roots go back at least to the Enlightenment. But the churches have only recently begun to take contemporary secular man seriously. They have only recently begun to acknowledge that the revolt of modern humanist, rational, scientifically trained man against the intellectual and moral tyranny of conventional religion represents a great gain for the human spirit and a new opportunity for the recovery of faith. For secular man has achieved a new stage of maturity, or adulthood, in his understanding of the world and of his freedom and responsibility for his own mundane destiny. He has become liberated from religiously imposed scientific and metaphysical theories, from the anti-intellectualism and otherworldliness of pietism, and from authoritarian forms of morality. This liberation from idolatrous forms of religion has brought with it the possibility of a new openness to the God of Biblical faith — to the One who is Lord of the future as well as the past, who works through science and technology as well as religion, and who has created man to be free and responsible in his life in culture.

In the past the churches have resisted the process of secularization, for they have viewed it as a threat to faith itself. Hence, they have tended to fight a holding action against the secularization of culture. They have been reluctant to recognize and accept the theological implications of man's increasing advancements in the physical and social sciences. In the name of Christian faith they have defended outmoded cosmological and metaphysical theories which once provided useful vehicles for interpreting the meaning of faith in different cultural settings. Similarly, they have often equated Christian faith and Christian ethics with particular economic and political systems that have developed in the West; hence, they have become the defenders of the *status quo* at home and the champions of imperialism abroad.

Moreover, when they have not actively opposed the liberalizing, humanizing forces that have brought about the breakup of Christendom, the churches have frequently responded to the increasing secularization of culture through a retreat into a private, spiritual world beyond the reaches of rational knowledge and scientific assault. In so doing, they have become irrelevant to secular man (including their own members), whose life is largely spent with mundane concerns outside of this spiritual retreat. In either case, the churches have opposed the secularization of culture because they have confused religion — that is, the outward form of faith — with faith itself. Consequently, in his revolt against the tyranny and idolatry of institutionalized, church-centered religion, contemporary man has rejected the possibility of faith without ever having understood the meaning of the gospel.

Increasingly in the present century, particularly since World War II, theologians and the churches have welcomed the advent of secular culture, and they have done so for two primary reasons. In the first place, they have recognized the judgment of God in the breakup of Christendom, for he has exposed the illusion and hypocrisy contained in the assumption that any society is *de facto* Christian. In the second place, they have seen in the advent of secular man the fulfillment of the will of the Creator who made man to be both free and responsible for his life in this world. God has endowed man with reason and set him in the midst of a community ruled by physical and moral law. God wills that man shall serve him with heart, mind, soul, and strength. Or, to say the same thing in different words, he wills a universal community of love (agape). Man's essential dignity is twofold: it consists of the relationship in which he stands to God as the Final Power from whom he comes and to whom he ultimately returns; it consists also of his capacity for responsibility vis-à-vis the neighbor in all the manifold relationships of man in culture. Secular society represents the protest of contemporary, enlightened, scientific man against the efforts of organized religion to deprive man of his freedom and responsibility vis-à-vis the created world. There is, of course, no guarantee that twentieth-century man will not misuse his freedom as an occasion for secularism, idolatry, and self-destruction, just as the first man used his freedom as an occasion for disobedience. But Christian faith understands God to be calling men to freedom and to responsibility as the content of love in both the personal and the impersonal relationships of modern life. The summons to freedom before God demands freedom from ecclesiastical imperialism and religiously sanctioned ideologies; and the summons to responsibility demands the use of all man's rational capacities to meet human need wherever, and in whatever form, it is found.

B. DIALOGUE AND INVOLVEMENT: PREREQUISITES
FOR RELEVANCE

The secularization of contemporary culture has been a gain both for secular society and for the churches. Bonhoeffer, for example, hailed it as a sign of the world's " coming of age," or passing from a stage of adolescence to maturity. More recently, Harvey Cox has celebrated both the secularization and the urbanization of modern society as great advances over earlier sacral and tribal forms of culture. For Cox secularization represents " the emancipation of man first from religious and then from metaphysical control." [1] Although Cox idealizes both the secularization and the urbanization of modern life, the process of secularization has been, in many respects, a liberating one both for society generally and for the churches. It has provided a new challenge and a new opportunity for the churches to enter into serious discussion with contemporary man about the meaning of human existence, about the nature of faith and the possibility of faith, and about the basic issues and problems that men face in culture. It has produced a new openness on the part of the church to the future, and also a new openness to the universal community of mankind.

In this new cultural situation, dialogue with secular man — both within and outside the church — has become a necessity if the church is to recover its relevance to modern life. The church must learn to speak in terms that are relevant to the life, the concerns, and the thought forms of contemporary man. But even before it can learn to speak in such contemporary language, the church must learn to listen to secular man, and *must learn to listen honestly*, sympathetically, and with a willingness to learn both about the world and about the meaning of the faith that it confesses. The church can no longer gain a hearing from secular man simply on the basis of authority or on the assumption of a commonly shared religious heritage. On the contrary, it must first listen to contemporary man's analysis of the needs and problems that he faces in the nonreligious sectors of society where he spends most of his wakeful hours.

The need for dialogue with the world is, of course, not new. Only the name and the cultural situation of contemporary man are new, for there has always been need for dialogue between Christians and non-Christians as the former have sought to communicate the gospel to the latter. Indeed, on the surface nothing seems much more natural than the need for dialogue in communication; but in reality genuine dialogue about man's relationship to the Ultimate that is honest and open is extremely difficult both for the church and for secular man. The former is tempted to dogmatism, smugness, and pride based upon its claims to special revelation; and the latter is also tempted to similar exclusivenes and pride — to secularism — based upon absolutist claims of reason. Prior to the breakup of Christendom, however, the church rather than nonreligious man had all the built-in advantages in the communication that took place between the two; and for this reason the church was able to superimpose its theology and its morality upon Western society in a way that is no longer possible either in the West or in the world at large. In this new cultural situation the church is forced to meet secular man in his new freedom; and, for its part, the church has begun to discover in this encounter a new freedom of its own from a massive burden of religious and ideological accretions to faith. In the process of participating in this dialogue many Christians have been forced to jettison many outmoded, culture-bound religious forms; and they have been led to seek contemporary, more universal symbols for interpreting the meaning of faith to secular man. From the standpoint of Biblical faith, this liberation of the church from conventional religion and morality is essentially a liberation from idolatry, from self-deification, and from pride.

In more specific terms, dialogue of the church with the world — as opposed to a monologue of the church to the world — means an openness to a new understanding of God's will and purpose for man in the world. It means openness to new disclosures of the majesty and grandeur of creation. It means openness to the discovery of new dimensions of human community, a new understanding of the unity of mankind in a common destiny, and a new understanding of who one's neighbor really is in urbanized, industrial mass society. It means openness to new insights into the meaning of love and justice; it means new forms of morality. Dialogue means the willingness and readiness to learn as well as to teach; it means the readiness to listen as well as to speak.

Stated in theological terms, the basic issue involved in the Christian's dialogue with the world has to do with revelation, that is, with the manner in which God reveals himself to man. To refer to our earlier analysis of typical church-world relationships, the withdrawal type of church tends to see revelation as exclusively channeled through Scripture and the institutional churches. Upon the basis of this view of the secular world, genuine dialogue between the church and culture is impossible. But, judged from a Biblical point of view, this concept of revelation is far too narrow; it fails to take seriously the work and purpose of God as the Creator, who has endowed man with reason and the capacity for culture. At the other extreme, the folk church represents a form of culture-religion, whose basic values are derived from culture and reason rather than from revelation. Such a church no longer exists in dialogue with culture, for it has essentially been transformed into the image of society, whether the latter be religious or antireligious. Judged from a Biblical point of view, this concept of the autonomy of culture and this final appeal to natural reason as the only path to truth concerning man's nature and destiny are idolatrous.

In both the foregoing conceptions of the church vis-à-vis the world, communication takes the form of monologue. In contrast to these, the pattern of creative tension is based upon a recognition of the mutual need for dialogue. On the one hand, as far as secular man is concerned, this need is grounded in man's universal tendency toward self-centeredness and pride and in his quest for ultimate meaning.

On the other hand, as far as the church is concerned, both the need and the possibility of dialogue with the secular world are grounded in the Biblical doctrine of Creation as the basis of culture, in the Biblical concept of the universality of sin, and in the New Testament understanding of the church as a community of faith.

Biblical monotheism represents the conviction that God confronts man in and through his life in culture and in his secular history just as much as through the church. The church, therefore, is not the exclusive — or even the primary — channel through which the divine will is disclosed. Rather, the church is that company of believers which confesses the Lordship of God-in-Christ over both the church and the world. It seeks to discern and respond to the divine will and action that it discerns in the totality of human history; and in its own history it has learned to understand the divine will in terms of a continuing pattern of creative, judging, and reconciling action with which all men are confronted. Faith discerns this threefold action of God upon both the church and the world. God is at work in the world wherever human need is being met, wherever pride and idolatry are being judged, and wherever man's alienation from his Creator and his fellowmen is being overcome by reconciliation.

Sometimes this happens within the churches, but sometimes also the churches themselves are "the enemy" that actively opposes God's will.[2] Thus, for example, the Hebrew prophets again and again saw God using the heathen nations to punish Israel and bring her to repentance. Centuries later Jesus declared that publicans and harlots would go into the Kingdom before the scribes and Pharisees; he accused the religious leaders of barring the Kingdom against men's efforts to enter it. The scribes and Pharisees were indeed zealous in their efforts to win converts, but in making converts they made men children of even greater damnation! (Matt. 23:13-15.) On the other hand, Jesus marveled at the faith of a Roman centurion, for he had not encountered such great faith before even in Israel (Matt. 8:10-12). The Children of Israel, he warned, could not rely on their religious heritage to give them a place of special favor in the coming age; for many will come from the East and the West and sit at the banquet table with Abraham, Isaac, and Jacob in the Kingdom while the sons of the Kingdom will be thrown into outer darkness. (Matt. 8:10-12.) Moreover, he used the example of a despised Samaritan to show the meaning of neighbor-love (Luke 10:29-37). Finally, he foretold the punishment of those who called him "Lord" while they remained indifferent to the hunger, thirst, nakedness, and loneliness of their fellowmen, but he promised eternal life to those who had spontaneously and unselfishly ministered to the needs of his brethren (Matt. 25:31-46).

C. GOD AT THE CENTER OF LIFE: THE RECOVERY OF THE PUBLIC WORLD

In order to engage in dialogue with man in secular culture, the church must turn its eyes outward from itself toward the world. It must learn to speak of what God is doing in and through history and contemporary culture.

Yet the churches are constantly tempted to turn their gaze

inward upon themselves. They are tempted to self-glorying, to pride, and to idolatry. They are always in danger of becoming more concerned about their own institutional advantages — about buildings, programs, finances, membership rolls — than about worship and obedience to God. In all these ways they tend to substitute religion for faith, and in so doing they witness to themselves rather than to God. In order to enter into dialogue with contemporary man about the meaning of faith, the churches must cease to talk about God as if he were their private or special possession. They must cease to speak of him as if he dwelt only — or even primarily — in religious institutions and as if he could be known only through participation in distinctively religious activities and only in the sharing of a common emotional experience.

Understood in Biblical terms, the vocation of the church is to point men to the God whom they encounter in the midst of their daily relationships and in the totality of human history. Its purpose is to witness to the manner in which God confronts men in the midst of all the conflicts, anxieties, choices, and creative possibilities of life — not merely, or even primarily, in the private, spiritual sectors of human experience. The vocation of the church is not to call men apart from life, but to point them to the presence, the power, and the will of God in the midst of human affairs: to the Creator who has given man dominion over the earth and commanded him to subdue it (Gen. 1:26-28), to the Sovereign over men and nations who metes out judgments upon the nations, and to the Deliverer who does "mighty acts" in history and delivers men from bondage, from meaninglessness, and from death. Its vocation is not to make men religious in some conventional sense, but to witness to the forgiveness of God as the ultimate context of all human relationships and as the center and ground of life's meaning.

In our day learning to speak of God at the center of life instead of on its periphery means, increasingly, to speak of what he is doing in and through the public, collective sectors of modern life — in science, in politics, in automation, in urbanization, in education — as distinguished from the private sphere of individual, personal relationships. With the growth of science, technology, and urbanization, the public sector has expanded to include a larger and larger portion of contemporary life, and the influence of these forces has become more and more determinative in shaping the personal lives of each individual.

Yet the churches have been largely irrelevant to the major forces of social change in modern society, and they have remained isolated from the real centers of power. This isolation has been geographical, theological, and ethical. Historically, this isolation has been related to the traditional emphasis of the churches upon the family as the primary agency in the formation of beliefs and values. They have failed to recognize the extent to which the role of the family has been affected by the changing character of public education, mass communication, and urbanization. Hence, the churches have remained almost exclusively family-centered in their ministry. Typically, they have followed their members to the suburbs in order to escape the problems of the cities, and in the suburbs they have confined their ministry largely to residential neighborhoods.

This geographical isolation of the churches has been defended theologically by interpreting religion almost exclusively in individualistic and pietistic terms (personal faith, worship, and beliefs). Salvation has been interpreted in individualistic and otherworldly terms to the exclusion of the divine demand for obedience to God in the midst of the public life of the community and the nation.

In their concentration upon the more intimate relationships of the family as well as the personal dimensions of religion, the churches have bypassed the problem of the responsible use of power. They have failed to comprehend the ethical significance and the far-reaching effects of power in every area of modern life. Hence, they have often failed to understand the importance of economic, political, and military power in the effort to achieve social justice; and they have restricted the meaning and relevance of the Christian ethic of love to the realm of individual, personal relationships. The private world has been divorced from the public world, and the former has been made the special sphere of religious concern.

In Bonhoeffer's phrase, the churches have pointed to God on the " periphery of life " rather than at its center. From the perspective of Biblical monotheism, a god who is limited to the private sphere of religion is an idol, and a god who can be edged out of the center of the world's history is not the true God. The God of Biblical faith is Lord of heaven and earth, and his power and his will are the ultimate realities that shape the final destinies of men and nations. He is the universal center of meaning; and he is sovereign over all that he has called, and is calling, into being. The great challenge to the church in our day, therefore, is to learn to speak meaningfully of the presence, the power, and the will of God in the public sector of contemporary life where modern man so largely " lives and moves and has his being." For the God of Christian faith is neither primarily a God of individuals in their private solitariness before him nor the God of humanity as a faceless, nameless mass. On the contrary, he is the God of individuals-in-community in this mundane world; and his creating, judging, and reconciling will is present to men wherever they meet one another in both their individual and their collective needs and potentialities.

D. WHERE CHURCH AND WORLD MEET: OUR COMMON HUMANITY

The vocation of the church, as we have said, is to point men to God at the center of life, and this means to witness to what he is doing in the public world. Its calling is to witness to the will and purpose of God in this world — whether men presently understand the latter in secular, religious, or atheistic terms — and to point to the tension between the divine purpose and what men are actually seeking and doing here.

But the church is called to witness to the divine will and

purpose in a world in which language about God is no longer meaningful for many people, particularly in relation to large segments of their experience. In this situation many theologians — including Paul Tillich, Dietrich Bonhoeffer, Bishop John A. T. Robinson, and Harvey Cox — have attempted to translate the gospel into secular, or nonreligious, language.

A few "radical theologians" have even maintained that the gospel has only a secular meaning — that is, only a nonreligious, humanist content. Paul M. van Buren, for example, using the tools of linguistic analysis, contends that the entire content of the gospel can be put into secular terms.[3] Love for one's fellowman, he insists, is the only kind of love there is; hence, the meaning of the first commandment of Jesus is included in the commandment of neighbor-love rather than the latter being comprehended in the first, as it is in Jesus' teaching. Certain other radical theologians, believing that it is impossible to speak meaningfully about God in the contemporary world, sometimes speak of "the death of God." Frequently what they mean by this phrase is not made clear. If the declaration that "God is dead" were intended only as an existential statement, meaning that modern man had ceased to experience the reality of God, it would obviously contain a great deal of truth. However, some of the writers — for example, Thomas J. J. Altizer — claim to be making an objective statement about God, namely, that he has died.[4] Moreover, they appear to affirm that God — or Christ — will be raised from the dead in the midst of the secular, profane (nonreligious) world. Used in this sense, the affirmation that "God is dead" is intended as a protest against religion (not against faith) and as an affirmation of the secular over against every form of world-denial. The difficulty, however, is that this form of world-affirmation ignores the transcendence of God, as Creator and Judge, over the whole created order. It substitutes faith in Christ for faith in the God to whom Jesus pointed men as the living Lord of heaven and earth. It separates the love of Christ from the power of God and thus undercuts the ultimate meaning of the gospel as good

news. It resolves the tension between the church and the world
by affirming only the secular world. Such an attempt to be relevant to contemporary culture does not provide a basis for
genuine dialogue with the secular world; on the contrary, it
substitutes a monologue of the world for that of the church. In
effect, it represents a new form of culture-religion which is essentially humanist and avowedly atheistic.

The need to find new ways of interpreting the meaning of
Christian faith to contemporary men whose lives have been
largely shaped by nonreligious forces is urgent. It cannot be
ignored, and it cannot be met by superficial or theocratic efforts on the part of the churches to impose faith upon an alien
culture and upon men who no longer see its relevance to their
daily existence. The simple fact is that the traditional language
of the devout is not universally understood in the world or
even in the churches. Moreover, the use of this language — as
Paul Tillich and Bishop Robinson, for example, have pointed
out — may itself create a barrier to understanding since, instead
of pointing men to God (the Ultimate One), it may in reality
point them only to an idol or to a great irrelevance.

But the existence of God is not dependent upon men's understanding of him or even upon their ability to speak meaningfully of him. Just as the Israelites often worshiped idols
even when they thought they were worshiping the Lord, so
Christians also worship idols when they worship tribalistic and
meaningless conceptions of God rather than the One beyond
all the polytheism and idolatry of popular religion, the One in
whom all things — individual and universal, private and public,
past, present, and future — cohere. The problem is not that
the " Lord of heaven and earth " — the Power and the Will
which calls all things into being and presides over their final
destinies — is dead, but rather that the idolatrous character of
much of contemporary religion has been exposed and is being
judged.

In this situation, it has been argued, dialogue between the
church and the secular world is a prerequisite for the recovery

out of man's wrestling with the basically human experiences of anxiety, dependence, freedom, responsibility, and death in the context of the history of Israel and the church. It is the conviction that God is the ultimate giver of all human existence. Man cannot finally escape him or wish him away, for he is the final Power and Will with which men and nations must in the end come to terms.

Dialogue between the church and the world takes shape, therefore, around all those relationships and decisions which affect the quality and potentialities of human life. It takes shape around all the values and choices that influence the possibilities and limitations of human life in both its private and its collective modes of existence. And it is only as the church engages in dialogue with the world about this common humanity that the meaning of faith becomes clarified both for secular man and for the believer.

This conception of man's common humanity as the meeting ground of church and world implies a recovery of the New Testament view of the world as the sphere of the church's work. It rests upon the New Testament understanding of the world as the place where the church is to be found. For the church is not primarily an ecclesiastical institution but a community of faith. This community does not come into existence when it gathers for corporate worship and then cease to be when its members return to their homes and daily occupations. On the contrary, as a community of faith the church exists more in its scattered than in its congregational form. Measured both in terms of time and in terms of the possibilities for witnessing to the world, the church exists primarily outside its ecclesiastical form. It exists as a scattered community of the faithful who, though scattered, share a common faith in the Lordship of Christ and seek to be his witnesses and his agents of reconciliation in the midst of an estranged, alienated, and Godless world. To be sure, the church also in obedience gathers together for worship — for cleansing, for praise, for renewal of its strength, and for rededication of itself; but it does

of the relevance of the church to the life of contemporary man. But how is such dialogue possible? Where can it begin? Is there any common ground for mutual understanding and discussion? Is there any common language that can be used? Must the church speak only in nonreligious — or, if one prefers, in nontheological — language? And if the church speaks only in secular terms, can it still point men to the God of Christian faith?

The clue to the answer to these questions lies in the Christian understanding of man's common humanity and also in the incarnation. In our day, at least, relevant dialogue between the church and the world must begin at the point of a common attempt to answer the question about the nature and meaning of human existence rather than the question about the nature and existence of God. In theological terms, it begins with anthropology rather than theology. In an age in which traditional language about God has increasingly lost its meaning for multitudes of people, it is pointless for the church to demand the acceptance of orthodox creeds and participation in conventional forms of worship on the basis of ecclesiastical authority. Rather, the church must learn to go into the world and establish a common ground with secular man by sharing the experience of those "outside the camp." Dialogue must begin with the identification of the church with secular man as he is, and with the Christian's being a "gracious neighbor" to his fellow-man in the midst of his secularity and estrangement from the church.

Before meaningful dialogue about God can take place, the church must, first of all, identify itself with secular man at the points of his aspirations and potentialities as well as his limitations and experience of guilt, alienation, and meaninglessness. But in so doing the church does not cease to be the church; on the contrary, this is the form of the church's witness to the world rather than to itself as a community of the saved. This is the form of the church in its proper role of a servant. In thus identifying itself with the world — by being willing to be unrecognized in conventional religious circles — the church is only following the example of its Lord in his incarnation and rejection and death outside the Holy City. For Christ too appeared as the incognito Messiah, thus removing every religious, theological, and human barrier to identification with his fellowmen — regardless of their faith, their reputation, their status, or their nationality — in order that he might reach them in their need and bring them to the fuller life of the Kingdom of God.

In the modern scientifically oriented world, identification with the neighbor means identification with contemporary man in his strength — in his ability to control and harness the forces of nature, to create a society of abundance, to control disease, and to unleash well-nigh unlimited quantities of power — as well as in his weakness. Identification with secular man means understanding the progress that the latter has made in science and technology; it means understanding why he has come to feel autonomous and able to control his own destiny. It means appropriating the knowledge of self which has been the fruit of the social sciences since Marx and Freud. It means participation in contemporary man's increasingly "mature" understanding of the natural world and in his expanding control over the external forces that affect human life.

The church must understand why contemporary man feels autonomous, but it cannot accept secular man's interpretation of this autonomy as final. The church ought to welcome the world's "coming of age," but it cannot accept the world's understanding of maturity as either adequate or realistic. The task of the church vis-à-vis the secular world is not to call the latter back into a stage of childhood and superstition; on the contrary, its task is to witness to the final dependence of secular man upon God and to the Lordship of God-in-Christ over contemporary man and contemporary culture. From the standpoint of Christian faith, the final measure of mature manhood is revealed in Christ, in whom both the divine will and authentic selfhood were perfectly united.

The question at issue between secular man and Christian

faith, therefore, is the question about the nat of human existence. It is not a question abo standing of empirical phenomena, but rather a the meaning and measure of man's true human it means "to be human" in the midst of this and in the ultimate context of man's life.

As the church enters into dialogue with cont about the meaning of our common humanity, it context of its participation in a community of fai itual roots go back to ancient Israel. The churc vorce itself from the history and the traditions of nity and from the understanding of human existe developed within the latter. Indeed, if the church itself off from that community of faith, it would ha to offer contemporary man that would make the sl ference to him. The church and the secular world r point of a shared humanity, but the two understand and final significance of this common life in radicall ways.

Man's common humanity is the point at which faith relevant to secular man. But the discovery of a ground of potentialities and needs is not the end but beginning of the church's ministry to the world. This the starting point for dialogue and communication, but not provide the sole content of that dialogue; for the quent dialogue centers around two quite different inte tions of the nature and meaning of this common hum istence. Thus, secular man seeks to find the ultimate me of human life in humanist, nontheistic terms, whereas (tian faith understands the secular to be the sphere of (activity.

Christian faith sees the secular world as being finally pendent upon the Divine Will. This is the ultimate and d sive relationship in which man, whether secular or religic stands. This conviction is not a matter of religious man's w ing that this should be so. Rather, it is a conviction wroug

so in order that it may go forth to glorify God in its scattered life of daily obedience and daily service.

For the church to be in the world in our day demands the discovery of radical new forms of the church and the recovery of the New Testament conception of the ministry of all Christians as "the people of God." It has become obvious to the leadership of even the most tradition-oriented denominations that institution-centered and clergy-centered churches cannot enter effectively into the world. Here the churches are being confronted with their greatest dilemma and their severest spiritual testing. Some form of institutional structure seems to be necessary to the ongoing spiritual life of the community of faith, but it is just as difficult for religious institutions to lose themselves in the service of mankind as it is for other institutions and organizations. The churches are constantly tempted to choose only those types of activities and programs which will foster their own growth in terms of membership, financial support, and building programs. It is hard for them to assume the form of a servant and minister to their fellow humanity simply as fellow human beings in need, as persons for whom Christ died, rather than as potential converts and potential members of the churches. But the renewal of the church depends upon its obedience in going into the world and spending itself in service of the human needs that it finds there.

For the church to go into the world in order to spend itself in love for the neighbor means that it must find ways of establishing community, or oneness, with men wherever they are found and particularly at the nonreligious sectors of their experience. It means identification with them in the slum, in the union hall, in positions of management, and in the dilemmas of politics. It means finding ways of interpreting the meaning of faith where men are involved in culture and in the community at large rather than calling them out of the real world into a withdrawn, spiritual community. It means identification with contemporary man in his alienation, his doubt, his false value systems, his narrow conceptions of community, and his depersonalized conception of himself. It means taking this secular man seriously; it means meeting him where he is and seeking to understand him. It means helping him to understand himself in the light of Christian faith. It means helping him to identify *his* problems and come to grips with them, within the context of a koinonia in which he is accepted, understood, and sustained by a community of faith and love.

For the church to go into the world means, increasingly in our day, that it must find ways of making its witness in the areas of public policy formation and public responsibility. It means being present not only among the victims of collective injustice, but also at the centers of freedom and power where human life is affected for good or evil. In a pluralistic society, for the church to be in the world means being present primarily in nonecclesiastical forms and in the midst of an essentially secular, or nonreligious, community. It means working through nonchurch structures and discovering new patterns of ministry.

It is not possible within this study to examine the variety of new, experimental forms of the church that have emerged in recent years; nor is it possible to analyze the emerging conceptions of a variety of ministries alongside the pastoral ministry. But regardless of whatever new forms the church may take as it seeks to become functionally relevant to contemporary society, it is clear that the church can really be present in the world only as it is there in its laity in their daily tasks; and it is also clear that the most adequate safeguard against the ideological distortion of the Christian faith — that is, against the culture-Christianity of the folk church — lies in a deepening participation in the ecumenical movement.

E. THE CHRISTIAN LIFE AS DEPUTYSHIP

If the church is to be present in the world, it must be present wherever human beings are related to one another in freedom and in responsibility. It must be present in the midst of all human relationships where belief struggles against unbelief and where human need and human potentiality are found. It must be present wherever human beings are related to one another either as individuals or as members of groups. Here is where the call to witness and to service comes to the church. Here is where the Christian, whether pastor or layman, is called to a life of trust, obedience, and love.

Due to the impact of both the physical and the social sciences, particularly in the fields of communication and transportation, modern man has come to a new comprehension of the social dimensions of human existence. No man is able to exist as an isolated individual. Each individual lives in many communities, beginning with the family and extending through a variety of kinship, residential, occupational, civic, and religious communities to the universal community to which the whole human family is bound.

The nature of these communities has changed as society has changed. Contemporary man has a fuller insight into the manner and extent to which the individual is dependent upon these groups and responsible for them. But the concept of the individual-in-community is not the discovery of modern science; it is deeply rooted in the Biblical understanding of man – of his nature, his dignity, and his essential humanity. The Biblical writers portray man as a being who exists in families and in a variety of economic, political, and religious communities; moreover, each person is responsible to and for the many neighbors whom he meets in each of these contexts. Each of these communities is grounded in the Divine Will. Each has its ultimate meaning and purpose in relation to God; for it is he who has created man to live, not as an isolated individual without companions, without language, and without culture, but as a social being, who not only is dependent upon his fellowmen but who also affects them for good or evil.

It is precisely in the midst of these relationships that a person confronts his fellowman as neighbor. This is the only place where the *real* neighbor – as opposed to some abstract, spiritualized, and, therefore, depersonalized conception of the neighbor – is present. And this is where the summons comes to love one's fellowman — namely, in day-to-day relationships where he lives and where his daily needs are being affirmed or denied. This is the concrete place where freedom and responsibility meet and where it is possible for the Christian to love the neighbor in a concrete, other-centered, human way.

Traditionally, Protestants have sought to interpret man's responsibility for his fellowmen in terms of " vocation." But, like " ministry," this concept has become so restricted in meaning that it is largely irrelevant for the laity in their understanding of their role as Christians in the secular world. Luther and Calvin, however, used the term to apply to the daily work, or occupations, of all believers. In so doing they were rejecting the medieval Roman Catholic notion that only the monks and priests had a divine vocation in their specifically religious forms of work. Against this view the Reformers insisted that every Christian, whatever his daily task, is called to serve God in and through his particular occupation. Thus, one's daily work is transformed into a divine vocation or calling insofar as it is done in faith and ministers to the needs of one's fellowmen. Whatever their occupations may be, all believers are called to subordinate their own aims and goals to the will of God precisely in their daily, secular life. In Calvin's language, a Christian's vocation is " the station " where, in God's providence, the believer stands in the world and where he is called to glorify God. In Luther's language, it is the place where the believer is called to obey the second commandment of Jesus by serving the neighbor in his concrete, mundane needs.

The Reformers tended to interpret the concept of vocation largely in occupational terms. Thus, in its emphasis upon work, the Protestant ethic, particularly in Calvinism, provided a major stimulus to the development of capitalism; but it has not generated an equal concern for economic justice, nor has it been able to cope with the problem of mass leisure in an automated society. Nevertheless, the Reformers did recognize that the Christian is called to serve his fellowman through his daily relationships *in the world* and that this call comes equally to all Christians, not simply or even primarily to the clergy.

In our day the concept of vocation needs to be extended to include all those relationships in which one person influences the well-being of other people, including the family, positions of community responsibility, participation in politics, and the formation of public policy in every area affecting the common life. Such relationships are the functional points at which love becomes relevant to human life. These are the places where men meet each other in some measure of freedom and, therefore, with some measure of responsibility. This is true whether the relationships are personal, as in the family, or impersonal, as in large-scale economic and political organizations.

Recognizing the variety of relationships of freedom and dependence in contemporary life, Bonhoeffer used the term *deputyship* to describe the *form* of Christian responsibility in realistic, concrete terms. This interpretation of the form of Christian responsibility was based upon Bonhoeffer's understanding of Jesus' entire life and ministry as a life of deputyship for all men as the incarnate Son of God:

> Jesus was not the individual, desiring to achieve a perfection of his own, but He lived only as the one who has taken up into Himself and who bears within Himself the selves of all men. All His living, His action and His dying was deputyship. In Him there is fulfilled what the living, the action and the suffering of men ought to be. In this real deputyship which constitutes His human existence He is the responsible person *par excellence.* . . . Whether or not life resists, it is now always deputyship, for life or for death, just as the father is always a father, for good or for evil.[5]

In his own life Jesus revealed the meaning of human existence at its deepest level as a life of freedom and of living in responsibility for one's fellowmen. Responsibility is possible, Bonhoeffer declares,[6] only if there is "complete surrender of one's own life to the other man." It is only the "selfless" man who lives responsibly, and this means that "only the selfless man *lives*."

Human life, Bonhoeffer held, is essentially a life of deputy-ship because man is a being who lives in many communities in which he must act in the place of, and for, other people. Thus, a parent acts for the children, working for them, interceding for them, suffering for them, serving as their guardians, and making decisions in their behalf relating to their physical needs, to their religious and educational development, and to the kind of society in which they will be destined to live. Similarly, the employer, the statesman, the judge, or any member of a group engaged in the formation or administration of public policy acts, for good or evil, in behalf of other people whose welfare he affects through his decisions and action. In all these relationships, one individual acts for other people who are in some way dependent upon him. He represents their various needs, potentialities, and interests in these concrete relationships, and in this very real sense he acts as their deputy. Although he may not choose to live in these communities, he cannot evade this responsibility through any effort to act as if he were not involved in them.

The fact that Jesus did not have the special responsibilities of marriage, of a family, and of a profession does not mean that he lived outside the field of responsibility; indeed, this very circumstance made all the clearer the meaning of his own special responsibility and his own special deputyship for all men.[7] Because of it he revealed all the more clearly the meaning of a life lived in complete obedience to God and in complete responsibility for all men. The Christian's deputyship is different from Jesus' deputyship because the former stands in concrete relationships different from those in which Jesus stood, but in his deputyship for all men Jesus revealed the fullest possible meaning of human freedom and responsibility in the universal community of mankind. This is the *quality* of life that he summons his followers to exemplify in their own special places of responsibility, including not only their daily occupations but also all those other positions — as parents, as citizens, as civic leaders — in which each person bears some measure of responsibility for his fellowman.

F. THE ECUMENICAL MOVEMENT AND THE CHRISTIAN'S SOCIAL CONSCIENCE

The ultimate human community in which our lives are set is the universal community of mankind. Morally and religiously speaking, the history of the race is the history of the discovery of the meaning of this common humanity. In particular, the story of Israel's spiritual development is the story of the emergence of faith in one God who is conceived to be the Lord of the nations and who wills the salvation of all peoples in a universal community of love. For Christians the fullest and most compelling manifestation of God's love and of his redemptive and reconciling purpose is found in Jesus Christ, who gave himself in life and in death for all men and who even in his death prayed for those who tormented him.

Viewed in negative terms, the history of mankind is the story of man's efforts to deny the essential unity of all men in one common humanity. It is the story of man's universal and persistent tendency toward self-centeredness rather than inclusiveness, toward alienation from his neighbor rather than reconciliation of the estranged. The tendency toward idolizing the interests of one's own limited group is found in all human communities, religious as well as secular. It is found in churches as well as in economic and political groups; and, indeed, the latter seek their final justification in religious and theological terms. Biblical faith, however, sees God's judgment falling upon all men's efforts to absolutize their closed societies and make them their final centers of value, their ultimate objects of loyalty. For beyond all men's exclusive groups, beyond their broken communities, God wills the creation of a Kingdom in which the essential humanity of all persons is fulfilled in justice and love.

As a community of faith which understands the unity of

mankind in terms of the creative and reconciling will of God, the church is sent into the world to witness to this oneness in acts of love and obedience in its common life. In the words of H. Richard Niebuhr, which were cited above, its mission is " the increase among men of the love of God and neighbor." In its very nature, the church is a community of believers who have discovered their oneness with each other in Christ and through him their oneness also with all of those for whom Christ died. It is a koinonia that transcends all barriers to love and brotherhood; it rests upon a common faith in one Lord who offers himself to all men and calls them into a common fellowship and a common service. Its ministry is a ministry of reconciliation in a world torn asunder by hostility, conflict, and war.

But the tragedy of the church is that it has oftentimes been itself an agent of division and conflict based, not upon the tension between the gospel and the world, but upon religious, social, and national pride and self-interest. The churches have set Christian against Christian as well as against Jew, pagan, and contemporary atheists; they have set class against class, race against race, nation against nation. They have set Christendom and themselves against the world. Instead of pointing men, all men, to their final dependence upon one righteous, sovereign Power and to love as the divinely ordained law of life, the churches have often been agents of economic and political warfare.

As we have seen, the churches in this country have become identified, to a very large degree, with particular class, racial, and even political groups. The result has been that the former have generally lost their power to be agents of reconciliation in healing the major social cleavages in American life. Their impotence in this regard has been most clearly evident in the area of race relations, but it is also evident in their tendency to view economic and political issues in terms of the special interests of their particular constituents. Instead of casting out the demons of prejudice, racism, nationalism, and economic injustice, the churches have themselves fallen under the sway of these same demonic powers.

For its impotence to do the reconciling deed and speak the reconciling word, for permitting the light that has been given to it to become darkness, for its inability to leaven the society in which it is set, the church is called to repentance: this is its humiliation and its summons to judgment. Yet, despite its unfaithfulness, it is not utterly forsaken: this is its glory and its hope. For despite its withdrawal, its self-seeking, and its schisms, it is never finally able to escape or deny its mission to exist in the world and for the world; it is never able finally to escape the summons to extend its compassion to the ends of the earth; and it is never able finally to deny the unity of all believers in Christ. It is never able finally to escape the mandate of its Lord to take, like him, the form of a servant and give itself for humanity.

Although there can be no final guarantee against the perversion of Christian faith into some form of ideology, the most effective safeguard against such a distortion of the gospel lies in a deeper participation in the ecumenical movement. As we have noted above, local congregations tend to be more exclusive than denominations in terms of race and class, but by far the greatest opportunities for churches to transcend not only racial and economic but also national and politico-ideological barriers are found at the ecumenical level of the church's life. In its earlier stages the ecumenical movement represented a growing effort toward cooperation and unity within Protestantism. Its most striking achievements in this period were the formation of the Federal Council of the Churches of Christ in America in 1908 (since 1950 the National Council of the Churches of Christ in the U.S.A.) and the World Council of Churches. A number of important ecumenical conferences, including the famous Oxford Conference on Church, Community, and State (1937), prepared the way for the formation of the World Council of Churches at Amsterdam in 1948. Representatives of a number of the Orthodox churches were present as observers at the Amsterdam Assembly, but both the Russian Orthodox Church and the Roman Catholic Church declined to be represented at that meeting. Subsequently, however, the positions of both these latter bodies have changed radically. The Orthodox church of Russia — along with the Orthodox churches of Rumania, Bulgaria, and Poland — was received into full membership in the World Council of Churches at its Third Assembly in New Delhi in 1961. The Roman Catholic Church was also represented at the New Delhi Assembly by a number of distinguished observers.

This new phase of the ecumenical movement, aimed at the exploration of means of greater cooperation and unity of Protestants and Roman Catholics, was dramatized in the Second Vatican Council, 1962–1965. This Council, inspired and convened by the late Pope John XXIII and continued by Pope Paul VI, constituted a major landmark in the history of the Roman Catholic Church, and it also marked a real breakthrough in the ecumenical movement as a whole.

Insofar as the theme of the present study is concerned, the Second Vatican Council represents a concerted and unprecedented effort of the Roman Catholic Church toward the renewal of that body by opening itself to the needs of the modern world. This purpose was symbolized by Pope John XXIII when he opened the windows of the Vatican to let " fresh breezes " blow into the church. More particularly, in its clearcut affirmation of religious liberty, in its greater appreciation both of man's achievements in secular culture and also of his responsibility for the historical future, and in its clearer recognition that the church exists to serve the world (all mankind), the Second Ecumenical Council reflected changes in the Roman Catholic Church similar to those which have been taking place in contemporary Protestantism.

In view of the New Testament understanding of the unity of the church as the body of Christ and as the koinonia, contemporary churches are called to manifest this oneness in their own life. They are called to take their stand within the larger community of faith to the end that the universal church of faith may become visible in the world.

This growing ecumenical movement is one of the most significant developments in the modern church. In a day when the secular world is being molded more and more into a single economic and political reality, it is imperative that the churches rediscover the universality of the gospel and the meaning of community which transcends ecclesiastical, racial, economic, and political boundaries. The church will be able to be truly universal only if it is able to draw peoples from all ideological backgrounds into a common fellowship of faith in which their differences are effectively overcome through the discovery of a more ultimate unity.

Every individual congregation and every denomination in every age is tempted to use the church and the gospel to sanctify its own most cherished cultural values. Christian faith is thus distorted into an ideology, the primary function of which is to provide metaphysical and theological sanctions for the prevailing values and patterns of culture. When this happens, the universal meaning and relevance of the gospel are lost. Instead of breaking through man's narrow groups and providing the nucleus of a universal community, such Christianity becomes captive to culture, and the real meaning of the gospel is obscured.

An incident in the life of the early church is instructive at this point. In Galatians, Paul describes a dispute that arose among the leaders in the Christian community concerning the requirements that should be placed upon the Gentiles who became converts to Christianity. The leaders of the church at Jerusalem held that the Gentiles should first be required to submit to circumcision before being received into the church. Paul, on the other hand, looked upon this requirement as a legalism carried over from Judaism, and he insisted that the gospel freed man from this requirement of the Law. Paul eventually won this struggle by taking Titus, an uncircumcised Greek convert, together with Barnabas, his fellow missionary, up to Jerusalem and presenting the matter personally to the leaders of the church. The latter were convinced by the results of Paul's ministry among the Gentiles that the gospel did in fact free the Gentiles from this requirement. To impose it in the name of the gospel, Paul argued, would deny the very essence of the gospel; it would be to subject converts to a new bondage instead of proclaiming to them their true liberty in Christ.

In essence the struggle between Paul and the Judaizers goes on in every generation, although it takes place in many forms. This debate is necessary because the faith of each believer and each denomination is a compound of gospel and culture (Law). Each church and each individual receives the gospel as a " treasure in earthen vessels." In our day the ecumenical movement provides a new, providential setting in which the continuing debate concerning the form and the content of the gospel can most responsibly take place. Direct, personal involvement in a fellowship that cuts across racial, class, and national barriers is indispensable for a radical understanding of the universality and the freedom of Christian faith. For it is in such an inclusive fellowship that the tendencies toward ethnocentrism which beset every group can most effectively be exposed. Here Christians from widely different theological and cultural traditions are drawn together into a single community with a common faith and a common loyalty. Here in our day they are discovering anew their *oneness* in Christ and through him with all men.

NOTES

NOTES

I. A Fellowship of Class

1. Joseph A. Kahl, *The American Class Structure* (Rinehart & Company, Inc., 1957), pp. 210 ff.

2. *Ibid.*, pp. 184–187. Other sociologists divide American communities into varying numbers of classes. W. Lloyd Warner and Paul S. Lunt, for example, found six major classes in Yankee City: upper-upper, lower-upper, upper-middle, lower-middle, upper-lower, and lower-lower. See W. Lloyd Warner and Paul S. Lunt, *The Status System of a Modern Community* (Yale University Press, 1942), p. 22.

3. Kahl, *op. cit.*, p. 201.

4. Leon H. Keyserling, *Progress or Poverty: The U. S. at the Crossroads* (Conference on Economic Progress, 1964), pp. 15–17.

5. *Ibid.*, pp. 22–23.

6. *Ibid.*, p. 15.

7. Barbara Ward, "World Poverty and the Christian Conscience." This address, delivered before the Sixth World Order Study Conference in St. Louis, Mo., was part of the second series of Dag Hammarskjöld Lectures.

8. Emilio E. Castro, "The New Threat: Rich Nations and Poor Nations." This address, delivered before the Sixth World Order Study Conference in St. Louis, Mo., was part of the second series of Dag Hammarskjöld Lectures.

9. Liston Pope, "Religion and the Class Structure," in *Class, Status, and Power,* ed. by Reinhard Bendix and Seymour Martin Lipset (The Free Press of Glencoe, 1953), p. 321.

10. Cf. Kenneth W. Underwood, *Protestant and Catholic* (Beacon Press, Inc., 1957), p. 203.

11. Donald J. Bogue, *The Population of the United States* (The Free Press of Glencoe, 1959), p. 703. These two nationwide polls included a total sample of approximately 5,000 households.

12. *Ibid.*, p. 705.

13. *Ibid.*, pp. 700–702.

14. *Ibid.*, pp. 699–700.

15. See E. Franklin Frazier, *The Negro Church in America* (Schocken Books, 1963), Ch. 4.

16. Gibson Winter, *The Suburban Captivity of the Churches* (Doubleday & Company, Inc., 1961), pp. 39–58.

17. Walter Kloetzli, *The City Church — Death or Renewal* (Muhlenberg Press, 1961), p. 185.

18. *Information Service*, Vol. XXXIV, No. 35 (Oct. 29, 1955), p. 2.

19. *The Christian Advocate*, April 21, 1955. Editorial, "The Church in Industrial Areas."

20. Earl D. C. Brewer, with the assistance of Marie Townsend, *A Study of the General Superintendency of The Methodist Church*, Part II (Religious Research Center, Emory University, 1963), p. 82.

21. "A Study Report on the Philadelphia Assembly: The Characteristics and Opinions of 800 Church Leaders," *Information Service*, Vol. XLIII, No. 15 (Sept. 26, 1964), pp. 1–2.

22. *Ibid.* The remaining 23.8 percent of the respondents did not indicate their family income.

23. David W. Barry in *Cities and Churches: Readings on the Urban Church*, ed. by Robert Lee (The Westminster Press, 1962), pp. 281–283.

24. Gibson Winter, *op. cit.*, pp. 55–56.

25. See Kenneth W. Underwood, *op. cit.*, pp. 189–206.

II. A Fellowship of Race

1. Kyle Haselden, *The Racial Problem in Christian Perspective* (Harper & Brothers, 1959), p. 29.

2. C. Vann Woodward, *The Strange Career of Jim Crow* (Oxford University Press, Inc., 1955), Chs. I and II.

3. Frank S. Loescher, *The Protestant Church and the Negro* (Association Press, 1948), pp. 51–63, 76–78.

4. Galen R. Weaver, "Racial Integration in the Churches," *Social Action*, Vol. XXII, No. 4 (Dec., 1955), pp. 11–12.

5. This was one of eight agencies that merged in 1950 to form the National Council of the Churches of Christ in the United States of America.

6. Frank S. Loescher, *op. cit.*, pp. 77–78.

7. It was estimated that approximately one third of the 300,000 Negro Roman Catholics in the United States were in mixed congregations at that time.

8. Frank S. Loescher, *op. cit.*, p. 79.

9. His survey of local churches was overweighted with denominations having predominantly northern constituencies and liberal traditions in race relations, and it did not include any southern denominations.

10. These, together with their respective memberships, were as follows: the National Baptist Convention, U.S.A., Inc. — 5,000,000; the National Baptist Convention of America — 2,668,799; the African Methodist Episcopal Church — 1,166,301; the African Methodist Episcopal Zion Church — 770,000; and the Christian Methodist Episcopal Church — 392,167. *Yearbook of American Churches*, Edition for 1962, ed. by Benson Y. Landis (National Council of the Churches of Christ in the U.S.A., 1961), pp. 249–253.

11. Alfred Kramer, " Racial Integration in Three Protestant Denominations," *The Journal of Educational Sociology*, Oct., 1954, pp. 59–68.

12. Galen R. Weaver, " Racial Practices in Congregational Christian Churches," *Social Action*, Vol. XXV, No. 5 (Jan., 1959), pp. 3–11.

13. Liston Pope, *The Kingdom Beyond Caste* (Friendship Press, 1957), p. 112.

14. David Loth and Harold Fleming, *Integration — North and South* (The Fund for the Republic, 1956), pp. 37–44, 91–96.

15. J. Philip Wogaman, *Methodism's Challenge in Race Relations* (Public Affairs Press, 1960), p. 10.

16. J. Oscar Lee, " Religion Among Racial and Ethnic Minorities," *The Annals of the American Academy of Political and Social Science*, No. 332 (Nov., 1960), p. 123.

17. S. Garry Oniki, " Interracial Churches in American Protestantism," *Social Action*, Vol. XVI, No. 1 (Jan. 15, 1950), pp. 4–22. Oniki noted, however, that while there are hundreds of Protestant churches in such areas, " one must comb the nation to find a score of significant interracial churches."

18. S. Garry Oniki, " Residential Desegregation: Confrontation for the Churches," *Christianity and Crisis*, Vol. XXI, No. 9 (May 29, 1961), pp. 91–95.

19. Cf. Will D. Campbell, *Race and the Renewal of the Church* (The Westminster Press, 1962), p. 9.

20. F. Ernest Johnson (ed.), *The Social Work of the Churches*

(Department of Research and Education of the Federal Council of the Churches of Christ in America, 1930), pp. 154–155.

21. See Kenneth K. Bailey, *Southern White Protestantism in the Twentieth Century* (Harper & Row, Publishers, Inc., 1964), pp. 147–148.

22. Ralph McGill, " Dynamics of Religious News," *The Atlanta Journal and The Atlanta Constitution*, Vol. 15, No. 19 (Oct. 11, 1964), p. 1.

23. E. Franklin Frazier, *The Negro Church in America.*

24. The NAACP reported, for example, that in 1963 at least one fifth of the presidents of its 941 branches were ministers. For an analysis of the role of the Negro church in the Negro revolution, see William Brink and Louis Harris, *The Negro Revolution in America* (Simon and Schuster, 1964), Ch. 6, " The Role of the Negro Church."

25. For an account of the work of this commission and an interpretation of the relationship of the churches to the civil rights movement generally, see Robert W. Spike, *The Freedom Revolution and the Churches* (Association Press, 1965).

26. *Ibid.*, pp. 86–87.

27. Ernest Q. Campbell and Thomas C. Pettigrew, *Christians in Racial Crisis* (Public Affairs Press, 1959), pp. 127 ff.

III.   Religious Pluralism and the Churches

1. Anson Phelps Stokes, *Church and State in the United States* (Harper & Brothers, 1950), Vol. I, p. 442.

2. William Warren Sweet, *The Story of Religion in America* (Harper & Row, Publishers, Inc., Rev. ed., 1950), p. 66.

3. Thomas G. Sanders, *Protestant Concepts of Church and State* (Holt, Rinehart and Winston, Inc., 1964), pp. 185–187.

4. M. Searle Bates, *Religious Liberty: An Inquiry* (International Missionary Council, 1945), p. 288.

5. *Ibid.*

6. Anson Phelps Stokes, *op. cit.*, Vol. I, p. 446.

7. Cf. Thomas G. Sanders, *op. cit.*, pp. 185–187.

8. Franklin H. Littell, *From State Church to Pluralism: A Protestant Interpretation of Religion in American History* (Doubleday & Company, Inc., 1962), p. 49.

9. Figures for the years 1850 ff. are taken from the *Yearbook of American Churches*, Edition for 1966, ed. by Benson Y. Landis (National Council of the Churches of Christ in the U.S.A., 1966), p. 218.

10. *Yearbook of American Churches,* Edition for 1966, p. 220.

11. Will Herberg, *Protestant-Catholic-Jew* (Doubleday & Company, Inc., 1955), pp. 32 ff.

12. D. L. Munby, *The Idea of a Secular Society and Its Significance for Christians* (Oxford University Press, Inc., 1963), p. 14.

13. Compare Harvey Cox, *The Secular City* (The Macmillan Company, 1965), pp. 18–21.

14. "America's Four Conspiracies," by John Courtney Murray, in *Religion in America,* ed. by John Cogley (Meridian Books, 1958), p. 40.

15. Will Herberg, *op. cit.*

16. John C. Bennett, *When Christians Make Political Decisions* (Association Press, 1964), p. 106.

IV.   The Faith of Israel

1. G. Ernest Wright, "The Faith of Israel," in *The Interpreter's Bible* (Abingdon Press, 1952), Vol. I, p. 389. Cf. G. Ernest Wright, *God Who Acts* (SCM Press, Ltd., 1952), Ch. 1, "The Church's Need of the Old Testament."

2. Cf. H. Richard Niebuhr in collaboration with Daniel Day Williams and James M. Gustafson, *The Purpose of the Church and Its Ministry* (Harper & Brothers, 1956), pp. 44–46.

3. See George E. Mendenhall, "Covenant Forms in Israelite Tradition," *The Biblical Archaeologist,* Vol. XVII, No. 3 (Sept., 1954), pp. 50–76. Compare his article on "Covenant" in *The Interpreter's Dictionary of the Bible* (Abingdon Press, 1962), Vol. I, pp. 714–723.

4. George E. Mendenhall, "Covenant Forms in Israelite Tradition," *loc. cit.*, pp. 50–76.

5. See Walther Eichrodt, *Theology of the Old Testament,* tr. by J. A. Baker (The Westminster Press, 1961), Vol. I, pp. 36–39.

6. Some of the earliest assertions of monotheistic faith are found in I Kings 8:60; II Kings 19:15, 19; Deut. 4:35; and Jer. 2:11. The concept appears repeatedly in Deutero-Isaiah — e.g., in Isa. 43:10; 45:5, 6, 14, 21 f.; 46:9.

7. H. Richard Niebuhr, *Radical Monotheism and Western Culture* (Harper & Brothers, 1960).

8. *Ibid.*, p. 63.

9. The author has dealt more at length with these themes in *Biblical Faith and Social Ethics* (Harper & Row, Publishers, Inc., 1960), Ch. 5.

10. H. Richard Niebuhr, *Radical Monotheism and Western Culture*, p. 37.

V.   The Church in the New Testament

1. Cf. Paul S. Minear, *Images of the Church in the New Testament* (The Westminster Press, 1960), pp. 28, 259, 268–269.
2. Cf. Paul S. Minear, " Idea of Church," in *The Interpreter's Dictionary of the Bible*, Vol. I, pp. 607 ff.
3. Although it is a matter of debate as to whether Paul actually wrote Ephesians and Colossians, these two letters are generally included in the Pauline corpus since their content agrees so largely with those writings of which Paul is the undisputed author.
4. I am particularly indebted in the ensuing discussion of " the body of Christ " to Prof. Edward Schweizer's treatment of this theme in *The Church as the Body of Christ* (John Knox Press, 1964).
5. L. S. Thornton, *The Common Life in the Body of Christ* (Westminster, London: The Dacre Press, 2d ed., 1944), p. 452. These references are as follows: Acts 2:42; Rom. 15:26; I Cor. 1:9; 10:16 (twice); II Cor. 6:14; 8:4; 9:13; 13:14; Gal. 2:9; Phil. 1:5; 2:1; 3:10; Philemon, v. 6; Heb. 13:16; and I John 1:3 (twice). Other scholars, basing their enumerations upon different texts, give slightly different numbers of references.
6. See J. Robert Nelson, *The Realm of Redemption* (London: The Epworth Press, 1951), pp. 53 ff.
7. J. Y. Campbell, " Koinonia and Its Cognates in the New Testament," in *Journal of Biblical Literature*, Vol. LI (1932), pp. 352–382, esp. p. 356.
8. J. Robert Nelson, *op. cit.*, pp. 53–60.
9. J. Robert Nelson, *op. cit.*, p. 58.
10. Dietrich Bonhoeffer, *The Cost of Discipleship* (The Macmillan Company, 2d ed., 1959), pp. 230–231.
11. Cf. Arnold B. Come, *Agents of Reconciliation* (The Westminster Press, 1960), p. 137.

VI.   The Church and the World in the New Testament

1. H. Richard Niebuhr, in collaboration with Daniel Day Williams and James M. Gustafson, *The Purpose of the Church and Its Ministry*, p. 26.
2. Pope John XXIII's encyclical *Ad Petri Cathedram* of June 29, 1959. Quoted in Hans Kung, *The Vatican Council in Action: Theo-*

logical Reflections on the Second Vatican Council, tr. by Cecily Hastings (Sheed & Ward, Inc., 1963), pp. 18–19.

3. H. Richard Niebuhr, *Christ and Culture* (Harper & Brothers, 1951).

4. C. R. North, " The World," in *The Interpreter's Dictionary of the Bible* (Abingdon Press, 1962), Vol. IV, pp. 873–878.

5. Rudolf Bultmann, *Theology of the New Testament,* tr. by Kendrick Grobel (Charles Scribner's Son, 1951), Vol. I, pp. 254 ff.

6. Cf. *ibid.,* Vol. I, p. 100.

7. Rudolf Bultmann, *Existence and Faith: Shorter Writings of Rudolf Bultmann,* selected, translated, and introduced by Schubert M. Ogden (Meridian Books, 1960), p. 220.

8. Dietrich Bonhoeffer, *Letters and Papers from Prison,* ed. by Eberhard Bethge and tr. by Reginald H. Fuller (The Macmillan Company, 1962), pp. 165–166.

9. *Ibid.,* p. 218.

10. *Ibid.,* p. 239.

11. Cf. Dietrich Bonhoeffer, *The Cost of Discipleship,* p. 42: " Luther's return from the cloister to the world was the worst blow the world had suffered since the days of early Christianity. The renunciation he made when he became a monk was child's play compared with that which he had to make when he returned to the world."

VII.   The Tension Between the Church and Culture

1. Cf. H. Richard Niebuhr, *Christ and Culture,* pp. 91 ff.

2. H. Richard Niebuhr, in collaboration with Daniel Day Williams and James M. Gustafson, *The Purpose of the Church and Its Ministry,* pp. 25–26.

3. *Ibid.,* p. 31.

4. Cf. *ibid.,* p. 39.

5. J. Milton Yinger, *Religion, Society, and the Individual* (The Macmillan Company, 1957), p. 229.

6. Cf. Lewis Killian and Charles Grigg, *Racial Crisis in America: Leadership in Conflict* (Prentice-Hall, Inc., 1964).

VIII.   Renewal Through Engagement with Culture

1. Harvey Cox, *The Secular City* (The Macmillan Company, 1965), p. 182.

2. Cf. William Stringfellow, *My People Is the Enemy* (Holt, Rinehart and Winston, Inc., 1964).

3. Paul M. van Buren, *The Secular Meaning of the Gospel* (The Macmillan Company, 1963).

4. See, for example, Thomas J. J. Altizer and William Hamilton, *Radical Theology and the Death of God* (The Bobbs-Merrill Company, Inc., 1966), and Thomas J. J. Altizer, *The Gospel of Christian Atheism* (The Westminster Press, 1966).

5. Dietrich Bonhoeffer, *Ethics*, ed. by Eberhard Bethge (The Macmillan Company, 1955), p. 195.

6. *Ibid.*, pp. 195–196.

7. *Ibid.*, p. 195.

INDEX

INDEX

Abrahamic covenant, 108 f.
Altizer, Thomas J. J., 219
Anti-Catholicism, 92, 98
Augustine, 206

Barry, David W., 45
Barth, Karl, 198
Bates, M. Searle, 86
Beecher, Lyman, 87
Bennett, John C., 99
Body of Christ, 140 ff.
Bogue, Donald J., 35
Bonhoeffer, Dietrich, 102, 153 f.,
    173 ff., 211, 218 f., 229 ff.

Calvert, Cecil, 83
Calvin, John, 82, 228
Campbell, Ernest Q., 78
Catholic Church. *See* Roman
    Catholic Church
Christendom, 14 f., 198 f.,
    209 ff.
Church
    definition, 171 f., 193 f.
    dialogue with secular world,
        96, 211 ff.
    New Testament conceptions,
        132 ff.
    purpose of, 173 ff., 191 ff.

relations to culture, 179 ff.
self-identity, 11
    See also Prophetic community
Church and state
    colonial period, 82 ff.
    federal Constitution, 85 f.
    separationism, 97 ff.
    transformationism, 99 f.
    See also Religious pluralism
Church and world
    "church" defined, 171 f.,
        193 f.
    dialogue between, 211 ff.,
        220 ff.
    isolation, 37 f.
    in New Testament, 156 ff.
    purpose of church, 173 ff.,
        191 ff.
    "world" defined, 172 f.
    See also Faith of Israel; Rele-
        vance of church to cul-
        ture; Tension between
        church and culture
Church literature, 45 ff.
Church membership
    and class structure, 31 ff.
    patterns of segregation, 59 ff.
    percentage of population,
        88 ff.

Churches and civil rights, 50 f., 72 ff., 201 ff. *See also* Commission on Religion and Race

Civil rights movement, 50, 70 ff., 201 ff.

Class consciousness in the U.S., 19 ff.

Class divisions
church leadership, 40 ff.
church literature, 45 ff.
church membership, 31 ff.
class consciousness, 19 ff.
dilemma of churches, 47 ff.
Jews, 34 f.
National Council of Churches, 38 f., 41 f.
Negro churches, 36
Protestant Episcopal Church, 41
Roman Catholic Church, 32 ff., 47
social classes in the U.S., 21 ff.
storefront churches, 38 f., 47
The Methodist Church, 41
white Protestant churches, 32 f.
World Council of Churches, 39 f.

Clergy and civil rights, 72 f., 77 f.

Commission on Religion and Race, 76

Common humanity, 218 ff.

Communism, 12, 194, 198

Constantine, 14

Covenant
Abrahamic, 108 f.
church as new covenant community, 116, 133 ff.
Israel as covenant community, 105 ff.
Mosaic, 109 ff.

new covenant of Jeremiah, 115

Cox, Harvey, 211, 219

Culture. *See* Church and world; Dialogue; Relevance of church to culture; Secular society; Tension between church and culture

Culver, Dwight, 64

Davis, Jerome, 40

Death of God, 175, 219

Delta Ministry, 76

Demerath, Nicholas J., III, 34

Deputyship, 226 ff.

Dialogue
ecumenical, 95 ff.
with secular world, 95 ff., 211 ff., 220 ff.

Disestablishment of churches
federal Constitution, 85 f.
states, 86 f.

Ecumenical movement
and social conscience, 231 ff.
Orthodox Churches, 233 f.
Roman Catholicism, 234
See also National Council of Churches; World Council of Churches

Episcopal Society of Cultural and Racial Unity, 75

Established church, 14, 82 ff.

Exodus of Protestant churches, 37 f., 47

Faith of Israel, 101 ff.

Fascism, 12

Federal Council of Churches, 70 f., 233. *See also* National Council of Churches

Fleming, Harold, 64

Folk church, 185 ff.

Franklin, Benjamin, 84, 88
Freedom of church
  external, 194 ff.
  internal, 199 ff.
  new dimensions of freedom,
    202 ff.
Freud, 222

Gandhi, 75
Gnosticism, 12
God
  center of life, 214 ff.
  as Creator, 123 ff.
  as Judge, 125 ff.
  as Redeemer, 128 ff.
  See also Monotheism

Herberg, Will, 91, 94, 97
Hitler, 173
Humanism, 12
Humanity
  church exists for, 173 ff.
  where church and world meet,
    218 ff.
Humphrey, Hubert, 76

Identity of church, 11
Inner city
  exodus of Protestant churches,
    37 f., 47
  See also Transitional areas
Isolation of church, 37 f., 217 f.
Israel
  covenant community, 105 ff.
  faith of, 101 ff.

Jefferson, Thomas, 84, 88
Jews
  immigration, 89 ff.
  in post-Revolutionary Amer-
    ica, 88
  See also Dialogue; Religious
    pluralism

John XXIII, 156, 234
Johnson, F. Ernest, 70

Kahl, Joseph A., 24 ff.
Kennedy, John F., 68, 81
Keyserling, Leon H., 30
Kierkegaard, Søren, 198 f.
King, Martin Luther, Jr., 74 f.
Kneel-ins, 65 f.
Koinōnia, 147 ff.
Ku Klux Klan, 70, 92

Laity, 168 ff., 173 ff., 215 ff.,
    227 ff. See also Church,
    New Testament concep-
    tions; Deputyship; Secular
    society
Lee, J. Oscar, 64
Littell, Franklin H., 89
Loescher, Frank S., 59 ff., 63, 65
Long, Herman H., 63
Loth, David, 64
Luther, Martin, 228

Madison, James, 88
Manichaeism, 12
Marx, Karl, 23, 222
Mason, George, 88
Missions, 201
Monotheism
  earliest appearance in Old
    Testament, 106, 119
  radical monotheism, 117 ff.,
    214 ff.
Mosaic covenant, 109 ff.
Muehl, William, 99
Murray, John Courtney, 95

National Council of Churches
  attacks on, 39, 73, 183
  class identification, 38 f., 41 f.
  Commission on Religion and
    Race, 76

National Council of Churches
(*cont.*)
  criticism of culture, 197 f.
  inclusiveness, 39, 233
  Sixth World Order Study
    Conference, 31, 50 f.
Nazism, 194
Negro churches
  and civil rights, 73 ff.
  class divisions, 36
  membership, 59
  rise of, 54 ff.
Negro revolution, 50 f., 72 ff.,
  201 ff.
Nelson, J. Robert, 152
Niebuhr, H. Richard, 121 f.,
  124, 157, 188, 192 f., 232
Niebuhr, Reinhold, 99
New covenant community, 116,
  133 ff.
New covenant of Jeremiah, 115
New Testament conceptions of
  church, 132 ff.

Old Testament, relation to New,
  101 ff., 132 f.
Oniki, S. Garry, 65
Orthodox Churches, 233 f.

Paine, Thomas, 84 f.
Paul VI, 234
Penn, William, 84
People of God, 136 f.
Pettigrew, Thomas F., 78
Pluralism. *See* Religious plural-
  ism
Poverty
  in relation to affluence, 28 ff.
  in underdeveloped countries,
    30 f., 39
  in United States, 28 ff.
Prophetic community, 180 ff.,
  194 ff., 207 ff. *See also*

Freedom of church; Rele-
  vance of church to culture
Protestants and Other Americans
  United for Separation of
  Church and State, 98
Purpose of church, 173 ff.,
  191 ff.

Racial divisions in churches
  at end of World War II,
    59 ff.
  changes: local church level,
    62 ff.
  changes: organizational struc-
    tures, 66 ff.
  Negro denominations, 54 ff.
  rise of racial barriers, 51 ff.
  Roman Catholic Church, 59,
    62
  tokenism, 67 ff.
  See also Churches and civil
    rights
Radical monotheism, 117 ff.,
  214 ff.
Ramsey, Paul, 99
Relevance of church to culture,
  11, 15 ff., 156 ff., 169 ff.,
  211 ff., 215 ff. *See also* Dialogue; Secular society; Tension between church and
  culture
Religious liberty
  in colonial America, 82 ff.
  in contemporary world, 194 ff.
  federal Constitution, 85 f.
  See also Church and state;
    Disestablishment   of
    churches; Freedom of
    church
Religious pluralism, 80 ff.
  aspect of secularization, 208
  disestablishment of churches,
    82 ff.

growth of, 87 ff.
implications of, 93 ff.
Renewal of church. *See* Prophetic community; Relevance of church to culture
Rich nations vs. poor nations, 30 f., 39
Robinson, John A. T., 219 f.
Rockefeller, Nelson, 203
Roman Catholic Church
and ecumenical movement, 234
anti-Catholicism, 92, 98
civil rights, 75 f.
class structure, 32–36, 47
in colonial America, 82 ff.
growth of membership, 90 ff.
Interracial Council, 75 f.
racial practices, 66 f.
See also Religious pluralism; Second Vatican Council
Roman Catholic Interracial Council, 75 f.
Russell, Richard, 76

Sanders, Thomas G., 85, 98 f.
Second Vatican Council, 81, 156 f., 234
Secular society
autonomy of, 222 ff.
dialogue with, 211 ff., 220 ff.
growth of, 208 ff.
meaning of, 94 ff.
relation of church to, 11, 15 ff., 169 ff., 179 ff.
See also Church and world; Tension between church and culture; World's "coming of age"
Secularism, 94
Secularization
meaning of, 208 ff., 211
resistance of churches, 209 f.

world's "coming of age," 211, 222
Segregation in churches
beginnings, 51 ff.
changes since World War II, 61 ff.
at end of World War II, 59 ff.
relation to patterns in secular society, 51 ff., 67 ff.
tokenism, 67 ff.
See also Racial divisions in churches
Sixth World Order Study Conference, 31, 50 f.
Smith, Alfred E., 92
Social classes in the U.S., 21 ff.
Southern Christian Leadership Conference, 74 f.
State church. *See* Established church
Stevenson, Adlai, 28
Stokes, Anson Phelps, 83
Storefront churches, 38 f.
Sweet, William Warren, 84
Synagogue Council of America, 76

Tension between church and culture, 181 f., 188 ff., 194 ff.
Thornton, L. S., 147
Tillich, Paul, 172, 219 f.
Tokenism in race relations, 67 ff.
Transitional areas, 60, 64 f.

Underwood, Kenneth W., 99
U.S. Supreme Court, 81

van Buren, Paul M., 219 f.
Vatican II. *See* Second Vatican Council
Vilakazi, Absalom L., 50 f.
Vocation. *See* Deputyship

Ward, Barbara, 30 f.
Washington, George, 88
White Citizens Councils, 92
Williams, Roger, 84
Winter, Gibson, 37
Withdrawal of churches from culture, 183 ff.
Woodward, C. Vann, 53
World, the
  "coming of age," 211, 222
  defined, 172 f.
  fallen, 161 ff.
  God's creation, 158 ff.
  object of God's love, 167 f.
  sphere of church's work, 168 ff., 173 ff.
  See also Church and world; Secular society

World Council of Churches
  Amsterdam Assembly, 156, 233 f.
  attacks on, 183
  Delta Ministry, 76
  Evanston Assembly, 156
  inclusiveness, 39 f., 233 f.
  New Delhi Assembly (1961), 156, 234
  relation to class alignments, 39 f.
World's "coming of age," 211, 222
Wright, G. Ernest, 104

Yinger, J. Milton, 199